Theology
from the
Spring

"There are some very important truths in life that every person, every Christian, should confront: order, unity and diversity, reality and perception, general and specific revelation. These can be dry and dusty unless you discuss them in a common experienced area. This is what Jacob Taggart does in *Theology from the Spring*. He indeed gives reflections of the Creator cast in nature. As Plato perceived shadows in the cave, as Augustine perceived the bending of an oar in water, so Jacob takes the simple experience of fishing and applies it to the realities in life. A relevant and enjoyable read for otherwise stilted and academic subjects. An unlettered person in theology and philosophy can get a head start by reading Jacob's blueprint."

–TOMMY NELSON,

Senior Pastor, Denton Bible Church

"As objective as I want to be, I own my prejudice about Jacob Taggart's new book. I love Biblical theology, the gospel of grace, the voice of creation, and the sport of fly fishing . . . a lot. As a tapestry of truth and grace, Jacob Taggart has woven all four together in *Theology from the Spring*. Whether or not you ever pick up a fly rod, you will be greatly encouraged by this creative presentation of our calling to know and love, enjoy and serve Jesus."

–DR. SCOTTY WARD SMITH,

Pastor Emeritus, Christ Community Church, Franklin, TN; Teacher in Residence, West End Community Church, Nashville, TN; Gospel Coalition Contributor

"Norman Maclean opened his book *A River Runs Through It* with these words, 'In our family, there was no clear line between religion and fly fishing.' And so it seems to be with most fly fishers. Their proximity to God's glorious creation, and the need to understand the complexities of aquatic ecosystems, bequeaths a nearness to our Creator that few other sports can offer.

"And, of course, water plays a powerful role on the fly fisher's life, from the fluid that harbors the trout, to the stream's siren song, to the lakes mirroring life. Springs have a special place in the fly fisher's arcane vocabulary, especially when one speaks of 'spring creeks.' Not seasonal phenomena, but springs large enough to form a trout stream right from their point of emergence.

"Weave together the fly fisher's reverence for spring creeks, their immediacy with nature, their near awe at the habits and habitats of trout, and the One Who created it all, and you have a good start at Jake's book. His theology is sound, and his stories of fly fishing revealing of the man, and his love of God and the out-of-doors. Even if you don't fly fish, or don't even fish at all, you will enjoy, and benefit, from this unique look at spring creeks as they reveal the truths of the Gospel."

–DR. GARY BORGER,

Best-selling *Fly Fishing* Author; Contributing Editor for *Fly Fisherman* magazine; consultant for the movie, *A River Runs Through It*; *Fly Fusion* magazine's top 7 most influential fly fisherman of the last fifty years.

"After reading *Theology from the Spring*, you will never again look at water in the same way. More importantly, you will see water's Creator in a refreshing new light. The One who called the seas into existence also poured Himself out for us by taking on humanity, thus offering us living water. Jacob Taggart has brought together his love of the outdoors, his fascination with science, and his love of Scripture in a way that helps us see the majesty of God revealed in the natural world."

–ROB PHILLIPS,

Strategic Leader for Apologetics, Missouri Baptist Convention

Theology
from the
Spring

Reflections of the Creator Cast in Nature

Jacob A. Taggart
Foreword by Dr. Owen Strachan

Ambassador International
GREENVILLE, SOUTH CAROLINA & BELFAST, NORTHERN IRELAND

www.ambassador-international.com

Theology from the Spring

Reflections of the Creator Cast in Nature

ISBN: 978-1-62020-701-7
eISBN: 978-1-62020-476-4

Library of Congress Control Number: 2018936821

Cover Design and Interior Layout by Hannah Nichols
Ebook Conversion by Anna Riebe Raats

AMBASSADOR INTERNATIONAL
Emerald House
411 University Ridge, Suite B14
Greenville, SC 29601, USA
www.ambassador-international.com

AMBASSADOR BOOKS
The Mount
2 Woodstock Link
Belfast, BT6 8DD, Northern Ireland, UK
www.ambassadormedia.co.uk

The colophon is a trademark of Ambassador, a Christian publishing house.

For the love of my life, Tiffany, you are the perfect personification of a mountain spring: Your natural beauty runs as deep below the surface as it does above, radiating outwardly with limitless breadth. You have an endless supply of life that naturally and genuinely flows into others. God put you into my life at a most crucial hour; something pure and real stood out to me amidst the hustling pace of a hollow superficiality. Like a spring that draws the deer to the life-giving water, God used you to draw me back to Him. For that, I am forever grateful. I love you.

And for my children, Abrah, Jonah, and Jobe, may this book, containing a lifetime of learning and truth I've been graced to receive, be a heritage to you and your children. Thank you for being my kids. My heart's desire is for this book to guide you in ways to know Christ through the things of nature we enjoy together, and may you always know Christ crucified through the pages of sacred Scripture.

ACKNOWLEDGMENTS

In his book *Fisherman's Luck*, Henry Van Dyke quipped, "The people who always live in houses, and sleep on beds, and walk on pavements, and buy their food from butchers and bakers and grocers, are not the most blessed inhabitants of this wide and various earth. The circumstances of their existence are too mathematical and secure for perfect contentment."[1] While much can and will be said in the following pages of the sort of existence Van Dyke pitied, I do believe I am most blessed and perfectly contented for the help a great number of people provided in bringing this project to fruition. My sincere gratitude goes out to the following people.

It sounds perfunctory, but no less genuine, that I should begin by thanking my Lord and Savior Jesus Christ for the privilege of producing a work to bring Him glory from a unique perspective. From the time You gave me the idea for this book in 2010, to the lifetime I've spent fishing in Your springs as You looked on preparing me for this work, I am grateful that is has been done by You and through You and to You.

I am indebted to my wife, Tiffany, who had to put up with my stammering, my self-doubt, my stacks of research books on the kitchen table, my floating of new ideas and directions, and my many fishing trips made in the name of "research." It's amazing that you can still read at all, given all the drafts and edits I pushed in your face when you had better things to do. You are the wisest person I know and exhibited what the consummate godly woman looks like through your patience and support. Most importantly, I would not be the man I am today without you.

To my editor, Kirk Anderson, without you, this project would have been like the quarter-miler who dies on the last curve. You were the holy trinity of editors, possessing the three attributes I needed: a professional English and grammar editor, a fellow fly fisherman, and a brother in the faith. Undoubtedly, Providence was at work pairing us together. I am grateful—not only for your work, which made this book possible, but also for the friend I have in you. Thanks!

Many people were gracious enough to lend their time for interviews and proofing this work. People like Kirk Farmer; Spencer Allen; Chris Gates; Jim Washabaugh; friends at Capital City Fly Fishers; Fish and Cross Ranch/En Gedi Retreat in Yampa, Colorado; my in-laws, Dan and Marcella Jordan; and Monte Shinkle and the pastoral staff at Concord Baptist Church, who provided great encouragement and feedback. I would like to also thank my dear friend Eli Burrell, the fly rod-breaking poet: while no fly rod is safe in your hands, much of my grammar and punctuation *is* safe due to all the grammar-checking text messages you've happily answered.

Thank you, Owen Strachan, for agreeing to the foreword of this book. I have long admired your work and took to heart your call to be a pastor/public theologian. Your participation cannot be overstated and shows the Lord's blessing of this work.

My mother, Becky Williams, a faithful mom, has always supported me and taken an interest in my fly fishing endeavors.

And, finally, to my father Mike Taggart, it was you who introduced me to the majesty of the spring, you who taught me how to fish, and as a means of giving back, it was you who I thought about as I wrote much of this book. Thanks, Dad, for investing in me. Let me reciprocate.

CONTENTS

FOREWORD   13

PREFACE   17

PART ONE
THE CREATOR'S EXISTENCE FOUND IN THE SPRING

CHAPTER ONE
THERE'S SOMETHING OUT THERE   31

CHAPTER TWO
THE ULTIMATE CAUSE: ALL SPRINGS FORTH   53

CHAPTER THREE
PURE CHANCE? DESIGN IN THE SPRING   83

PART TWO
THE CREATOR'S IMMANENCE FOUND IN THE SPRING

CHAPTER FOUR
REFLECTIONS OF THREE IN ONE:
THE TRINITY IN THE SPRING   125

CHAPTER FIVE
LIVING WATER: DRAWING AND SUSTAINING
THEOLOGICAL AND PHYSIOLOGICAL LIFE   165

CHAPTER SIX
LIVING WATER: DRAWING AND INITIATING
PSYCHOLOGICAL AND SPIRITUAL LIFE   193

PART THREE
THE CREATOR'S COMMISSION
FOUND IN THE SPRING

CHAPTER SEVEN

CATCHING FISH, PART ONE: CALLED
AND EQUIPPED TO CATCH FISH   221

CHAPTER EIGHT

CATCHING FISH, PART TWO: STRATEGIES
FOR EFFECTIVE FISHING   251

CHAPTER NINE

EATING OUR OWN: ECCLESIOLOGY
IN THE STREAM   291

CHAPTER TEN

SLIPPERY ROCKS: WHAT ARE YOU
STANDING ON?   319

ENDNOTES   337

BIBLIOGRAPHY   353

DISCOGRAPHY   363

FOREWORD

I GREW UP WHERE THE salmon run wild. This was no ultra-plugged-in environment. Coastal Maine has a solid number of folks who live there, but not in the boisterous, see-and-be-seen way familiar to modern urbanity. Many go out of their way to avoid discovery; they build cabins in the woods and quietly pass along ideal fishing spots to their children, so as to escape, and generationally so. The people of Maine seem, in retrospect, a people apart, communities who hide together.

Jake Taggart understands such a mentality. In *Theology from the Spring*, he evinces a thick affection for hours of solitude in the outdoors. He is obviously a man of deep passions—chief among them theology, fishing, and the world God has made. This book is—like the mythic fish outdoorsmen talk about years later—one of a kind—a blend of apologetics, doctrine, scientific observation, and reminiscence. I commend it to you, whether you are entirely new to the Christian faith or have been searching the grace-dappled streams of God for a lifetime. Taggart is a sharp-eyed guide, and his thoughtful exploration of the faith once-for-all delivered to the saints enriches, instructs, and creates praise to our all-wise God.

One of the strengths of this book is that it does not generalize what the Bible renders in detail. This is true of the various springs in the heartland; this is true of the work of the Holy Trinity, each Person of the Godhead filling His role, playing His holy part in the drama of creation, redemption, and ultimate restoration. A large part of sanctification is seeing these threads that run throughout Scripture, threads that remind me of the treasure chest of flies that the best fishermen store in preparation for the big catch. Unity in diversity sums up the Godhead; we marvel at the oneness of the Father, Son, and Spirit, even as we savor the three-ness, the celestial harmony that the Divine Persons produce.

Theology from the Spring beckons to us to come and learn the wonders of God's Word and world. Conversion does not kill curiosity; conversion stimulates the heart and mind, creating a sense of awe and a desire to plumb the depths of this place. I see echoes of the musings of America's theologian, Jonathan Edwards, in the observations of Jake Taggart. Now, more than ever, we hear that faith and science are opposed, but we do not accept the terms. This book offers abundant evidence of the way that regeneration renews the mind and frees it to think after God. This—and not rebellious "inquiry" that denies Divine design—is why God gave us intellect. God's special revelation teaches us the very mind of the Ruler of the cosmos; God's general revelation shows us that He is a many-splendored Lord, One who takes delight not only in making sinners brand new, but also in forming the river-probing senses of the salmon.

Some may wonder about the unique linkage of outdoorsmanship and faith. What do these two pursuits have in common? I am reminded of John one. When Christ begins to gather leaders of His new covenant people, He does not go first to the rabbis, or the political class, or the philosophers. He goes to the fishermen. He gives them little prologue, little backstory, little glimpse of where He will take them. He calls them to follow Him, and they do. From that point forward, He molds these outdoorsmen into apostles—men who will not only preach the truth, but die for it.

We have no record of what the first disciples thought of their former career, fishing. But I wonder if they sometimes thought back to the days when the sun caught the sea, and the wind drove at them with gusto, and all the world seemed alive. Perhaps we can surmise that their engagement with the natural beauty of this realm prepared them elegantly for their engagement with the spiritual beauty of Christ's kingdom. If that is the case, it just may be that this rich book will do the same for many readers, including those who now love nothing more than retreating to the wild, saying few words, and casting into streams, rivers, and lakes formed by the very hand of God.

—Dr. Owen Strachan

Associate Professor of Christian Theology, Midwestern Baptist Theological Seminary

Author: *Risky Gospel: Abandon Fear and Build Something Awesome*

cpt.mbts.edu

PREFACE

A Return Home

"Jesus said to her, 'Everyone who drinks of this water will be thirsty again, but whoever drinks of the water that I will give him will never be thirsty again. The water that I will give him will become in him a spring of water welling up to eternal life.'"

– John 4:13-14

WATER PREACHES THEOLOGY. IF THERE is anything you should know about this book before turning a single page, know that it is about three things: fresh water springs, fly fishing, and God. While a plethora of works have been written on each topic individually, it's the convergence of these three into one medium—the spring—that warrants a composite treatment. Simple, yet didactic. How the spring teaches us, preaches to us, and reaches us in subtle ways provides the long-forgotten remedy of living water for a spiritually-parched culture.

Water. How often people take the compound—two simple atoms of hydrogen bonded with one atom of oxygen—for granted. At least, that seems to be the case in western culture, where our lifestyle is centered on technology and gadgetry as its core "needs." Even in something as mundane as driving across a bridge during a daily work commute, guided by our navigation systems, we seem incapable of looking beyond the wheel to catch a glimpse of the stream running below. What fills that stream is the precise compound necessary to sustain our lives. It's a sad indictment when we can't live five seconds without glancing at the circuitous devices that now own us, yet we are wholly indifferent when encountering the compound that sustains us in

17

its most natural expression. Water is that compound essential to our physical life. However, most of us have never once considered how water, particularly spring water, bespeaks a supernatural expression of life beyond physical constraints.

Water is viewed much differently in other parts of the world, where it is seen as both value and vice. Its presence, or lack thereof, is wholly conspicuous. Take, for example, a region of western Africa. It was on a mission trip to Senegal that I saw for the first time what it means to live at the mercy of liquid—how water can legitimately be christened with the superlative, "living water." The climate is so dry that even the rocks are brittle from dehydration.

Senegal is a predominantly Islamic country in northwest Africa. Its residents generally aren't hostile to Westerners, or even Christians, for that matter. While the people are friendly, the country is not a developed nation, as its "roads" would attest. "Decrepit" would not even begin to describe their road system, as they are often forced to go off-road altogether, meandering through ditches, dodging animals, and avoiding pot holes large enough to swallow a car.

Our destination was one of the most remote areas of the country. It was a distant village called Dhakatelle, located in the southeast corner of the country, just two miles from the border of Guinea. One of several anxious moments occurred as we were going off-road and had to cross a dried-out streambed. This very streambed dictated the time of year that we could make our trip. The only way in or out of this isolated village is through this streambed, which is impassible during the three-month rainy season. Access to this village is subject to the whims of the water. As a vice, water not only cuts off ties to the outside world, but it threatens to drown anyone who dares to cross the boundaries it has established.

The stream had dried out at this time, and a crossing ford had been semi-formed by vehicles. Only a jeep or four-wheel drive truck could make it across the stream bed, where years of water erosion had left a steep incline at the point of egress. To make matters worse, the path was essentially like trying to drive up a wall of rip-rap, scaling forty-five-degree hills while dodging rocks larger than basketballs. Water not only subjugated humanity's maneuverability to a halt when it was flowing, but it also left some glaring reminders of its sheer power when it was absent.

We arrived at the village after a twelve-mile, off-road adventure that took nearly forty minutes. Pulling up in a cloud of dust, we were quickly greeted with an enigmatic climate. The landscape was dead and scorched, devoid of any semblance of green. The terrain appeared to have been run through a massive dehydrator. The grass was dead, with scant patches here and there. The trees looked like raisins with their shriveled trunks. Livestock roamed the village aimlessly with their "six-packs" on display—emaciated ribs that stuck out so far you could have played a xylophone on them. But the scenery of death contrasted to a wellspring of joyous faces. People readily rushed up to us, complete strangers speaking in an unknown language, but with lively flowing smiles, springing from a deep-rooted heritage of hospitality.

Everything about this area appeared dead, except for its affectionate and affable people. What fueled their ebullient esprit? After spending time in the village, the source of their vibrancy was clear in both a literal and metaphorical sense: deep, hand-dug wells maintained within each individual family compound. Peering down into one of these wells on a sizzling, 114-degree day and feeling the cool air rising up was intoxicating. The well delved approximately fifty feet down before hitting the water table. And if the well runs dry, the people execute an old-fashioned sense of community—the paradigm utilized in early Israel, Mesopotamia, and westward European expansion. Basically, the compounds that still have water in their wells share life by taking in those whose wells have run dry. As primitive as these people are, they understand the essential nature of two things—life provided by the water and life provided for their neighbor.

I still can't fully assimilate how these people, who live in abject dirt and poverty, were the happiest people I've ever met. They were innocently content with whatever the environment gave them. We came to teach them about Jesus and the Life that He came to give for them to live more abundantly. But as I left, I realized there was much these uncultured people could teach Americans about our flippant disregard for the element essential to sustain the human body—water. The lesson cuts even deeper, though, considering we take for granted, almost smugly, not just the water, but also the One Who orders and sustains every water molecule. And it's not just the water molecule itself we take for granted, but also the ordering of millions of water molecules, intelligently fashioned together to comprise the human body.

It is no coincidence how—in lieu of the gifts we brought these primeval villagers such as food, oil, and toys for the kids—the one item they seemed to treasure above all others was our trash. We brought our own water bottles for the week-long stay in the village, knowing that our bodies weren't conditioned for the natural bacteria present in their well water. When we'd finish off one of these large, 2.5-ounce, plastic water bottles, the children of the compound would swarm to it like a group of fish in a hatchery darting to a feed pellet. It sounds inconceivable to us Westerners that the most valuable thing we could give them was an empty, plastic tube that better enabled them to transport their most valuable possession—water.

The reaction of these village children offered a bit of a dichotomy—candidly artless, yet surprisingly mature. It wasn't the little toys we brought them (which they certainly enjoyed and beamed after receiving) that were of most value to these kids, but rather plain, empty, plastic water bottles—something we deem completely dispensable. To these kids, who lacked even shoes to cover their feet, this was not just a bottle, but a vessel that secured the most essential, life-sustaining element available. These native children demonstrated wisdom by elevating a container that holds that which gives them life—water—over the toys made by man that sustain entertainment and silently indicted our Western system of values without even saying a word. I saw a raw purity and innocence in Senegal that's hard to describe.

The eight-hour flight back to Washington, D.C., allowed plenty of time for reflection. I was so tired I couldn't sleep, suspended in a semi-lucid state. In that state, my mind was bombarded with ironies and contrasts inferred from the trip. There was the irony of how we came to reveal the true nature of God the Son to these Muslim villagers, but it was God Who revealed Himself to us, in manifold ways, through the medium of nature. There was also the irony of how utterly lost these primal villagers were; yet abiding in the desolate abyss of nature, they held a clearer perspective of God's hand in the natural world than those of us in "civilized" cultures.

And still, there was the irony of traveling across a rickety bridge on our way into "work," where I finally observed a stream and its glistening water below. Back home, I drove across far more modern bridges every day without noticing the underlying water. Evidently, I required the vantage point of another country to see the water that anchored the bridge's foundation. Removed from the syncopation of civilization and Western distraction, I was finally able to see facets of God's natural truth that had been staring at me all along.

Trying to make sense of things on the return flight, I couldn't shake the feeling that there was something familiar about God's fingerprints observed in the bush country of Africa. I couldn't fully place it, but it was similar to some place where I've seen God's indescribable majesty on display, a place where ancient waters flow—waters that transform us, baptizing our agnosticism and quickening our spirits.

Then, an epiphany occurred. Seated next to my friend who had organized this mission trip, it suddenly dawned on me that this was the second time he and I had taken refuge in a tent together, roughing it in the extreme outdoors. The first excursion was a fishing trip campout we took with our two oldest boys at Bennett Springs State Park near Lebanon, Missouri. On that trip, we logged a couple of days without the comforts of electricity. We pan-fried our dinner, fresh rainbow trout, and slept in a tent in ninety-five-degree heat. The instant this memory came to mind, a connection was made between God's natural revelation observed on this African mission trip and His palpable presence at the place of unrivaled, innocent beauty, where we camped with our boys. And this tranquil presence is the reason I've been innately drawn to Bennett Springs since my childhood. It all, now, made sense.

I struggle to assemble the adequate words to describe what Bennett Springs means to me. There is no place on earth that evokes a more wistful and safe aura. Everyone has a sanctuary in their life—their place of tranquil asylum. Their place of refuge when the chips are down. Their place of protection—like the Bat Cave for Batman or a fort built out in the living room for would-be superheroes. Perhaps it was underneath the front porch of your house, like Vern in the movie *Stand by Me* (although, if you remember, that safe place ended up becoming a land mine of frustration). Jesus even had a safe sanctuary for prayer in the Garden of Gethsemane. Bennett Springs was my sanctuary.

Bennett Springs holds "sanctuary status" to me for nostalgic reasons, among others. A line from the classic J.B.F Wright song, "Precious Memories," perhaps says it best:

> *Precious father, loving mother*
> *Fly across the lonely years;*
> *And old home scenes of my childhood*
>
> *In fond memory appear.*
>
> *Precious mem'ries, how they linger,*
> *How they ever flood my soul.*
> *In the stillness of the midnight,*
> *Precious, sacred scenes unfold.*[2]

You see, Bennett Springs was that special scene from my childhood where everything was right in the world. I hold vivid memories of camping there every summer. School would be out, which was certainly a positive memory. Mom and dad were still married. My little brother was an innocent boy, unmarred by the byproducts of divorce or the snares of the world. S'mores and hot dogs were roasted over a camp fire. My grandpa, the most loving man I've ever known, was still alive to over-zealously praise my catch of the day. I remember laying in their camper at night, when they'd turn on their TV—a camping luxury for a boy—which seemed incapable of picking up anything other than old black and white episodes of Rod Serling's *The Twilight Zone*.

There is no better show for a young boy on a campout than *The Twilight Zone*. If the darkness of the unknown wilderness outside our tent or camper wasn't spooky enough, *The Twilight Zone* exacerbated every little noise we heard. The show itself was a metaphor for the feeling of being exposed to the unknown of nature. Watching *The Twilight Zone* on campouts wrought ambivalent emotions of fear and enticement. It's similar to how we pursue being scared, but only up to the point where we *are* scared—the sensation where we can't resist watching, but are too scared to watch at the same time. That was *The Twilight Zone* for me, viewed from the safe comfort of grandpa's lap, under a cover and within his camper parked out in the Ozark hills. Such is also the reaction of one confronted with the holiness of the God Who created nature.

During some ugly stages of my life, marked by uncertainty, transition, or the struggle to find my identity, I could always retreat to Bennett Springs for safe harbor. The crisp air and ethereal fog, ascending from and descending down the stream, had a cathartic way of wiping away the stresses of the day. Just the sound of water running in its natural effluence or the distinct smell of fresh spring water provided a natural sedative that blanketed the fears left behind in the "real world." Similar to how I felt as a child, everything was right while in its presence. Unsurprisingly, then, when it came time to depart, I would brood out the window as the car pulled away, consoled with the assurance I would be irresistibly drawn back again.

As an aside, parents, if you've never taken your children camping, please do so. Please understand you don't have to grow a beard, live with a survival knife, or morph into a Bear Grylls, feigned tough-guy in order to enjoy camping. It really isn't about the machismo of "roughing it," or even about getting away, for that matter. More importantly, it's about doing without. Camping creates that sense of being in a foxhole together, where we are sequestered away from the conveniences of life that we've become so dependent upon, to be exposed—to an extent—to the elements of nature. We camp *together*, spending time with those closest to us, who are then able to see us from a different angle. This different angle occasionally shows people putting their intrinsic resourcefulness on display, such as the time I embarrassed my kids by using a cast iron skillet to hammer down tent pegs. It is an angle, such as awakening to the entrancing hymn of a cardinal calling you to rise and rekindle the crackle of last night's campfire, that the advancements of technology can't duplicate. Angles like these, whether seen in state or national parks or private retreats like Clydehurst Ranch in Montana, embed themselves in the core of our humanity.

Aside from bringing us together, camping also enables us to see the cosmos and its Creator from a different angle. We obtain a license to slow down and view the natural tapestry of creation, untainted by man. Such a venture is not unlike that of Jacob, who, around 1950 BC, returned to Bethel to commemorate the moment when he wrestled with, and ultimately yielded, to God's plan for his life and, on an even bigger scale, God's plan for redeeming His creation. There, Jacob ceased being his own god and humbly postured himself toward God's Lordship over the cosmos. Today, modern culture would do well to exercise similar humility. Like Jacob, when utterly exposed out in nature, our once-jaded eyes become better-equipped to see the Creator's hand orchestrating the universe. When those elements of nature surround us, we're forced to confront them on their own awesome terms. As result, a trip to the spring strips us of the synthetic anesthesia of not only technology, but also of the fast-paced routines that dominate our lives. Dehumanization is supplanted by re-humanization, as humanity is reacquainted with its original roles as keepers, gardeners, and even priests, to a degree, of this natural world.

For me, Bennett Springs has always possessed a supernatural allure—one that has provoked a sense of awe and draw for many other people as well. Ultimately, I believe Bennett Springs, or most any stream, possesses a natural attraction for three primary reasons. First, it is pure and natural. The superlative purity of an object makes it stand apart as holy from the common, manmade elements of modern life. The striking quality of natural streams is that they often seem frozen in time, as if impervious to the vicissitudes of the world around it. Second, the spring is peaceful. Its pure and orderly ambiance delivers an element of peace that soothes the soul. Seeing creation in its unadulterated form has a pacifying effect on the observer. And finally, the spring is rational—that is, it makes sense. One can observe the organic interactions of life sustained by the spring, and deduce its truths in a manner that can be applied to our daily lives. The stream ambushes our senses with the impeccable harmony of natural laws found in its crystalline waters. The spring's purity, peacefulness, and rationality point to its Creator.

So, for whom, then, is this book written? Christians? Non-Christians? Fishermen and nature enthusiasts alike? Actually, the answer is all the above. Such a broad target is simple when you consider that all of these groups invariably encounter the spring's tales woven above their heads and below their feet.

This book applies to Christians because it offers a practical, yet profound, perspective on their faith from an angle they likely haven't explored—one lying right before their eyes. Illustrations will be extracted from the natural order so that the Christian reader can deduce God's unequivocal working in creation to guide him or her in their ongoing walk with Him. Many believers have become numbed to the fact that God has not only called them to illuminate the world with the light of their Creator, but also that their Creator, Himself, permeates the entire world with His light. Everything that we take in by our senses, with each passing second of our existence, speaks to its Creator.

Christians, also, are often those most guilty of getting swept away by the tide of busyness and technological dependency. Often, with the best of intentions, Christians can unknowingly substitute busyness for holiness. Many get so concerned with being "relevant" in the eyes of the world through gadgets and technological advances, they lose focus on the very thing they were called to do—loving God and loving people in a pure, unqualified manner. This book is an aid to prevent us from falling prey to glorying in self, or self-made creations, by instead directing us to natural truth revealed by the natural world's Creator. Christians are very often the audience in need of stepping back to refresh and recalculate their lives through the lens of the spring.

This book is also germane to non-Christians—for those who are fishermen, hikers, canoers, or campers, who simply want to enjoy nature without having to worry about dogmas and ordinances. This book is for you as well, because this book's focus is something you already love. Not only will you find scenes you identify with, but it may also point you behind the scenes to a novel way of seeing things you may have never considered. The book is framed within the parameters of logic and natural laws that are innately present within those things that you so treasure. May the stories and rational deductions found in this book lead you to a greater appreciation of your current passions and, in the process, point you to a transcendent presence inevitably reflected within them.

As noted above, most people have an innate draw to natural springs. Let this book, then, draw you to the spring for your own enjoyment. Beyond that, this book is about history, logic, theology, hydrology, geology, ichthyology, and many other "ologies"—all of which are fact-based, objective disciplines. At worst, you just broadened your perspective. Besides, if what you already believe is really true, then it would remain true in spite of anything found in this book. So, what do you have to lose?

To be clear, this book is not intended to rail against technology or to suggest that *simple* is more pious. Rather, it's about taking a step back to reevaluate the proper context and relationship of the Creator and His creation. It's about the natural adornments we seem to have forgotten—whose treasures and truths we've been derelict to pass on to our children—and how their timeless lessons—*His* timeless lessons— are still there to behold if we would just take time to examine them. These are lessons that don't require you to be a theologian or teacher to pass along. The Creator has already written the lesson for you. Your job, as a parent or one who simply loves the outdoors, is twofold—to use this book's discourses to further your insight, appreciation, and stewardship of the natural world and to share these lessons with others.

Simply put, this book is about natural theology distilled through the allegory of a freshwater spring. More specifically, it is about how God *gives* life through nature and how He *reveals Himself* through nature. The word "theology" can be an intimidating word. Don't let it. While this book will not delve into highly-technical, theological treatments, it will challenge you and stretch your mind a bit, as theological topics are integrated and contextualized within the central motif of a natural spring.

The spring gushes forth homilies with much to say about its Creator. The heavens declare His glory, the earth is His handiwork (Psa. 19:1); and if He is the beginning and end of all things, then it's time we humble ourselves to read what His cosmic declaration says to those graced to observe it. After all, He doesn't need us spectators; even His revealing of Himself in general, natural ways, is grace we don't deserve. To Him be all glory, forever.

Part One

THE CREATOR'S EXISTENCE FOUND
IN THE SPRING

CHAPTER ONE

THERE'S SOMETHING OUT THERE

"Remember to extol his work, of which men have sung. All mankind has looked on it; man beholds it from afar. Behold, God is great, and we know him not."

—Job 36:24-26a

"JAKE, LOOK OUT THERE!" IF you want to immediately command the attention of a teenage boy, look no further than this simple, four-word formula. Embossed in my brain is the memory of walking by a stream with my father on a reconnaissance mission to find trout stacked up in the current. The late-morning sun rained down upon the riffle upstream, producing a shimmering background vignette. A boulder in the water impeded the fast-flowing current, creating an eddy as the stream floor sank into a deep, azure pool. The color spectrum unfolded before us in a manifold display of olive green to cobalt blue. Yet, in spite of the glorious hues, it was these four words from my father that suddenly possessed me in a rapt, hypnotic fervor.

As simple as these four words appear to be, they convey three significant things. One, something has been perceived or discovered which was previously unknown. Two, this perception is independent of our control or ability to affect its presence. And three, this "thing" has meaning or importance to us; it is no trivial find. The latter point is especially true for a teenage boy who has not caught a fish all day, as this "thing" might be the remedy for growing impatience with an empty stringer. So, upon hearing of my dad's discovery, I would have done anything—eaten onions or cleaned my brother's room—for him

31

to share this revelation. My dad leaned toward me in full "coaching mode," his voice shifting to a whisper, and said, "Out there in that deep pool . . . There's something out there." After a pause that seemed like half an hour, Dad finally delivered the news I'd been waiting for: "There's six trout suspended out there." I could hardly contain myself.

My head swiveled around to the pool of water quicker than Linda Blair's head in *The Exorcist*. I looked, and looked, and looked. Nothing. Dad pointed in the general vicinity, but still I could see nothing but a deep, blue abyss. Sure, the sun was bright, causing a slight glare on the surface, but my adrenaline and pent-up anticipation should have given me x-ray vision by this time.

"Here," my dad said, sensing my irritability about to boil over. He pulled off his polarized sunglasses and slipped them onto my under-sized head. Immediately, it was as if scales clouding my vision fell off, and I had new eyes to see. Polarized sunglasses possess a filter to help eliminate glare and the opaque haze caused by light reflecting off high-luster surfaces, such as water. With the aid of these "new eyes," I could now perceive something that had been out there all along, however imperfect this perception might be. It was like a spiritual awakening. With this revelation, I had been given eyes to see what had always been there.

Needless to say, now I never go fly fishing without polarized sunglasses, as learned through this object lesson. I will do so for the rest of my life. But perhaps even more necessary is the deeper, eternal meaning this story points toward, well beyond the finite scope of my life on earth.

I suspect if you are reading this, you have at one time questioned, if not sensed, there is "something else" out there. Something transcendent behind the constraints of the physical reality we perceive. Something beyond the limitations of a contingent, created order. The sensation might hit you while fishing, or in a moment of solitude upon reaching a precipice on a mountain hike, or after the loss of a loved one. Such human experience bears witness to the innate sense that there is something out there. The joys and the anguish of life, its beauties and horrors, the order, logic, and precision of the melody of physical reality all grip us with the imperious sense that something is out there, something far transcending our finite existence. For now, we'll refer to this mysterious thing as "the Transcendent."

To not sense "the Transcendent" out there is to have never lived. To deny "the Transcendent" is to be a liar. That might sound like extreme hyperbole, but that is exactly what one of the greatest philosophers of all time, the apostle Paul (formerly Saul of Tarsus), said about the matter. Identifying "the Transcendent" as God, Paul writes, "For what can be known about God is plain to them, because God has shown it to them. For his invisible attributes, namely, his eternal power and divine nature, have been clearly perceived, ever since the creation of the world, in the things that have been made. So they are without excuse" (Rom. 1:19-20). This indictment was preceded in verse eighteen by Paul's charge that unrighteous men have suppressed the truth of the universal awareness of God's existence. Paul argues that an eternal Being, with the concomitant power necessary to bring about a cosmos ever-compliant to His laws, is evident from an examination of the physical world. Undeniably sufficient proof of His existence is present in nature. Paul reasons that to deny God's existence is not a matter of ignorance but a matter of morality; those who deny Him are suppressing a deeply felt truth.

Suppose, if you will, we are able to pause the scene that began this chapter and create a still frame. Bright sunshine raining down unfolds a beautiful homogeny of spring colors as a stream cuts through the meandering ravine of uplifted rock and lush foliage lining either side. Alongside a deep pool, a man and his son cast their lines into the water. Six trout, perceived only by the father, are placidly suspended in the depths of the pool. The remainder of this chapter demonstrates evidence of "the Transcendent" through the lens of the scene we just described. This evidence gives us an indication of the nature of this awesome Presence—even if we cannot perfectly comprehend it.

NATURE AS A MEDIUM

In the story from my youth, nature is the agent of "mediate revelation," meaning it is the medium by which the Transcendent communicates its presence to humanity. On a much less grandiose scale, this book is the medium of revelation between me, the author, and you the reader. Mediate revelation differs from "immediate revelation," which is revelation that requires no medium for information to be exchanged. For example, I naturally know I ought not lie to people. This general and universal immediate truth requires no medium in order for me to know it. I have never met a rational human being who needs to be told we ought not lie, nor, inversely, have I ever met anyone who enjoys being lied to. That truth universally resides within every human being immediately, through what we call "conscience."

I believe a natural spring is one of the purest and most dynamic mediums to find the presence of this "Transcendent" in nature. Note that I am not calling this Transcendent "God" just yet, though the title at least warrants capitalization as attributes associated with God are coming to light. Obviously, the created order functions apart from us as finite humans. We did not create the physical and metaphysical necessities that were present the day my dad pointed out the six trout in the stream. Therefore, the animals themselves, the matter making up the stream, the intelligence imparted within the animals, the variant light spectrums, the colors absorbed and reflected that make vision possible, and the constants of physics (e.g. laws of density, inertia, nuclear forces holding each water molecule together, etc.), all point to something beyond our mediate senses.

Philosophically, however, if this Transcendent is the Creator of all these things, would it not be illogical if the creation did not bear His stamp and reflect His ordering? After all, it is impossible for any created thing to not convey some fingerprints, some clue, as to the nature and character of its Creator. Even an amoral world would say something about values, or lack thereof, of the One who brought it to be. Our cosmos points to a Transcendent Creator unbridled in power and intelligence, Who brought about its governing truths—some we understand imperfectly but can never replicate. Gravity and density, for example, are things we can't manufacture.

Without consciously thinking, let's do a bit of word connotation. What do you think of when you hear the word "pure"? How about "pristine" or "immaculate"? There is something enrapturing about the allure of a natural stream, particularly when we ascribe these adjectives to it. Its pristine setting and impervious flowing purity are enough to make the most sophisticated skyscrapers and technical marvels wilt in envy. However, they pale in comparison with those same attributes shared by its Creator. For who could know purity, let alone create it, but that which is the source and utmost fulfillment of purity? A something (or Someone) that possesses unadulterated purity as its natural being. Thus, like an artist that reveals something of his nature through his art, so, too, does the Creator of pure, "living" water reveal its perfect and pure essence through the medium of the creation. And even in this case, as vibrant and enrapturing as the stream may be, it is a creation and, as such, nothing but an incomplete facsimile and imperfect reflection of its Creator. Logic would agree that a created thing cannot reach a higher level of being than its source. (It cannot both depend on its originator for its being while mutually subjugating the originator to a state of contingency or dependence for its continued being.)

We call this kind of rational inference from creation to creator "induction." Consider even the most simplistic example, where one might take a sheet of paper and draw a five-inch vertical line on it. What does this simple line convey to its viewer? What can you rationally infer about its author? For starters, a psychologist might look at the location of the line on the page. Is it drawn in the middle of the page, indicating someone who is orderly and conservative? Maybe it is a bit off-center, representing one who might exhibit a fear of crowds and prefers the outside for a quick getaway—a loner perhaps? A psychologist might also examine the weight of the line drawn and pay particularly close attention to the depth and intensity of the pen's indentation. Perhaps the indentions into the surface of the paper lack consistency, reflecting an author who lacks confidence. And even yet, a neuroscientist might examine how straight the line is, or how much longer or shorter the line was drawn with respect to the five-inch rubric, formulating theories of how deliberately the artist works with the creative faculties he's been endowed. But most importantly, and this fundamental truth cannot be underscored enough, it tells you that this creator is relational and freely makes himself known. The creator, with full autonomy over pen and paper, could have decided not to create anything, eschewing any relationship with prospective viewers of the medium.

You can also apply the same creator inference analogy in other categories. Imagine you freeze your DVR or television during a baseball game just after a batter hits a home run. The screen displays only the ball landing in the stands beyond the outfield wall. What does this picture say about the hitter, the one who caused the ball to land in this location? He must be somewhat powerful to hit a ball over 400 feet. He must be intelligent to know how to perfect his swing and decide within milliseconds whether or not to start the process of swinging a bat at a ball coming at him at over ninety miles per hour from sixty feet away. He must be highly coordinated and precise with his movements. But the still image of the screen, of this ball landing over the fence, is not the person who hit it over the fence. It can't give us a perfectly clear understanding of the person responsible for the blast. But it can tell us a good deal about this person, and through inductive reason, we might very well conclude him to be Albert Pujols. We can also conclude it certainly is not Jacob Taggart.

Let's return to the portrait of the stream presented earlier. What clues or evidences are found within this vista that reveal, albeit imperfectly, marks of its Creator? Some Christians might refer to a biblical passage that affirms the clarity of God's authorship upon the created order from the book of Psalms. (*Psalms* simply means "songs," which are typically hymns of praise, thanksgiving, lament, etc.). The psalm-ist wrote, "The heavens declare the glory of God, and the sky above proclaims his handiwork. Day to day pours out speech, and night to night reveals knowledge" (Ps. 19:1-2). The most common applications of this Psalm are viewing the beauty of a sunset, observing the constant precision of each sunrise, and enjoying the enchantment of gazing up on a starry night to take in a canvas that the mortal observer could never recreate. All of those spectacles leave us in awe of a Being that had the power and intelligence to create them. So how, then, does the aforementioned Psalm apply to our picture of the spring? How is the glory and knowledge of its Creator revealed?

The sheer beauty of the scene tells me there is an even more beau-tiful Creator of the scene. The swaying of the flora to the rhythm of the wind, the contrast of warm air and cool water, the diamond-esque reflections of the water, and the raw power surging through the spring all converge to form a glorious beauty that no human or finite being could reproduce. However, beauty is, as they say, in the eye of the beholder. Beauty is subjective. So, while the splendor of streams like the Elk River, that gallantly cascades through stone diadems in west-ern Colorado, is sufficient for me to convey unrivaled glory due to its Creator, it may not be for someone else. Thus, we'll need to drill down a little deeper for more objective fingerprints of this Master Artist.

Three clear deductions can be made from this scene of the spring that point to the necessity of something Transcendent. These deduc-tions demonstrate what scientists call the laws of nature. First, consider the reliability exhibited by the water. Every drop, within every gallon, within every pool of this water exhibits the same properties. Every drop is consistent in its root elements, in its viscosity, and in its homog-eny. One doesn't see water droplets separate from one another—like sand, for instance. And deeper than that, the physics of the water mol-ecule reflects perpetual consistency in how the hydrogen and oxygen molecules always cohere together and never fall apart. This reliability and constantly predictable behavior of the perpetually-flowing water points to some standard that ordered it this way, something far more potent than I. I'm just a co-actor in the picture with the water.

Second, while density is something one seldom considers, it actually plays a vital role in this scene. Density, if you recall from middle school or high school science class, has to do with the mass of an object in relation to its volume, or how much space it consumes. Objects with the same volume but different masses will demonstrate different densities. Thus, my float/strike indicator (or "bobber," as my kids say) buoyantly rides along the top of the water, while my lure/fly (called a "woolly-bugger") sinks. Without constancy in density, I would never be able to get my fly down for the fish to observe and would be wasting my time even attempting to fish. If density were not orderly, it might result in my fly floating atop the water surface, while my strike indicator drifts five feet below it!

Third, without the consistent laws of gravity and inertia, fly fishing would be impossible. Casting in fly fishing is an art in itself, involving timing, balance, wrist force, aim, potential and kinetic energy, and varying degrees of tension. If there were no gravity, my line would take off endlessly into the sky when I lift my wrist. Too much gravity, and I could not lift the line into the air. If the laws of inertia were not static, then the tension and force required for the sudden 180-degree change of direction in trajectory from my backcast to my forward cast would be impossible to calibrate. The energy loaded into my rod and the kinetic energy awaiting a deployed fly line would be unusable without consistent forces of inertia.

All of these examples pointing to the necessity of the Transcendent fall under the umbrella of what can be regarded as the uniformity of nature. It is mightily fortuitous that the uniformity we find in nature allows us to confidently predict interactions in the natural world. The laws of nature do not capriciously change but give us certainty that water molecules always hold together, that people sink in the stream while strike indicators float on top, and that gravity and inertia act upon my line consistently every time I cast. These are just three obvious ways that this mental portrait of the spring declares the glory of its Creator. Ultimately, there must be something orderly to account for this order—some Transcendent source of this order that exists outside of its own design.

SENSING CONSCIOUSNESS THROUGH THE STREAM

Our particular portrait of the stream establishes that the order we find must be attributed to an Order-giver, just as the stream's beauty reflected the beauty of its Creator. Our next step is acknowledging that it is one thing for order to exist, but quite another for limited creatures like us to recognize it.

Let's attempt to tackle this concept by involving you, the reader, in an exercise. Imagine you are transported into this chapter's opening scene with my father and me. What is the first thing you would do? While you might consider walking to the water or snatching a fly rod for yourself, you would first assess the scene in your mind. That is, you would exhibit consciousness. Maybe you would begin by mentally asking, "Where am I?" Perhaps, upon perceiving the temperature, you would think, "It's hot." Next, after perceiving the unrivaled splendor of the stream, you might think, "Why aren't there more people here?" Before even making a move toward the scene, you intuitively determine whether it is safe to approach this father/son duo. Deeming them as either friend or foe is itself a conscious assessment the mind must make before you *can* move. Said another way, the will must be moved by exercising a conscious decision.

If we survey the scene sufficiently, we can eventually surmise that self-consciousness is a gift unique to us. The rocks do not wonder where they are. Even if consciousness is not determined by an object's physical actions, a nominal examination would conclude rocks don't actively respond to any stimuli, nor have any brain waves flowing. The flowing stream does not complain that the water's too cool and call back to the fountainhead of the spring to raise the thermostat. And the fish, even if they do display some degree of intuitive intelligence and are conscious of their surroundings, don't contemplate their responses as a means of the self-awareness requisite for self-consciousness. The fish might demonstrate general conscious awareness, such as the contemplation of a potential food item, but even a last-minute rejection is more akin to a tiny microprocessor that rapidly scans images of legitimate food stored in its database-like brain, but finds no matches. The fish don't stop and consciously wonder why the fly at the end of my line they rejected isn't included in their "safe food database." Nor do the fish rationalize their existence or weigh the morality of behavioral options.

Self-consciousness is not innate to, or restricted by, our physical existence. Therefore, if we die, the physical composition of our bodies remains the same, even if our consciousness is gone. Our dead bodies would become inanimate matter, similar to the rocks and the water.

One truth we can deduce from this portrait is that because consciousness does not have a material existence, the consciousness we display did not come from ourselves. Matter, by its nature, is inanimate, being defined as "physical or corporeal substance in general, whether solid, liquid, or gaseous, especially as distinguished from incorporeal substance, as spirit or mind, or from qualities, actions, and the like."[3] Logic would contend that we are imparted with this gift of consciousness from a Giver of consciousness, who must be conscious Himself. Moreover, if we examine the source of our consciousness from a logical and *onto*logical perspective—"onto," the Greek word for *being*, meaning, the existence or essence of something—we eventually discover all roads lead to this Giver of consciousness as the cause of *all* consciousness. That sounds like a big leap, but, in actuality, it's a necessary one.*

---

* Only an ultimate Being who is eternally conscious (i.e., unlimited in consciousness) can account for derivative consciousness exhibited by creatures who are, by definition, created beings brought into existence. Consciousness cannot exist independent of a being. All beings that come into existence in space and time are not only limited in power, knowledge, space, etc., but are dependent on something else for their consciousness, thus, possess a limited consciousness.

Consciousness is the starting point of knowing any kind of revelation or reality, but our knowledge, as creatures, is not eternal. Therefore, without eternal knowledge we cannot have eternal consciousness, and must derive our consciousness from an ultimate, eternal Consciousness. In addition to the self-consciousness that human beings uniquely practice, the general consciousness of other creatures through which they engage their environment must also be derived from a Consciousness-giver.

One might ask if it is logically necessary that there be one ultimate Source of all extant consciousness, positing whether there could be multiple sources for the consciousness we see exhibited in the physical world. However, the prospect of multiple eternal beings providing multiple origins of consciousness is a logically impossible one. The reason for this impossibility is that an eternal being is an unlimited being; and if there are multiple "eternal" beings, then they all are limited by the others, rendering them all no longer eternal. All the consciousness we find in the spring—whether it be humans, fish, or caddisflies—is limited on account of when it began, what it can know, etc. Therefore, our portrait of the spring does, in fact, beg for a sole Fountainhead of the consciousness we see.

I love the way the great theologian John Gerstner put it: "While in the stream of life, we are yet spectators of it. Now if matter could not produce plain life (mere animation), how could it produce a thinking being? How could matter, which has no life in itself, actually produce a life which can reflect on matter and tell it that it has no life in itself?"[4] Gerstner goes on to make the case, one we will visit in the next chapter, that matter is simply an effect. Likewise, our being and consciousness are not self-existent and are, instead, dependent upon an ultimate cause. For now, we will leave this first step by acknowledging our own consciousness is the fundamental building block to awareness of the Artist of the stream.

Consciousness alone paints a very opaque picture of the stream. Mentally, we can conceive the most beautiful spring imaginable, but it is not an actual spring in physical reality. Not only does it lack means for our senses to assess it, it lacks "being" altogether. Without our senses, a vehicle to perceive and appropriate the truths presented in the spring, we are like the men in the ancient philosopher Plato's allegory of the cave. In Plato's illustration, a group of people were bound to a wall of a cave in near utter darkness, with only a faint flicker of light available. They journeyed through life, able to see only their shadowy reflections on the wall of the cave. This limited experience formed their perception of who they were and what they looked like. Only when the allegorical cave-dwellers were finally freed and illuminated by way of the revelation of stepping into the light could they gain a greater perspective of their reality as human beings and that of the world around them. Unlike those prisoners of the cave, we've been gifted with illumination, whereby our consciousness, through means of the senses, manifests the revelation of the world around us.

Perhaps we can conceive of the most beautiful freshwater stream in the world. Or maybe we take it a step further, making a pilgrimage to what are reported to be the most beautiful streams in the world: the Green River in Utah, or the streams of South Island, New Zealand, or (according to my Twitter friend, Jordan Allen) the canyon stretch of the South Fork of the Snake River below Swan Valley in Idaho. But in order to assess the Transcendent nature of the stream reality before us, or even to deduce something ontologically greater, such as its source, some presuppositions must be inherently present.

First, we must possess senses to receive reality of this stream. Second, we must trust that the information being revealed to us is rational and reliable. And third, amongst other requisites, we must be equipped with means to categorize the revelation we receive in order to classify it as rational, as well as to assess the object of the revelation, the stream, as superlative in a comparative sense. In short, the fact that we have been created to reason and assimilate knowledge coherently begs for an intelligible Source of knowledge and, thus, to place our trust in that Source for the intelligible information it reveals.

During the eleventh century A.D., Anselm, the Archbishop of Canterbury, England, was heavily concerned with demonstrating the congruence of faith and reason. Anselm argued that revelation lies at the epicenter of truth, particularly those transcendent truths which precede human ordering and categories. Only by trusting in the revelation provided by an ultimate reality, Anselm postulated, would humanity be able to discern its coherence with the physical world.[5] Admittedly, this can be easier said than done. Anselm even conceded humanity's struggle to comprehend the holy Transcendent "because of God's brilliance and because of the soul's darkness."[6] Due to both our fallen nature that is inclined toward the unholy, and the finitude of human thought, the being of every human is so far-removed from anything holy that our cognitive conception of a perfect, holy essence is impaired.

Anselm contended, however, that just because humanity is clouded with unholiness, the rationality of revelation gleaned from the world around us is not negated. For example, that which causes motion or change, such as flowing streams, cannot be subject to motion or change itself. Our senses perceive the changing stream, and our minds, in spite of our fallen nature, can apprehend the rationality of an unchanging reality behind the stream. Nor do our human limitations mean that just because we cannot have a comprehensive knowledge of the Transcendent, we should simply hold to a childlike fideism (i.e., just believing something with no regard to intellectual understanding). What God reveals, according to Anselm, is never irrational, but is to be understood in an intelligible manner.[7] If we can trust in rationality, we can trust in its Source.

Anselm wasn't the first to wrestle with these issues. Before Anselm, the great Aurelius Augustinus, better known as Saint Augustine, was also occupied with demonstrating the validity of our senses, as well as the revelation and existence of the Transcendent. Augustine's theological and philosophical works are massive, and much of western thought to this day has been influenced by him.

In Augustine's day, many intellectuals and philosophers were concerned with the study of epistemology—that is, the study of knowledge—and how one acquires it. The school of thought known as skepticism was experiencing a resurgence. The skeptics held as a core tenant the belief that any ultimate truth could not be known, and nothing could be known with any certainty (which is a self-defeating argument, given that it states so *certainly* that nothing can be known with *certainty*). The skeptic also maintained the conviction that because our physical bodies are the mind's only connection with the external world and because we perceive the external world through our limited senses, our understanding of our context is flawed. After all, the skeptics argued, our senses are not perfect—vision, hearing, and touch are dependent on outside variables that can change relative to different persons—and they are, therefore, unreliable. Because our senses are untrustworthy and our perceptions might be illusions, skeptics claimed the only way of knowing anything is exclusively by our thoughts.

The skeptics' error is evident: a person could never increase in knowledge without a conduit transferring it to the mind. Augustine countered the skeptic's argument with the famous depiction of an oar used for a row boat. He compared the fluidity of our visual senses with an illusion that results from partially submerging an oar into the water. As the end of the oar is immersed in water, a mysterious phenomenon seems to occur: the oar appears bent! Of course, the oar is not actually bent, as it can be pulled out of the water to prove so. But as soon as the oar returns to the water, it appears bent again, an illusion created by the water refracting the light that informs the human eye.

Augustine marvelously used the illustration to note that, while his perception of the oar's shape can be wrong, perceiving it as bent in the water, he can still be confident that he understands the true nature of the oar. In other words, Augustine was saying, "the content of my perception may not be perfectly accurate, but I can still know I'm perceiving it."[8] And so, Augustine won the day by indicating that we can know truth through our senses, even if our perception is imperfect, and our understanding is not comprehensive.

Augustine's example easily applies to the stream. I have wasted many a moment in awe dipping the end of my fly rod in the water. Rather than appearing bent, the thin rod actually appears disconnected in the water. I know that image is not reality, that the rod is one contiguous piece—as is proven when I lift it out of the water. Stick the rod back in, and two separate pieces reappear. As Augustine pointed out, I know my rod is intact, even though my perception of it changes.

My youngest son, Jobe, like many eager kids in the stream, has much first-hand experience with this perception. Often when one wades in public streams, the trout see so many anglers that they lose their fear of the unknown and grow tamer. These trout, exhibiting some of the instinctive intelligence noted earlier, will come and suspend themselves immediately down-stream from anglers' legs because this placement enables them to expend less energy. At the same time, ironically, some fish sense protection and cover from the large object towering beside them.

On bad fishing days, the presence of these trout loitering in close-quarters appears tantamount to taunting. It can be maddening when the hunted taunts the hunter, especially for an eight-year-old boy who sees trout, right within reach, virtually begging him to grab them. But as soon as he reaches with the eager reflexes of youth, he ends up empty-handed and frustrated. Not only is the fish better-equipped and designed for an aquatic confrontation with a land creature, but the fish also holds an advantage, due to its actual physical location being slightly different from the location where Jobe perceives it from above the water. Thus, the place where he sees the fish and where he aims his mad grab is not the actual physical location of where the fish resides at that moment. Jobe knows the fish are there, as he can occasionally feel them as he gently kicks at them in frustration, but he falls short of grabbing one, partially due to the principle illustrated by Augustine's bent oar metaphor.

SIX FISH THAT POINT TO ETERNAL TRUTH

Augustine was not content to rest his case of only perceiving, albeit imperfectly, the presence of a Divine Being he called "God" inductively through the senses. Desiring a case that was airtight against his critics, Augustine understood that a higher degree of certainty existed in rational knowledge beyond sensory perception. Therefore, Augustine declared that there are certain truths that are always necessarily true, regardless of the existence of the physical or perceived world—truths like mathematics and logic. And thus, if the mind can recognize that these rational truths are eternally necessary, such as two fish plus four fish always equals six fish, then there must be a foundational source for these eternal truths, one that eternally sustains the truths that infuse and order the universe.

The sheer fact that people cannot avoid operating by these eternal truths given by an eternal mind means that while mankind can deny God religiously, it cannot deny Him philosophically.[9] Whether it be using math to determine the change the grocery cashier *ought* to return to us or using calculus to figure the dimensions for constructing a skyscraper, we have no choice but to affirm in practice the God who gives us logical and mathematical constants. The skeptic may attempt to use logic as a tool to disprove the existence of a Creator but, in doing so, defeats his case from the moment he places logic in his toolbelt—as logic itself requires a Creator. A chance, irrational universe cannot produce logic. This refusal to recognize the Transcendent's existence, despite affirming its everyday truths, demonstrates the apostle Paul's argument in Romans chapter one for the suppression of Divine reality. Thus, Augustine's appeal to the cognition of transcendent truths, particularly math and quantitative reality, can be easily applied to our portrait of the stream. Applying these truths will enable us to elevate the earlier sensory perceptions in the stream to quantifiable proof—proof that Something is, indeed, out there.

Going back to the opening scene where we receive our first sense of the Transcendent, you may recall that my father spotted six fish in the stream on that sunny day. But did six fish really exist? Prepare yourself because if you don't have a migraine yet, you might get one now. While we can rely on our senses that the fish were there, recording this historical fact as "six" fish is not real. Why? Because "six" does not exist; it is a number. Numbers are an abstract concept that possess no physical properties or physical existence. Thus, if I write in my daily fishing report that I saw "6" fish, the six on that page does not refer to something actually perceived; it is merely a symbol representing a quantity—in this case, a quantity of fish. I can touch these fish individually, but I can't touch the number "six," nor would deleting this symbol "6" negate the reality of the quantity of fish I observed. The point is, mathematical truths are real and constant, even if the symbols used to communicate this truth are not real in the visual sense.

Laws of mathematics, though not physical and tangible, exist as eternal truths that quantify relationships between objects. Thanks to the laws of mathematics, we know that the two fish plus the four fish equaled six fish, even before my father and I entered the scene. The sum is true whether or not there are people to count them or whether or not the objects being quantified are fish or rocks. That being the case leads us to the fact that laws of mathematics are eternal and immutable (not subject to change), given their independence of the physical world. Mathematics, like the aforementioned laws of physics and consciousness, points to a sole, foundational source.

Suppose I was to weigh one of the fish and the scale reads, "Three pounds five ounces." How is this number at all meaningful? Numbers function here as the non-physical truth, describing the relationship between two objects—in this case, the individual fish as a creature and the force imposed by gravity on the collective matter comprising the fish. But even if we are able to determine a weight, this number is useless, unless we have some means to objectively compare it. Is this weight small, average, or large? Should we brag about this one or throw it back and hope no one sees it? Thankfully, the laws of mathematics are consistent and able to be applied to other objects—in this case, other fish. By being able to use the constant laws of math and numbers, we can have some comparative perspective between objects such as fish.

Dr. Jason Lisle helpfully breaks down the laws of mathematics with greater clarity. Lisle deduces four corollary truths about the laws of mathematics: "They are (1) universal, (2) invariant, (3) absolute, and (4) abstract."[10] Math is universal in the sense that it is the same everywhere; two fish plus four fish equals six fish, whether in Bennett Springs State Park in Missouri or the Lower Redgorton on the River Tay in Scotland, or as it would be if there were fish on the planet Mars. Furthermore, whether the formula "two plus four" is depicted with English numbers or Chinese symbols, the answer is still the same.

The laws of mathematics are invariant; that is, they are immutable. The sum "two plus four equals six" is as true now as it was before people existed. It will be the same tomorrow and doesn't evolve. For that reason, Eratosthenes' calculations of the earth's circumference are just as accurate today as they were 2,000 years ago. Or consider seventeenth century astronomer Johannes Kepler, who applied mathematical formulae with remarkable precision to discover the orbits of planets before the planets themselves were ever discovered!

Mathematics are absolute in the sense that "two plus four" will not sometimes equal six but will *always* equal six, making calculations reliable and reproducible, such as the example of weighing different fish. And finally, numbers are abstract and merely represented by symbols, which is true regardless of the symbol used to represent "two," "four," or "six;" using Chinese symbols to represent these numbers does not alter their logical truth.

Lisle argues that when all of these factors are considered, it points to the undeniable conclusion that "mathematics were *discovered* by people and written down by people, but were not created by people."[11] Math and logic alike, then, are not products of the human mind as they precede human experience. Ideas and things invented by humanity across different regions of the earth exhibit variation in the design, pattern, utility, etc., but math and logic are constant. The consistency and objective truths of mathematics, which are uniformly obeyed by the entire universe, point to an absolute, self-existent Truth-giver—One Who is immutable. This One, as Augustine put it, eternally "speaks" the truths by which the universe is bound—analogically akin to the way a spring perpetually issues the water that encompasses its stream channels, binding the life therein.

The objective, rational truths of physics and mathematics further support our certainty of the perceptions of the Transcendent extracted from our opening portrait of the stream. In our earlier illustration, the medium of the spring pointed to three specific signs of the Transcendent: properties of water, density, and gravity/inertia. Using the uniform laws of mathematics in conjunction with the properties of water, density, and gravity/inertia, one can analyze the precision of the laws of nature to see how incredibly improbable it is that the universe came about by chance.

First, consider our observation about the properties and consistent behavior of water, how the atoms of a water molecule always bond together. For this to be possible, there must be some cause for the universal constant. Scientists have determined over 200 known parameters that must be met for a planet to support life.[12] Of the necessary parameters, physicists identify four fundamental forces that must be calibrated just perfectly—both individually and in harmony with one another—to permit these constant ratios that make life on earth possible. One such force is called the "strong force," the thing that holds the nucleus of atoms together. The universe operates with a constant strong force value of 0.007, a number that precisely allows for the existence of hydrogen, an element vital for water, amongst other things. If the strong force were just 0.001 more or less, hydrogen, water, and life, therefore, would not be possible. But the forces are also inter-dependent with each other. Consider the extreme fine-tuning necessary for the relationship between the strong force and the electromagnetic force (the force that bonds atoms and molecules together). If this ratio were to deviate by just .0000000000000001, the universe could not exist, let alone water molecules form. Just multiply 0.001

by 10^{16}, which is how mathematicians combine probabilities, and our number necessary for the universe becomes even more infinitesimally precise. This can be no accident.

Consider the matter of density, how it enables our fly to sink and our strike indicator to float. According to renowned physicist Stephen Hawking, if the density of the universe were to change by just 0.0000000000001 percent, the universe could not exist.[13] Talk about your strike indicator going under! Consider further how the laws of density impact elements differently, which, in the case of water, permits the formation of six-sided crystals when it freezes. This leaves symmetrical gaps, which causes ice to be less dense than water, which then makes pools freeze from the top down rather than bottom-up. A scenario of water freezing from the bottom-up would prohibit any life from surviving a winter in the stream. This can be no accident.

Finally, consider how the physics of gravity and inertia not only act upon our fly line, enabling us to cast, but also enable life itself. If the surface gravity of the earth were just 0.001 more, our atmosphere would trap excessive levels of ammonia and methane, precluding life. If this number were just 0.001 less, the atmosphere would be unable to retain enough water to sustain life.[14] But the kicker is the necessary relationship between the gravitational force we are presently concerned with and the electromagnetic force. Author Eric Metaxas indicates if this relationship was off by just one part in 10^{40}, ten followed by thirty-nine zeroes, the universe could not exist.[15] When all of these mutually dependent factors are taken into account, the quantifiable calculus necessary to produce our portrait of the stream is staggering. John Lennox, a mathematician from Cambridge, likened this precision to "the kind of accuracy a marksman would need to hit a coin at the far side of the observable universe, twenty billion light years away."[16] This could be no accident.

We could present countless more objective evidences of the fine tuning of the universe, but doing so would be superfluous. We have clearly grounded our earlier perceptions and deductions of the stream in eternal truths

The portrait of the stream at the beginning of this chapter reveals many truths: the intuitive truth of beauty; the truth of human consciousness; truths from our senses that we can consciously perceive; truths of the laws of physics that envelop us; truths that are rational, mathematical, and logical. These truths all converge to demonstrate there is something out there—some Master Artist at work on the canvas of our reality—the truth of a Transcendent.

The truths we speak of reflected in the stream are those truths "made clear to all," to which the apostle Paul referred in Romans chapter one. The evidence of these truths reveals that humanity cannot fully suppress this Transcendent Truth-giver. In ancient times, an "apostle" was sent out as an emissary of a royal figure to deliver a message. Rejecting the message was akin to rejecting the king. Likewise, an apostle, as used in the Bible, stems from the Greek word meaning "one sent out." While the term carries different meanings, such as the once-for-all office of twelve apostles commissioned by Jesus, it also, in a general sense, indicates one charged with delivering the message of Jesus. In a sense, objective, eternal truths like logic and mathematics function like apostles themselves, presenting a message from their Creator. This message, "shown to all," reveals the "eternal power" that has been "clearly perceived ever since the creation of the world," so that all who deny the existence of the Transcendent are "without excuse."

The motif Paul gives us reminds me of a story about a group of divers that, after removing some debris obstructing flow, set out to plumb the origin of one of my favorite places in nature, Bennett Springs near Lebanon, Missouri. Using every ounce of strength they had, descending eighty-five feet to the spring's orifice, the divers were unable to proceed due to the enormous current and pressure. However, they were able to partially view a submerged cavern, representing the spring conduit.[17] They aborted the mission, knowing the beginning of this spring lay beyond what they could physically perceive—a beginning they no less knew must exist.

I'm now forty years old. I'm now an adult and a father myself. Still, I cannot shake the memory of my own father sensing something out there in the stream but, to this day, refusing to see that Something beyond the stream and greater than the stream—the Master Artist to whom the spring points. My heart splinters into a thousand shards seeing my father suppress the truth about the Creator of the spring he so loves—the Transcendent that is wholly pure as it is purely holy. And like the polarized sunglasses my father gave me, providing me with "eyes to see," I pray that my Heavenly Father, the Transcendent I know and love as God, would clear my earthly father's eyes to undeniably see the truth.

Do you know someone like that? Somebody you love dearly and grieve over? Perhaps a trip to the stream together would do you both well to take in the truth declared by the theology of the spring.

Reflection Questions

1. Think about a time when you were confronted with a profound sense of a greater Being's existence (i.e., the Transcendent). Describe this experience and how it impacted you.

2. Which means of discerning the Transcendent is more convincing to you: sense perception from the beauties of nature; consciousness; or rational truths, such as mathematics and logic?

3. What can be found in nature that best declares the glory of its Creator to you?

4. How do intangible, yet rational, concepts like numbers and math make the case for a Divine Being? Is it possible for rational, absolute truth to exist in the universe without an absolute Truth-giver?

5. What are some works or things you have created that uniquely bear "your stamp" as the creator behind it?

CHAPTER TWO

THE ULTIMATE CAUSE: ALL SPRINGS FORTH

"The mountains rose, the valleys sank down, to the place that you appointed for them. You set a boundary that they may not pass, so that they might not again cover the earth. You make springs gush forth in the valleys; they flow between the hills . . . From your lofty abode you water the mountains; the earth is satisfied with the fruit of your work."

—Psalm 104:8-10, 13

"THEOLOGY!" THIS LONE WORD LEFT my mouth in a drawn-out gasp, like the remnant of steam slowly wafting off a pressure cooker. My fingers pulsated uncontrollably with a soon-to-be-released neurotic ecstasy. Strangely, just as the day's much-anticipated activities were set to begin, I stood momentarily paralyzed, wholly incapable of engaging the stream until first offering an oblation as a subtle act of worship. Squinting my eyes to a gradual close, I gently gripped my tool of artistry, my fly rod, in one hand while extending the other out toward the water, slowly swiveling my palm down to the surface. The stream rippling through my fingers gave me an instantaneous charge. Its touch and fragrance quickened my soul. My eyes opened. The bracing reunion between man and spring, weeks in the making, had finally commenced.

A man can lose himself in that stream. And in no time at all, time itself ceases to exist, relinquished into the image of its timeless Creator. Contact with its waters is a natural tonic. I've long felt that there is no greater way to observe the natural theology revealed by the Transcendent than through the living discourse of a natural spring. This chapter continues to examine the sheer beauty and theological truths exuded by our freshwater streams. Hopefully by the end of this chapter, readers will feel compelled to go discover those truths for themselves.

Now, upon reading this chapter's opening scene, you might reasonably ask, "If you believe a god or transcendent type is responsible for everything, including this pristine stream you so cherish, it seems silly not to just directly acknowledge this being as your act of exaltation. And why exclaim your devotion with a vague term like 'theology' if you've been chomping at the bit for two hours to start fishing? Just skip the ritualistic mumbo-jumbo and have at it!" These questions may resonate even more if you don't believe some other Being is responsible for the universe and everything in it, including this magnificent stream. These are fair questions. Allow me to address them before you go adrift.

First, we need to understand that the word *theology* comes from the combination of two ancient Greek words: *theos*, meaning "God," and *logia* or *logos*, meaning "utterance, sayings, discourse, or word." As *theology* developed into English, it came to mean "the study, word, or discourse of God."[18] Although there are many branches and systems of theology, "theology proper" refers to the study of the nature and attributes of God, the Ultimate Being. And as the Ultimate Being with no limitations, this Being reveals Himself in unlimited ways.

Someone wading into a stream joins himself to a natural canvas of sorts. Stepping into the mural of the stream, the fisherman unknowingly assents to becoming the subject of the artist. The subject then becomes encompassed by the artist's diverse handiwork of color, dimensions, and brush strokes. Similarly, I am moved to exclaim, "Theology!" upon entering the stream precisely because I clearly see the fingerprints of the spring's Artist all around me. However, I understand many readers are not convinced that there is a God, much less that He created this stream. This chapter will allow the spring itself to address these presuppositions.

I exclaim the word "theology" upon entering the stream as an invocation of thanks, worship, and praise to both the Artist *and* His art. Rather than a more wooden salute by simply saying "God"—granted, we aren't to the point of conferring this Transcendent the status of God yet—the address of "theology" issues a more elastic ode to the living God, given the abundance of natural treatises the spring declares about Him. It would seem rather myopic, perhaps even less worshipful, to generically acknowledge His being—a common act *all* men do. Instead, I revel in His multifaceted Authorship before enjoying His creation.

Concerning the second question: why even bother wasting time to offer praise for the Creator of the spring? The fish are rising in momentary frenzy, willing to hit anything, and may soon shut off like a light switch. Why not strike while the iron is hot? Why not simply begin fishing and enjoying the stream immediately, given the pent-up excitement garnered during the two-hour trip? The latter response would seem more practical.

The short answer is because I can do no other. The kind of effusive praise that begins the delight of a day spent in the spring could never express itself as a perfunctory sort of gesture or be regarded as a silly waste of time. Rather, it boils over as an inevitable procession from a heart filled with love for the object of its affection. When that object has a Transcendent source behind it, One that creates and perpetually sustains the pleasures I enjoy, I find that these pleasures reroute me back to their source. I cannot help but spout my delight in both the object of my pleasure and its Source.

The inexorable gushing of praise contained in the word "theology" is a microcosm of the spring that envelops me as I wade into its malleable realm. The stream's constant flow pours forth the sustaining power of the reality that abounds within its breadth, continuing without pause. Its nexus commands a rapt mystique from man, whose finitude prevents him from viewing it all with his eyes or grasping it all with his hands. Within me wells a limitless joy and delight from these "living waters." The beauty of this spring portrait holds my thoughts captive, viewing a masterpiece through the prism of creation that casts an indelible reflection of its Creator.

The spring and stream proceeding from it possess an organic way of fostering fellowship among its participants. There is a kind of dichotomous interest most fly fishermen display if fishing within eye/earshot of one another. On one hand, as we engage the stream, we activate our peripheral vision out of a genuine interest in the stream, like an unspoken duty of stewardship. On the other, if we are honest, we are looking around to see if others notice what we're hauling in. Or we're observing the haul of others. As proud creatures, we'd be lying if there wasn't even the most infinitesimal seed of envy behind our glances. But in between these two poles, those called by the theology of the spring understand the splendor of the stream and want to share the experience with others. We position ourselves not so close as to smell what the other had for breakfast, but neither so far away to obscure the visual purview of the success enjoyed by our fellow man or woman and, by extension, to determine what fly or lure they are using.

Not long after my moment of initiatory praise, I found myself in that kind of *koinonia*, or joint communal fellowship, one morning at Montauk Spring, a fly fishing stream that is the headwater for the Current River. I noticed a gentleman standing about twenty yards downstream, who was having about as much success as I. If you've never been fly fishing, mutual success is typically a disarming stimulus to conversation. But in our cynical minds and regardless of the other's true intent, we fishermen often consider it an outlet of proud patronizing when another who's been having success strikes up a conversation. Unfortunately, in my moments of frustration, I have been "that guy" who clams up and won't respond. I reached out to this gentleman— we'll call him Jerry—with the usual pleasantries, such as, "Where you from?" "How long you been down here?" "What are you using?"

Finally, after accumulating a bit of relational capital, I asked the man, "Jerry, you seem like a reasonable guy, who enjoys the true beauty in front of us. What would you say to someone if they told you there was no beginning for this stream—no source of this water, no fountainhead or spring where it all originates; it all just springs forth from nothing?" Jerry's eyebrows undulated with surprise, yet he didn't even move his gaze from his fly line before responding, "I guess I'd say they're crazy and then try to move away from 'em."

"Oh, I agree," I said, mending my line so as not to look too dogmatic and then, after a long pause, I asked him, "So why isn't it equally crazy when educated and common people alike claim that all complexities of nature surrounding us right now, all of the created world and all that is, came into existence without a Creator, Source, or cause?"

This question got Jerry's attention. He sharply turned his head over to me and, after momentarily struggling for words, he said, "I dunno . . . Sounds like you're talking religion, and that's a whole different area. Especially if you believe in some god."

Sadly, Jerry, and many like him, misunderstand that while the effects in the two analogies differ, we are not using a different argument. Rather, both analogies apply the same rule of logic concerning causation, or the law of causality that says that every effect (not every *thing*) must have a cause.

We will spend the rest of this chapter exploring this matter of causation. Just as everything that exists within the stream is dependent upon the spring's fountainhead, whose effluence delivers every point of physical presence, this parallel also speaks to the universe's ultimate existence and cause. Jerry is not alone. There are many like him who are inconsistent in how they selectively affirm logic. The logic inconsistently affirmed in this case is that *everything* that begins to exist has a cause.

One of the most fundamentally important questions anyone could ever ask is this: "Where did I, and all that exists, come from?" Sadly, as civilization increases in knowledge, many of the great thinkers of our day continue to offer nebulous answers to this question, dressed up in esoteric language and steeped in academic condescension that is devoid of common sense. The answer to this question, whether we consciously know it or not, penetrates the very core of our being.

The way we answer the question, "Where did I and the rest of the created order come from?" dictates our thoughts, our desires, our actions, our relationships, and our purpose for living.[19] The answer given most often today is some form of, "Everything that is, such as the universe, popped into existence from nothing." But does it really make sense that the most "sophisticated" scholars of our day, in all their hubris, would give such an irrational answer? It was against this kind of thought that ancient philosophers such as Parmenides asserted, "Ex nihilo nihil fit!" which, translated from Latin, means, "Out of nothing, nothing comes." As ancient as this axiom is, its truth is all the more eternal: if ever there is a point when nothing exists, then nothing could ever exist. Nothing can't produce anything but nothing. Make sense?

At this point, we'll zoom out of the spring portrait and our conversation with Jerry, while keeping the spring as our focus, as it provides an exceptional analogy for our question of causation and the source of all that springs forth. We will proceed by first studying the fascinating science behind the formation of springs in a field of study known as hydrology. This foundational instruction will allow us to better understand the spring as the cause of the ecological world that proceeds from it, serving as a springboard to examine causation at a larger level that develops a further basis for the necessity of an ultimate Creator (i.e., the Transcendent).

FRAMING THE PICTURE

Genesis literally means "beginning." We can determine our direct genesis by going back to our parents. We might take it back further and consult a family tree to discover the genesis of their parents and ancestors. We can even determine the genesis of reading this book by tracing our purchase back to the store (or, more likely, an online vendor), who can trace it to a storage warehouse, who can trace it to the printers, who can trace it to a publisher, who can trace it to my laptop. We can be certain that this book, like ourselves, had a genesis.

But the genesis of those things whose substance is beyond our creative capacity is more of a mystery. Take rocks, for example. Certainly, mankind didn't invent rocks. Nor did we invent the elements comprising rocks—such as calcium, magnesium, carbon, or oxygen; those particular elements comprise rock types such as limestone and dolomite that are the ingredients for "preincarnate" springs. The genesis of rocks and the matter they consist of could be rationally deduced to have come from a Creator. One might even argue that they had no genesis and are eternal. But what would be irrational, if not plain silly, would be to posit their genesis came from nothing.

Rocks are a part of nature. We demonstrated in chapter one the presence of the Transcendent revealed through the medium of nature. While the irrefutable truths of the Transcendent permeate nature, what it doesn't explain is how that nature got here. Using our earlier illustration, we might ask how the portrait of the spring made it to the canvas. In this chapter, we take it a step further by examining the genesis of this dazzling spring as a metaphor for answering humanity's most significant question: "What is the genesis of the universe?"

Imagine the closest thing on earth to nothing. I realize this sounds close to a contradiction, because one cannot imagine nothing without attributing some sense of being to it. But imagine a place of desolation—perhaps at the bottom of a barren valley. The air is still and bleak. If "apocalypse" had a color, this would be it. The only color contrast seen is varying hues of grey. It is motionless and lifeless. There is nothing around but rocks, thousands of lifeless rocks.

Suddenly, you sense the slightest quake from a couple of the rocks. A moment earlier, there was nothing but "sleeping rocks," as the great theologian Jonathan Edwards would say. There were no signs of movement, just a bleak landscape devoid of life or physical capacity. Nature had no pulse. Nothing. But instantly, out of nowhere and initiated by nothing on this side of reality, a couple of small stones quiver, and an orifice beneath is called to open by something on the other side. Out of this orifice oozes a slow trickle of water. Slowly, momentum builds, and this trickle begins to crawl further away from the opening along the valley floor.

The crescendo of this trickle builds as the Transcendent side, or the Transcendent that is there supplying this water, compounds its intensity and force. The clear fluid contracts and squirms, fighting with itself to be the first drops that breach the portal. A new reality shudders. A landscape, previously primordial and listless, now brims with motion, sound, color, and life. Then, like the scape of a spring lily emerging from the clutches of winter, the Transcendent sees the potential beauty this orifice can provide and blows it wide open. The pebble-sized outlet grows to the size of a softball, then to the size of a basketball, and, ultimately, to an aqueous cavern large enough to drive a car through. A spring has been born.

The birth of this spring, though simplified and expedited, was first perceived via the fracture, or pebble-sized portal, that connected our physical reality with that of another realm lying on the other side that supplied and sustained it. Consider this spring, from the perspective of the life that will flourish within it, as a kind of universe of its own. On one side of this confined universe lies space that is inflating exponentially—a new realm ballooning with water flow that forges its domain. On the other side is a relatively infinite mass of living water, supplied by a perpetual recharge cycle fed from far-off, unknown caverns, funneled to the portal where the never-ending flow of this pure matter exudes life to the other side of the orifice.

The analogy to our universe ends there. The water doesn't have "pure being," meaning that it doesn't exist by its own power. Instead, the water relies on a chain of causal events for its being. But the water's derivative being isn't the only thing that distinguishes its genesis from that of the physical universe, given there is more than just water on the other side of the portal. Other rudiments, such as rock and air and debris, also exist. On the contrary, the other side of our physical universe must be nothing but pure Transcendent, that wholly other Being that has being in Itself, infinite in space and unlimited in power to create the world on this side of reality according to Its perfect will.

HYDROLOGY AND THE FORMATION OF SPRINGS

The classic and technical definition of a spring is, "Any natural discharge of water from rock or soil onto the surface of the land or into a body of water."[20] While the discharge—or "resurgence," as it is also called (evoking a more theological tone)—is defined as a natural profusion, springs have fascinated humanity for millennia with their almost-supernatural mystique and ethereal connotations. Oft idyllic in setting, springs have nurtured the physical needs of people in almost divine ways with their unexpected emergence, appearing as a providential oasis to those nourished by its waters.

But how did this natural discharge begin? Many a child gazing deep into its blue void has asked this question. The point observable to the human eye where the water emanates is called the spring orifice, but like the cosmos itself, the source and power from this beginning point lies beyond what the eye can observe. The stream can metaphorically be considered a sort of a cosmos of its own, given all life abiding in it is contingent upon the orifice from which the life-giving water springs forth. The spring is the source of a self-contained, ecological universe.

It is not farfetched to say that the water boiling up from the spring comes from the heavens. Surface water from oceans, lakes, and rivers evaporates, bringing moisture into the atmosphere. Moisture also comes from trees and plants through a process called transpiration, where water that has been purified in the plant through photosynthesis is released back into the air by its leaves and branches.

Eventually, the moisture in the air condenses, forming clouds, and falls to the earth as rain. As the raindrops fall from the sky, they come into contact with carbon dioxide present in the atmosphere, which is dissolved in the raindrops.[21] Once the rainwater hits the ground, it will either percolate into the ground through multiple fractures beneath the soil; or, for those surfaces impermeable to water, such as rock and clay, the rain becomes runoff water that washes into streams, lakes, etc.

Gravity causes rainwater that does not run off to seep through the soil. As it passes through the soil, further absorption of carbon dioxide occurs through contact with decomposing organic material found in the soil. The chemical reactions produce a weak carbonic acid that is capable of dissolving certain minerals that act as bonding agents within areas of certain insoluble rocks, such as limestone and dolomite.[22] The most conducive topography for spring formation, such as those in Missouri and Florida, contain abundant limestone and dolomite layers of rock. The Salem Plateau, the geological formation of surface rock layer topography that encompasses most of southeast Missouri, contains the largest concentrations of springs in the United States.[23] It should be no surprise that the Salem Plateau—where marvels such as Blue Spring, Big Spring, and the White River in northern Arkansas are found—is laden with karst topography, rich in dolomite and limestone rock layers, extending thousands of feet beneath the earth's surface.

Karsts are areas characterized by porous surface rock and surface fractures, accompanied by subterranean rock that is easily dissolvable. The terrain of Israel, considered as one of the cradles of civilization from which much of humanity and world history has proceeded, exists with karst topography not too dissimilar to the Salem Plateau. Places laden with springs—such as Israel, Florida, and the Ozark Plateau—owe much of their geological makeup to the karst topography that undergirds them.

As the carbonic acid seeps further down through fractures in the rock, it dissolves a downward sort of tunnel through different rock layers. At the point it reaches a layer of non-dissolving rock where it can no longer flow downward, it begins to move and dissolve sideways in what becomes a sort of "rock highway" along this bedding plane. This begins another "genesis," a process called speleogenesis, or the beginning of caves.

Eventually, as more and more water infiltrates this rock corridor, its dissolution creates open cavities and pore spaces in the rock, permitting it to hold water. This formation is known as an aquifer. An aquifer is a water-bearing rock that is full of many holes that can absorb and hold water. Think of it as a hard, mineralized, underground sponge. The top level of the rock's pore spaces becomes air-filled, while lower levels become water-saturated as more water enters the aquifer. The point where these two saturated and aerated zones meet is called the water table.

Within an aquifer, often along bedding planes where two layers of rock meet, small, horizontal cracks are gradually dissolved and expand to the point of essentially becoming underground caverns and streams. As the stream dissolves and hollows out more rock, it creates enough air space to become an underground cave. While speleogenesis is a long process, often believed to take thousands of years, a number of variables influence the dissolving power, the most important of which is the level of carbon dioxide in the water. Steven A. Austin, for example, has demonstrated conditions present in the Cave Upland area of central Kentucky where a cave one-meter square and fifty-nine meters long could possibly form in just one year.[24]

The ground water contained within these underground aquifers moves constantly. Under typical conditions, this groundwater will flow in the direction of lower elevation. Ultimately, a spring arises when these aquifer "expressways" meet a point of entry on the land surface. This often arises when two land masses meet, such as when a valley intersects with the water table. Water from the aquifer is forced through this natural opening on the ground, rising to the spring orifice, and becoming the visible manifestation of the flowing stream. According to Paul Blanchard, Stream Program Coordinator with the Missouri Department of Conservation, the two primary means of water hydraulics are elevation (water moving downhill) and pressure (the sheer force of new water entering the aquifer moving extant water, sometimes even uphill or miles away, through its spring orifice).[25] Thus, we can now see all the necessary, causal events behind the orifice of the spring and sit in awe as water, and the world contained therein, springs forth. It is these causal events that mine the aquifer of natural minerals that are displayed in the spring basin like a natural gem factory. The vivid aesthetics captivate spectators as aqua, blue, and emerald hues rage from the deep. A spring's colors are dictated by the light absorbed and reflected by the natural minerals basking and shimmering in the pool.

The water springing forth from the spring may have taken days, weeks, or even years to reach the orifice from the time it entered the ground. Many springs have an extensive range from where they pull the water that eventually emerges. The overall surface area that feeds water to a spring is known as its recharge area. A recharge area extends beyond the typical watershed of streams. Just one inch of rainfall on one acre of ground can provide 27,192 gallons of water out of the spring. Paul Blanchard indicates, as a general rule of thumb for larger springs in the Salem Plateau, that the average discharge of a spring in cubic feet per second is roughly equivalent to the number of square miles of recharge.[26] So a spring like Big Spring near Van Buren, Missouri, with a discharge of 470 cubic feet per second, has a recharge area of around 470 square miles![27] Dye testing conducted by scientists has traced water emergence in Big Spring from sources forty miles away.[28] This pervasive breadth of a spring's recharge is all the more reason that stewards of this magnificent resource should be vigilant against pollutants.

Pause for a moment and consider the raw power that emanates from a spring orifice that has been channeled from the collective volume of a 470-square-mile recharge area. But it would be shortsighted to see the spring as proverbially "all brawn with no brains." It is nothing short of a stroke of brilliance on the part of the stream's Designer to utilize the brawn exploding from the origin of the spring to ensure its eventual survival downstream. In a confluence of mind and might, one of the sediments dissolved and dispersed through the dolomite aquifer is a flint rock called chert. Fortuitously, chert is not water-permeable. As pieces of chert exit the aquifer and are blown out of the spring, the spring's force distributes them downstream, where they settle in the streambed as a buffer to prevent any downward erosion or water loss affiliated with so-called losing streams.[29] Thanks to the chert acting as the water-proof pavement of the stream, fishermen are given many points of access to a sprawling natural amphitheater.

TAXONOMY OF STREAMS

Spring-fed streams can be organized in a myriad of different ways. For example, these streams can be classified by means of output type, output volume, the hydraulics influencing output, and even the temperature of output. A substantive examination of each type of stream falls beyond the purview of this book. However, due to the fact that streams can be enjoyed by all in numerous forms, a cursory treatment of stream types will follow.

There are four basic types of spring-fed streams categorized by their means of water discharge relative to their orifices. A seepage stream, also called a filtration stream, is a stream that is not a flowing, gushing stream (as the name implies) but appears as a pool of water pervading the ground due to perforations in permeable sections of the terrain. Thus, often after periods of rain, water percolates up and seeps into areas of the surface where these two layers (ground and water table) most closely intersect.

Conversely, the opposite of the seepage spring is what is known as a "losing" stream or "sinking" stream. In this case, the stream is drained by its orifices instead of fed by them. Losing streams become pirated when flowing over a porous layer of ground, which filters its water downward into an aquifer.[30]

A third type of spring is a fracture spring, which owes its opening to fractures in the rock near the earth's surface. Movement underground, due to plate tectonics or pressure from nearby fault lines, can cause surface and rock layer cracks that conduct water. As rock strata intersect, water contained within these fractures will flow from a joint in the rock to a fracture on the surface. Fracture streams generally emit a larger discharge than seeping streams.

The fourth type of spring—and the one that will serve as our exemplar for the remainder of this book—is called a tubular spring. A tubular spring emerges from a cylindrical-shaped orifice, fed by a vast network of conduits, carved through the aquifer. Essentially, underground caves, conjoining themselves to aquifers that can house enormous quantities of water, supply tubular springs with the splendid orchestration that channels sources from many miles beyond the resurgence. Renowned springs—such as the majestic surging power of Big Spring in Van Buren, Missouri, the largest spring in the United States, or Wakulla Spring in Florida—are tubular springs.

Springs can be classified by the volume of water they discharge, either in cubic feet per second or gallons per day. The largest springs are classified as first magnitude springs, which discharge over one hundred cubic feet per second (or 64.6 million gallons per day). The smallest magnitude in terms of discharge is an eighth magnitude spring, which discharges 0.00028 cubic feet per second.[31]

A spring may also be classified by its surface temperature as a thermal or non-thermal spring. Non-thermal springs maintain a surface temperature at or around the mean temperature of their sub-surface climate, generally around fifty-six degrees. Thermal, or hot, springs are springs with water that exceeds ninety-eight degrees.[32] These hot springs—such as those at Hot Springs, Arkansas, or the warm springs in the mountains of Colorado—result from water being heated as it descends through layers of subterranean hot rocks, where it ultimately surfaces before it has time to cool.[33]

The natural hydraulics present at a spring also provide a basis for classification. Artesian springs are typically marked with a fervent boil at their orifice, which is attributed to the pressure pushing the water through the aquifer to the confined exit point. A classic artesian well entails layers of impermeable rock both above and below the aquifer, and the pressure of the water entering the aquifer is so great that it forces water "uphill" through a spring orifice, exiting in well-type fashion.[34] So-called gravity springs occur when the water moves downhill and the water table intersects with an opening in the ground, such as that found on mountain sides. But the springs clamoring with the utmost mystique are ebb-and-flow springs, which have enamored onlookers for centuries; some have even attributed divine motives for their flow. They are known for sporadic water bursts and unpredictable surges of intensity where the water boils through the orifice. The pool of Bethesda, mentioned in the Bible in John 5:7, has been corroborated by archeological excavation and was likely such an ebb-and-flow artesian spring.

Regardless of the type of spring, they all have sprung forth due to a series of connected events on the other side of their orifice—causal events we can't see. I do concede that for all their exotic beauty, variety, and subsurface machinations, it seems almost crass to simplify the formation of these wonders of water as we have in this chapter for the sake of brevity. However, the question I posed to Jerry, standing in the flow of that tubular spring that is Montauk Springs, remains: "Does this water have a source or beginning?" From the waterdrop that evaporates, to the rain that falls, to the organic compounds in the soil with which it interacts, to fortuitous topography, to the crevice from which it seeps, to the aquifer through which it flows, to the minerals it liberates, to the caverns it digs, to the orifice from which it is released, a spring owes its existence to a far-reaching sequence of causal events working itself back. But who provided the raindrop to begin the cycle? That is where this near-perfect analogy fails on account of its finitude.

COSMOLOGY AND THE NEED FOR A CREATOR

There's Something out there. The chorus line of nature sings as witness to the truth that all springs forth from this Something. Things that have a beginning, logically, must have a cause. The spring had a beginning. Therefore, we may conclude, syllogistically, that the spring has a cause. Such is the classic Kalam argument for the existence of God, formulated by ancient Islamic philosophers. Variations of this logical expression have arisen, with the most notable being the cosmological argument for the existence of God developed by preeminent Christian theologian Thomas Aquinas. Aquinas developed his own argument that he felt, from an epistemological sense, afforded greater a priori knowledge of an Eternal Being. His cosmological argument can basically be summarized as follows:

The universe exists;

The existence of the universe has a cause; and

God is the cause.

Both forms of argumentation, Kalam and Aquinas, can be applied to demonstrate the causality necessary for the existence of the spring. Conversely, given the natural, inanimate elements that comprise the spring are also elements that make up the matter that fills the universe, the argument can apply to the existence of the entire universe. Let's wade in.

The spring exists. We know this from our senses. As philosopher Rene Descartes famously asserted, we *must* exist because we can think about whether or not we exist. You can't contemplate not really existing unless you actually exist in order to do the contemplating. You may contemplate a headache just thinking about that! But because we exist, we can also perceive the universe around us. We can feel the wetness and cold sting of the stream through our senses. We can identify the spring's unduplicated scent with our sense of smell. Our senses are our only connection to the universe around us that can tell us about it. Thus, to deny that the stream or that the universe exists would ultimately deny that we physically exist, making everything just an astral delusion.

The transcendent truth of logic also demands the truth we asserted earlier in the phrase *ex nihilo nihil fit*: that nothing can produce only nothing. As noted earlier, if there was ever a point in the plane of physical and metaphysical existence where nothing existed, then nothing could ever be. There would be nothing there to cause anything to come into being. Thus, the fact that you exist or the fact that you are reading this book means you and this book came into being, logically making the necessary case that *Something* had to exist before you and the book. This something must be infinite—to have always been there—in order for anything to be. Therefore, this Something must be self-existing.

Notice, however, we didn't say Something had to be "self-creating." Inexorably, that word is often used to describe how the universe came about. But upon closer examination, we can see that the idea is absurd because to be self-creating, the self would have to exist in order to create itself. This non-sequitur proposes that there is an identity associated with a being, which is necessary in order for it to come into being. It would have to be an effect without a cause and would be, and not be at the same time, a logical contradiction.

The rational dictum that most honest atheists and Christians alike would agree upon is that anything that begins to exist must have a cause. This is quite different than saying, "Everything must have a cause" because, as has been demonstrated, there must be Something beyond everything that exists that has always existed, Something that has the power of being in Itself. It must possess the attribute of *aseity*, existing in and of itself.[35] If it didn't, then It would be brought into being by another cause, which would make It an effect, thus which puts us back at the same starting place of determining the Being that must be infinite and the self-existing Cause of everything else. So, no, the point is not that every *thing* must have a cause, but rather that every *effect* must have a cause. And everything that comes into existence is, in essence, an effect that was brought about by a cause.

Equipped with this logic, we have before us the origin of the spring—or the universe, for that matter. We've shown why we can rule out the options proposing that they either really don't exist at all like a Matrix-esque illusion or are self-creating. We are then left with only two options: either the universe and the stream began to exist (and thus have a cause), or they have existed eternally. So far, this chapter has chronicled the origin of springs "in time"; thus, springs, being comprised of matter, are hereafter dismissed from exploring the proposed argument that matter exists eternally. So, can we find evidence that the universe began to exist, or is it eternal? The lynchpin lies in the answer because if the universe is not eternal, then as John Gerstner argues, "There would have been a time when it was not and when something or someone brought it into being."[36]

Hardly could a more profound question be asked than, "Where did I come from?" That question runs as deep as the bluest of hues sighted from the depths of all the ocean and springs combined. We will examine the eternality of the universe from three perspectives: philosophical, scientific, and last, so as not to be accused of begging the question right out of the gate, theologically.

Let's start from a philosophical perspective to examine whether an eternal universe is even possible. By "philosophical," we are not referring to the relationships between things and phenomena observed within the universe and then extrapolated back into time to formulate a speculative theory (despite the fact that no one was there to observe it). Rather, we mean applying certain propositions that *must always* be true, according to universal truths.

One is the law of non-contradiction. For example, a fish cannot also be a dog. Another is the law of cause and effect, which says that every effect has a cause. Casting your fly into the water (cause) creates a wave that ripples across the surface (effect). When I wade into the stream (cause), water is displaced from the space I now occupy (effect). I typically take a mid-morning breakfast break when fly fishing and have been known to displace more water after breakfast than before.

The philosopher William Lane Craig argues that logic itself precludes the actual existence of an eternal sequence of events. Dr. Craig couches his explanation using the term "collection," which is to say it is impossible to develop an infinite collection of things by adding to it because you would never be able to reach the end point and, hence, form a collection.[37] This impossibility applies to the future and the past. The events that have occurred in the universe that culminate in the present day, hour, and second are a collection and, thus, indicate the universe cannot be eternal.

Dr. Craig presents this argument in the form of the following syllogism:

The series of events in time is a collection formed by adding one member after another;

A collection formed by adding one member after another cannot be actually infinite;

Therefore, the series of events in time cannot be actually infinite.[38]

This argument can be rather difficult to grasp in our minds, given its esoteric terminology and our unfamiliarity with the concept of infinity. Two items of clarity may be helpful to better comprehend the argument. First, think of prior history as a sequence of events unfolding in a forward progression. Second, given anything that has a history exists as a collection, or series, of prior sequences that occurred one after another, it could not have just come about instantaneously as a whole. An actual infinite could not have a past.

Consider the following analogy using slack fly line. One of the cardinal rules of fly fishing is to control your slack line for the benefit of a fly's future presentation. The fly naturally unfolds from the slack as it drifts downstream. Suppose you spooled to your reel fly line that was infinite in length. The line extended on forever, all the way up to your reel. But with each passing day, you were required to release a bit more slack in order to "keep up with infinity."

The logical impossibility of this scenario is striking. If the infinite fly line comes to an end at the point in which "you hold the strings," then it cannot be infinite. The same is true for the universe. If the universe were infinite and eternal, then the present end point could never arrive. Or think of it this way: every time you snap your fingers, it marks the end point of all history. Nothing has ever come after it. Nothing, except for when you snap your fingers again three seconds later, which is now the new end point of all history. Nothing beyond this sequence, up to this point, has ever been observed. And so it goes . . . The end of our infinite fly line, just like the end of history that comes each time we snap our fingers, indicates that the universe can neither be eternal or infinite.

Eventually, philosophy and science intersect. However, materialists propose that matter itself is the pinnacle of transcendence—the stuff that is eternal. This belief avails itself to criticism, given the very nature of matter. Theologian R.C. Sproul aptly notes, "We know that the chief characteristic of matter is its *mutability*—it changes, and it changes from one state into another so that it is not stable, eternally, and therefore it is in *process*; it is in a state of becoming and not in a state of pure *being*."[39] Take, for example, the element of oxygen. It can change from a gaseous state to a liquid state and on to a solid state. Its state of becoming something else is predicated on outside variables and forces, which demonstrates the element's contingency (to use a philosophical term); that is, it is dependent on something else for its present existence. Everything in the observable universe is contingent upon something else for its present state of existence.

Before developing this necessary truth philosophically, let's back up from Dr. Sproul's comment for a second to understand, by way of logical necessity, why that which is eternal must also be infinite. Consider what must be true if Something is eternal: not only must It possess the power of being in Itself (i.e., is self-existent); but also, if eternal, It must be independent. We use the term "independent" to mean that this Being is not dependent upon anything else to exist; It is not contingent. If this Being were ever dependent upon something other than Itself, then it would be temporal and not eternal. This example illustrates why it is logically impossible for a deity to make a second deity to exist: one would be contingent upon the other for its existence, and by definition, could not be considered "god."

We are now able to make the logical progression that a Being that is wholly eternal and independent must be infinite. Infinity is necessary for this Being because an independent Being could not be limited by something else, lest it then be revealed to be dependent. If this Being were limited in any way by anything, it would be finite. Inherent with finite beings, there is an element of its being that is dependent upon something else. Finite beings are also limited by other finites and, like all finites, are not eternal.[40]

This discourse now brings us back to Dr. Sproul's point about the mutability of matter—how its quality of changing or becoming necessitates that it is finite and not eternal. But not only does matter fail to escape the quality of mutability, it cannot escape the reality of being brought into time, because there was a time "when it was not." Matter is subject to time and aging, but that which is eternal doesn't grow older. You can probably figure out the reason for this on your own: that which is eternal cannot age because it is beyond the confines of time. But we know matter decays and demonstrates signs of age. Therefore, matter cannot be eternal if it becomes lesser than it previously was. The corollary is Dr. Sproul's point that an infinite Being cannot change because It has nothing to change into. There is nothing greater to become, and there is nothing unknown to acquiesce toward.

Medieval philosophers took these truths and established an argument for an uncaused first cause of the universe. Applying the fact established above—that every object we have observed in the universe is contingent—the following syllogism was developed:

All objects observed to exist are dependent on some cause to exist.

An infinite sequence of causally dependent causes cannot be infinite, or else nothing would ever exist.

Therefore, there must be an uncaused first cause.[41]

Thomas Aquinas produced a well-known conception of this argument. The important philosophical point made is that a circular, infinite cycle of contingent (think "created") objects is a logical impossibility because they could never come into existence because there can be no beginning point for their causality. For example, people cannot indefinitely trace back their ancestors person by person without end because in such a scenario, the people doing so would never come to exist! There can be no infinite regress. While the argument stops short of ascribing the uncaused cause to be the God of the Christian Bible, it does use philosophical reasoning to dismantle the argument of an eternal universe, or eternal matter, as a byproduct.

Many scientific laws contradict the idea that matter is eternal. These universal laws transcend human or creaturely intervention. The laws of physics help explain through proven hypotheses, interactions between matter and energy within the universe, including "space and time configuration."[42] We cannot tinker, say, with the laws of centrifugal motion, so that an action may not arbitrarily require an equal and opposite reaction. These immutable laws not only require an immutable Lawgiver, but they must have been in place for human life to even be possible, let alone perpetually sustained.

Take, for instance, the First Law of Thermodynamics, which says that matter cannot be created or destroyed. Matter and energy can only be converted or changed, so this law clearly explains there is no new energy or matter coming into the universe. There is exactly the same amount of matter and energy in the universe now as when it began. Easy enough, right? The epiphany comes when the Second Law of Thermodynamics is introduced. The Second Law of Thermodynamics reveals that all forms of matter and energy will continually proceed to lower levels of usefulness.[43] Thus, the universe is in the process of winding down its supply of usable energy; and if the usable energy is decreasing, then science and logic intersect to conclude that the universe cannot be eternal. Such a construct is completely rational, given laws of causality are affirmed by effects *becoming* lesser than their cause. As demonstrated above, what is eternal is never "becoming"; it simply "is."

Therefore, since matter and energy cannot be created nor destroyed, it only devolves to a lower level of utility. As British philosopher Samuel Clarke once remarked, "Matter only has the power to continue in motion or rest,"[44] which is to say that matter cannot act or will. For example, a carbon atom, via its nature as contingent and dependent for its existence, does not have the inherent power to cease its decay. Such contingence does not discount other processes, such as ionization or atoms gaining or losing protons and electrons. But even in those instances, atoms do not move to a higher level of being. The fact that matter observably deteriorates evinces it is finite and has a beginning.

The aforementioned reality of the universe's regressing energy also coincides with observations of astronomers and physicists about the expansion of the universe. The theory of an expanding universe was introduced by Albert Einstein within his theory of relativity and later proven to be true, via new insights yielded by the Hubble Space Telescope. The significance of the discovery was what the expansion of the universe implied about its origin. If the universe is expanding, then the corollary must be that it had a beginning. Said another way, for something to move outward, it must have a nexus. Einstein concluded his finding by commenting, "I now see the necessity of a beginning."[45]

If Einstein's work helped lend empirical credibility to the logical conclusion that matter is not eternal, what if other scientific evidence exists to facilitate the cosmological shaking hands of philosophy and science? Einstein is not the only genius physicist to deduce a beginning of the universe from the physical and meta-physical evidence at hand. Arno Penzias won a Nobel Prize for his discovery of cosmic background radiation that pointed to a locus of creation for the universe. And what was Penzias' comment? "What I ought to find I did find—a finite universe."[46]

Even as recently as January of 2016, an article appeared in the *BBC News* titled, "Largest Ever 'Age Map' Traces Galactic History." A colorful map of the galaxy traced the movement of stars. One line in the article says it all: "It confirms what was already suspected about our galaxy's growth: it started in the middle and grew outward."[47] As recent as the news was, it confirmed the same truth Einstein found decades before: an expansion necessitates a beginning.

Perhaps the most compelling evidence comes from theoretical physicist Stephen Hawking. In the late twentieth century, astrophysicists began to observe that the universe has been outstripping the gravitational counter force, which has resulted in an accelerated rate of expansion. Hawking sought to make sense of this data and began applying it to Einstein's field equations of general relativity. Hawking's data led him to conclude that if one could go back far enough in time, there was a point in the universe where there was zero spatial volume. At this point in the beginning, no matter or energy could have fit into a "universe container" because it had zero spatial volume. A physical reality with zero spatial volume means that neither time nor space could exist. Curiously, we are left with a point where there was no universe. We are left with nothing.

Hawking's findings provide a segue as natural as a mountain spring to our third means of evaluating the eternality, or causality, of the universe: the theological perspective. Fittingly, Hawking's conclusion ends where the Bible begins. If one is to talk about the origin of space and time itself, logically, one needs something that exists outside of space and time. The theological perspective presents, through the sacred text of the Judeo-Christian Bible, a paradigm that has always perceived God this very way. At this point, the theological perspective must be admitted, like a strike indicator floating atop the water keeping your lifeline from sinking.

On its very first page, the Christian Bible establishes the foundation that all its subsequent truth claims are predicated upon. This first page answers the primeval questions, "Who am I, and how did I get here?" The Bible begins in Genesis 1:1 with the statement, "In the beginning God created the heavens and earth." The statement implies that time, just like the physical order, is a created thing that came into being by God acting as the first cause (cf. Titus 1:2). The Bible does not ask, "Who made God?" It assumes from the beginning that such a question is irrational, that a self-existent Being that has always been there is implicitly necessary. Later, in the New Testament Gospel of John, God is described as a spiritual, non-physical Being (Jn. 4:24) that has the power of self-existence (5:26)—attributes matching the profile established earlier by logic. Therefore, this theological perspective, thus far, squares with what our philosophical and scientific reasoning has concluded: that a self-existent Being, One that we cannot observe, given He is spiritual and not physical, brought the created physical universe into existence at a point in time as the first cause for all that we observe.

The Christian Bible proceeds to personalize the self-existence of God through His self-disclosure—that is, how He reveals Himself. Obviously, God existed before humans and, therefore, before language. An eternal, independent Being must also, by necessity, be omniscient, meaning "all-knowing." There can be no language that God cannot understand. How telling and profound, then, is the name of God as first revealed in Exodus 3:14—enigmatically translated as a first-person, present-tense verb (meaning that it is not completed)—"I AM WHO I AM," or "I am the ONE who is," and, later, shortened to "I AM." The English language equivalent is the imperfect verb "to be." In the original Hebrew tongue, pronouncing the third-person form of "I am" (which would be "He is" in English) makes the sound of the word "Yahweh," which was revealed to Moses as the ineffable proper name/noun for God—although, the Hebrew language didn't use vowels, which were inserted later). To the Hebrew, the meaning in changing a verb form "to be" to a proper noun was clear: God is that which just *is*.

So, God giving His name as an infinite, uncompleted action conveys the heart of His very being as self-existent. Rather than communicating a name for Himself as a noun, such as "Creator," or an adjective, like "Mighty" or "Powerful," He more accurately reveals a name that is, basically, "Is" or "He Is," a verb connoting an uncaused, unending, and unchanging action. By way of revealing Himself using a term wholly different from traditional human nomenclature, the name of the God of the Bible, though awkward linguistically, speaks to the very essence of His being. God's name proclaims the very necessary eternal Being that must exist outside and above the universe, fittingly similar to what we concluded earlier must have always existed in order for it to be possible for anything to exist now. Therefore, we can conclude that the theological perspective has much to contribute to the discussion of what caused the universe to spring forth.

With a barrage of reasoning flowing as seemingly forceful as a first magnitude spring, we can safely concede the evidences presented point to a universe that is not eternal. But given the universe is all we observe and given it requires a first cause, how do we explain its existence if out of nothing, nothing comes? Something eternal has always had to exist in order for something as massive as the universe to be here now. We need that Something to explain us—Something not like us finite creatures.

God is that Something. He cannot be like us. He cannot be finite. Therefore, God cannot be physical. He must be infinite, eternal, independent, omniscient, and omnipotent. Encapsulating all of these descriptives is the overarching essence of God; He must be holy. But in order for these attributes and essence to be deduced by us, in order for you to read the words in this sentence, He must be. The Transcendent must exist.

We have now come full circle in the discussion with my friend Jerry that opened this chapter. We have seen how irrational it would be to posit that the stream did not have a beginning, demonstrated from multiple perspectives. The stream, in all its grandeur, is not eternal. There was a time when it was not. And then, beyond the realm of observation, where creative forces were orchestrating the spring's arrival via subterranean machinations unbeknownst to us, the spring came forth in an instant. The universe, like the spring, has been demonstrated to not be eternal and, thus, followed the same script: One second, there was nothing. A second later, all springs forth. To suggest the universe came from nothing would be irrational. It would also be irrational to suggest it did not have a cause. And at this point, we have no rational basis to continue cloaking the source of all that springs forth as an abstract Transcendent and will begin referring to Him, hereafter, as "God." May the theology of the spring teach us more about Him in the pages to come.

Reflection Questions

1. Jonathan Edwards said, "Nothing is what sleeping rocks dream about." What do you think he meant by this? What do you picture if you close your eyes and try to imagine nothing?

2. I described the colors of the spring rather poetically, saying they "rage from the deep." Describe a time and place where you have seen a beautiful array of colors "raging"?

3. I indicated there cannot be an infinite regression. How far back can you trace the "cause" of your personal existence through ancestral lineage? If you could trace your family line back to the first human, would it give you greater confidence in the existence of a Creator?

4. How does the truth that every effect must have a cause help you understand the necessity of a Creator? Does this truth give you comfort or trepidation?

5. Where and when was the last time you took in the raw splendor of the spring? How would you describe the natural spring you visited? To help ensure you and your family and friends don't miss out on one of these natural wonders, I have ranked the top ten freshwater springs to visit in the United States on the following page. If you live near or are traveling in the vicinity of one of these marvels, do yourself a cathartic favor and visit one. (Note: rankings are for large magnitude, cold-water springs only. Springs were ranked based on factors such as raw beauty, history, wildlife, flora, activities, and distinctive naturalistic elements.)

Top Ten Springs to Visit in the United States

(in Ascending Order)

10. Coldwater Springs—Minneapolis, Minnesota: The first American settlement in Minnesota, the site was originally home to Native Americans. A remnant of the original springhouse remains. A blend of quaint antiquity meeting natural aura.

9. Alley Spring—Eminence, Missouri: Known for its pristine setting as the epicenter of a community, only a historic, old millhouse remains as a lasting picture of a spring's vitality.

8. Blue Hole—Wimberly, Texas: A botanical fantasyland, this natural swimming pool is guarded by Cypress trees that line its banks and entice visitors to swing from their ropes before making a splash.

7. Kitchitikipi—Manistique, Michigan: The name, given by Native Americans, means, "Mirror of Heaven." You can walk out onto a dock to gaze down to the emerald floor of Michigan's biggest spring.

6. Giant Springs—Great Falls, Montana: One of the country's largest springs hosts abundant bird life, hiking, fishing, and nature tours. Panoramic, breath-taking scenery abounds.

5. Manatee Springs—Chiefland, Florida: Get lost scuba diving within the liquid terrain of turquoise that flows into the Suwanee River. Whether you are watching deer from a nature trail or fishing from a kayak, this spring seems to have escaped the clutches of modern, commercialized accoutrement.

4. Big Spring—Van Buren, Missouri: A spring iconic for its power and might, you won't find a gushing water boil that compares to it. Few wonders of nature will leave its spectators with such ambivalence of intrigue and self-frailty. If you seek to take in the raw, unbridled power of the spring, this is the place to go. A walk-in cave adds to its mystique.

3. Mammoth Spring—Mammoth Spring, Arkansas: As family-friendly a spring as you'll find, its sprawling stream branches slice through grassy plains, manicured like a golf course. Whether fishing, strolling through the herb garden, or viewing the old train depot, you won't want to leave.

2. Niagara Springs—Hagerman, Idaho (Thousand Springs State Park): From the incredible scenery of cascading waterfalls, to legendary fishing spots brimming with steelhead, to the scintillating mountain air feeding your lungs on a horseback ride through the mountains, this spring and the outflowing Snake River will make you question whether you've truly lived.

1. Wakulla Springs—Wakulla Springs, Florida: Looking into this azure spring will leave you believing its floor is lined with jewels. The deepest spring in the world unpacks huge fun from its orifice through the myriad of aquatic activities it provides. A perfect blend of aesthetics and attractions. Diverse wildlife, such as manatee and alligators, complement a diversity of recreational activities, such as snorkeling, fishing, and boating. A burgeoning population to the north, however, threatens to rob this spectacle of its glory.

CHAPTER THREE

PURE CHANCE? DESIGN
IN THE SPRING

And God said, "Let the waters swarm with swarms of living creatures,
and let birds fly above the earth across the expanse of the heav-
ens." So God created the great sea creatures and every living creature
that moves, with which the waters swarm, according to their kinds,
and every winged bird according to its kind. And God saw that it
was good. And God blessed them, saying, "Be fruitful and multiply
and fill the waters in the seas, and let birds multiply on the earth."

—Genesis 1:20-22

I EXHALED A SURVIVOR'S SHAKEN breath upon finding solid footing. My face, anemic in fear seconds earlier, quickly rebranded itself
to a full-orbed hue of triumph. I felt a resurgent victory after crossing
the stream. Most fishing excursions worth the effort must be this way,
it seems. Whether accessing the south fork of the American River in
California, the west fork of the Black River in east central Arizona or,
in my case, maneuvering to a ripe location on the Eleven Point River
in south central Missouri (home to some of the best blue ribbon fly
water in the Midwest), the reward requires the risk.

One could say this was treasure hunting of a different kind. The
reward in this hunt was a natural-born rainbow trout in spawning
season, its coloration a radiant brilliance not normally seen in nature.
The risk was crossing the stream to reach the side of the river that
afforded a covert perch to launch my stealthy approach in hopes of
landing one of these beauties. The kind of real estate along the bank

necessary for such a staging area isn't overly common, making it, too, an object of the hunt.

I had hiked about three-quarters of a mile through head-tall weeds and jungle-thick brush. There was no trail, so I was left to swat branches out of my face with one hand and protect my fly rod with the other while trudging through marshy sloughs. But just reaching the stream was not the end point; then I must choose to go up or down stream in hopes of finding a riffle shallow and narrow enough to cross.

On this particular day, I had traveled along the bank upstream about a quarter of a mile to a spot where I had crossed in the past. The crossing point was at a bend in the river, where the current was swift but not overly deep—at least not according to my perception. Herein lies one of the fisherman's cardinal rules of thumb, one that is not unlike the high-paced technological world in which we live and are exhorted to escape from time to time: the river is always changing. I found that out the hard way, challenging the river to surrender the other side of the bank to me.

If you've ever seen the movie A River Runs Through It, the scene where Paul (played by Brad Pitt) "goes all in" to land the catch of a lifetime was not unlike my crossing the Eleven Point. In this particular scene, Paul hooks a lunker of a trout and follows it into the bosom of the stream, cascading over rocks and deep pools to keep up with the fish before it can outstrip his line. You see Paul completely disappear into the current, fully submerged, and you think all hope is lost, until a right hand penetrates the water's surface to keep his fly rod intact. At other moments during the epic pursuit, you see only Paul's wide-brimmed Stetson floating down the stream, until his head miraculously pops up attached to the hat. Ultimately, he lands the giant fish, and his brother, Norman, concludes he had just witnessed perfection.[48]

My crossing of the Eleven Point on this day was far from perfection. I certainly did not recall the current being as fast and strong as it was. More importantly, I didn't recall the water being belly-button high; when I crossed before, it was only knee-deep in the same spot. I struggled with each step to gain the balance and footing necessary to advance one step closer to the other side. Like Paul, I held my fly rod high above the water to protect my only weapon. My fishing vest swung frantically from my neck like a grandfather clock, the pendulum swinging with each step. With the slick-stone bottom as an accomplice, the sweeping stream finally got the upper hand, catching me in mid-stride and sweeping me off my feet.

I went under once but managed to uncoil my feet beneath me (all the while keeping my rod unscathed) and launched myself into a series of lunging jumps, until I landed in ankle-deep water, where I staggered off to the bank. Freighted with saturation, I felt water sloshing my toes in the bunkered feet of my waders as I keeled over to catch my breath. I used the moment to take an inventory of vest supplies that might have survived the deluge. My only loss was one of my four fly boxes. This unplanned bath reinforced an axiom that Matt Moline, fly fishing guide for Steamboat Flyfisher in Steamboat Springs, Colorado, once told me: "There are two kinds of fly fishermen: those who have swum and those who are about to."

Regaining my composure, I steadily crept upstream, scouting for an ideal location, where the stream could be harboring these wild trout. My reconnaissance had to take place from a bit of a distance, given how easily wild trout are spooked. Their acute eyesight enables them to see upward and outward at a ten-degree angle above the water's surface. I eventually sighted an eddy formed by a boulder in the water. Crouching by the bank, I decided to dead-drift a Brown Harvester midge impersonation right into the eddy. Once I was close enough to see the depths of the stream while remaining hidden from the fish, I made three fruitless casts. Then, I adjusted my strike indicator to drift the fly five feet below the surface to approach the fish at their deeper holding level.

Knowing the challenge of landing wild trout, I wasn't expecting immediate results. But on the first cast after my harvester fly sank five feet, it hit. Bam! In an instant, the strike indicator was sucked fully beneath the surface, and the fight was on. Like an unbridled horse, the wild rainbow trout fought relentlessly for its life. Three times, it jumped out of the water, flashing its scarlet splendor with the smooth, powerful grace of a pirouetting figure skater. My heart pumped so hard with frantic fear that the fish might spit the hook with each jump that it could have flushed all the water from my flooded waders. But three minutes later, the fish was spent, landing placidly in my net.

The real treasure I had sought was now uncovered. Surrendered in the net was a marvel of nature, a creature designed with an unfathomable precision matched only by its exquisite coloration. The green top of the fish took on a forest hue that conjures the lushest of vegetable gardens. The color gradually transitioned to the middle of the fish, where its jaw-dropping beauty was on full display. True to its name, the fish glowed like scarlet plasma had been spread across its body. The ruby color looked all the more pronounced this time of year as the males become more vibrant in appearance to attract a mate. Glistening in the morning sun, this sight was the treasure I had come seeking. This was my witnessing of perfection. However, as perfect as this rainbow trout was, it spoke all the more about the perfection of its Designer.

TAXONOMY OF TROUT

The purpose of this chapter is to move from the abstract and theological/theoretical to an up-close, tangible examination of the life within the spring and how it bears definite evidence of a Designer. Conveniently, we don't need to travel to some exotic location to find some rare creature, equipped with some extraordinary design feature. We need only zoom in and pause the picture of the preceding scene on the Eleven Point River. Within this still frame, we can view the undeniable purpose uniquely programmed within each creature that can be spotted. In short, the reader is exhorted to get out of technological idleness and get up close and personal with the creation bearing the unequivocal design of its necessary Creator. This chapter will provide bountiful evidences of design within the residents of the spring, some so fascinating in their intricacies that it boggles the mind to consider how what we consider "lesser life forms" possess such biological specificity. The best place to start is with the "crown prince" of the spring: the trout.

There is no dearth of treasure found within our natural streams. However, the trout—an aristocratic animal in both manner and reputation—certainly has a claim on the top prize. Both sleek and strong, the trout utilizes both red and white muscle types at different times for the utmost swimming and breathing efficiency. As tenacious fighters, they are an adventure to watch every time a lucky angler hooks into one. A most scrupulous feeder and adherent to a natural diet, it is not easily fooled. This predator entails brains, beauty, and brawn. Trout can also live in community with non-competing fish in a symbiotic manner that serves their self-preservation. Treasured for numerous reasons, trout are found all across North America in different species.

Their sleek, missile-esque shape, relentless fight, dietary cunning, and array of colors make trout a favorite game fish across North America. A person's location in North America often dictates the species of trout that can be found, given the multiple types of North American trout that are often localized. A salient starting point before delving into the interesting characteristics of the design of my most beloved trout, namely the rainbow trout, would be a short introduction to the primary types of trout found in North America.

Brook trout were once the only native trout of the eastern United States, and they still flourish in the smaller streams. They are known by their green backs, which can vary from olive green to dark green; yellow spots; and orange/red bellies. Brook trout are native to many eastern states in the United States, evidenced by the fact that nine states designate the brook trout, or some sub-species of it, as their state fish: Michigan, North Carolina, New Hampshire, New Jersey, New York, Pennsylvania, Virginia, Vermont, and West Virginia. However, "brookies" have been introduced in a number of western states, sometimes at the detriment of local trout in those areas. A beautiful fish—thanks in part to its contrasting colors—brook trout are not generally among the hardest trout to catch, and do not grow as large as other species. A typical decent-sized brook trout will be seven or eight inches long.

If measured by the number of states claiming it as their state fish, the cutthroat trout would be the second most popular trout, as six states claim it as their state fish: Idaho, Montana, New Mexico, Nevada, Utah, and Wyoming. As can be seen from the states claiming it, the cutthroat trout is primarily a western and Rocky Mountain trout. The cutthroat gets its name from the red, horizontal line running below its jaw; ruddy gill plates; and an oft-red or pink underbelly. Cutthroats are adorned with black spots sporadically splashed across their tan body. Many sub-species of the cutthroat exist, giving it a very wide range in size from twelve inches (Rio Grande Cutthroat) to commonly over thirty inches (Lahontan Cutthroat).[49] A favorite of the Yellowstone and Snake River communities, the cutthroat has long-served as an indigenous western fish, identified as early as 1541 by the Coronado Expedition in Northern New Mexico on the Pecos River.[50] The Lewis and Clark expedition in 1805 also identified the cutthroat. Meriwether Lewis, camped near Great Falls, Montana, described cut marks under the lower jaw in "trout 16 to 23 inches in length."[51]

Perhaps the most powerful and difficult trout to catch is the brown trout. It is not native to the United States but was imported in the latter part of the 1800s from Scotland and Germany.[52] Brown trout have been introduced in various parts of the United States and can be found in most states—particularly the Midwest and western states—but also in the larger rivers of the East. Their bodies are a yellowish-tan with lighter-colored bellies, decorated with almost psychedelic black spots, eclipsed within larger, reddish-orange spots. Known to prefer nocturnal feeding, browns can tolerate warm waters with less effluence, like the White River in northern Arkansas or Lake Taneycomo in Branson, Missouri. They are even found in large lakes like Lake Michigan. Brown trout commonly reach twelve to fifteen inches and can exceed forty pounds.

Some consider the golden trout to be the most beautiful of all trout. A high-altitude mountain fish that favors cold water, golden trout are indigenous to only two small regions within California's Kern River basin in the Sierra Nevada Mountains.[53] The golden, a descendant of the rainbow trout, has since been introduced to other high-altitude areas, such as the Wind River Range in Wyoming and some mountain lakes of Montana and Colorado. A seamless blend of coloration starts as olive brown on its back and turns to golden brown near the belly. The fish also mixes in a coral stripe and a large mass of crimson covering its gill plate with relatively few spots. The arduous task of just getting to golden trout makes them a favorite among sport fishermen who love a good challenge. Most natural golden trout rarely exceed nine inches.

Another highly localized trout, found only in the White Mountain stream system of Arizona, is the Apache trout. The state fish of Arizona, the Apache is also considered a sacred animal by the White Mountain Apache Native American tribe. The introduction of rainbow, brown, and brook trout in the early twentieth century decimated the Apache Trout population, but conservation protections have preserved the fish to a stable population. The Apache looks similar to a brown trout, though it has fewer black spots and is a more homogeneously tan or brown. Apaches rarely exceed nine to ten inches.

While the Apache trout population is rare, but stable, an endangered, but beautiful, trout is the bull trout. It resides in the Pacific Northwest, British Columbia, and Alaska. The bull trout looks somewhat similar to the brook trout, with its dark-green-to-deep-blue back, yellow spots, and orange-to-red belly. However, bull trout, while rare and considered to be a threatened species, grow considerably bigger than brook trout, often exceeding twenty pounds in lake environments. Bull trout can be voracious predators, using their large, torpedo-shaped heads to ambush smaller fish.

Similar to their bull trout cousins, the lake trout is prevalent within the northern latitudes in lakes of Canada and in the colder glacial lakes of the northern United States. Lake trout spend much of their lives in deep water, one hundred to 200 feet below the lake's surface, coming into shallow water of twenty feet or less only to spawn. The dark charcoal coloration of their backs illustrates the depths where they dwell receive little sunlight. Yellow-to-white spots speckle the fish, including the belly. Lake trout commonly reach twenty pounds but can reach fifty; and given their size, they are often sought as a commercial food fish.[54]

Our final trout species commonly sought and observed in North America, the muse and inspiration for this chapter, is the rainbow trout. The rainbow trout, as one can deduce, gets its name from the dark-to-light rainbow coloration of the fish. The rainbow takes many forms, and color can vary by diet and habitat, but their chromatic brilliance typically runs from deep forest green, with a hint of deep indigo, to an alkaline violet, to a broad pink band that runs the length of the fish down its side, dissipating to a white belly. While the derivation of the fish's common name is obvious, its scientific name has its etymology from Russian nomenclature, as the rainbow trout is native to eastern Russia, where they were scientifically specified in the early 1700s.[55] Rainbow trout are also native to the Pacific Northwest, though they have been robustly introduced in locations throughout the Rocky Mountains and as far southeast as Georgia. Rainbows can further be found in Mexico, South America, Europe, Australia, and even Iran and Turkey, which have become the fastest-growing trout producers in the last twenty years.[56] When mixed with other trout species, such as brook or brown trout, rainbows are consistently observed to exert dominance.

Rainbow trout are prolific fighters, known to jump several feet out of the water several times after being hooked. They tend to prefer swift water. Their grit, fastidious appetite, and culinary appeal have made them an extremely popular game fish. Seafood Watch considers rainbow trout a best choice for consumption.[57] The rainbow has become a bastion of commercial freshwater fisheries, as their ability to easily propagate in hatcheries makes for an ideal "anchor tenant" within state-sponsored and private trout parks, lakes, and streams alike, as well as fish farms for restaurants. Rainbow trout commonly reach twelve inches, and fish exceeding three pounds are generally considered large.

Even larger than the rainbow is the anadromous (sea-faring) version of the fish called steelheads. They are the same species as rainbow, the difference being that they leave freshwater streams, where they are hatched, and migrate into the ocean, where they adapt to salt water by a process called smoltification. Steelhead spend most of their lives in the ocean, only to return to the freshwater stream, where they were born, to spawn. Naturally, steelhead, with larger prey in the ocean to eat, grow bigger than rainbows, as some can exceed fifty pounds. Moreover, the salinity of their environment also dictates a different coloration than rainbows, with steelhead leaning toward a more metallic silver color.

In a cursory manner, you've just been introduced to eight members of a family. All eight members were introduced from afar in the pages of a book, instead of inspecting them close-up within the pools of their home waters. There are more than these eight species of trout, but these are arguably the most esteemed in North America. All eight are uniquely crafted to operate within the natural abodes in which they are created. And in spite of their unique nuances, their commonalities not only point to a head of the family, but also to a Head Designer. To better see the hand of design and calibrated intellect required to make the labyrinthine components of a trout function, we now turn to an up-close examination of one member of the salmonid family: the rainbow trout. Upon review, it will become clear that the fish didn't think of its exquisite design on its own, nor could its complex, interacting specifications result from chance.

DESIGN OF THE RAINBOW TROUT: MADE FOR ITS ENVIRONMENT

By now, you've probably noticed that this book has taken you on a tour through various "ologies." We've studied hydrology, geology, ecology, and cosmology, with an over-arching emphasis on how they all relate to theology. We now continue our trek through the "ologies" by venturing into another "theology" that I love: ichthyology, the study of fish. That only sounds natural, using ichthyology as a platform to connect to theology, right? In fact, we're not even done invoking Greek philosophers, since ichthyology began with Aristotle over 2,300 years ago.[58] During our short digression on ichthyology, we'll make a brief stop at an ancillary, yet connected, "ology"—entomology, the study of insects—given the vital role insects play in the spring and to trout. Along the way, you'll probably pick up some fun facts about fish and other life supported by the spring that you never knew. Let's begin!

We explored the life-giving quality of water in the previous chapter, making it an ideal entry point to the manifest specifications of life engineered within. For starters, you can't have rainbow trout without water. Water is not only a biological prerequisite for trout, but the physics of water make it the most amenable environment for them to flourish. For example, because water is denser than air—800 times denser—fish are able to move through water with minimal obstruction from the forces of gravity. In fact, trout are buoyant-neutral, meaning they have the same density as water (thanks to self-regulating, internal equipment, such as swim bladders) and, therefore, have no wasted motion in counteracting gravitational force, blessing them with precise mobility to avoid predators, find food, and navigate the stream.[59] Fish can generate more force swinging their tails and fins against water than what they would create pushing against air. What a fitting environment for a creature to live!

Another physical property of water that is beneficial to fish is its incompressibility. Air compresses as an object moves through it—think of a car barreling down the highway. All of the air occupying a space right before the car doesn't have to be completely shoved out of the way, but, rather, some gets compressed along the hood and sides as the car moves through it. Water, on the other hand, does not compress like air and must be displaced for something to occupy space within it. The incompressibility of water, however, creates turbulence and carries waves, which fish use to their advantage. Water's greater density and incompressibility explains why sound carries faster in water than in the air (4.8 times faster) and also explains how fish are "serendipitously" equipped to live in water. Why? Because fish have such an acute sense of hearing that they can detect any sound or vibration through the water. A clumsy fisherman clomping along the bank sees trout scatter before he even reaches the water. The crashing of his feet onshore passes from the ground to the water, where fish are sensitive enough to detect its vibration.[60]

One might ask that if fish don't have ears, how do they hear or detect sounds and movement in water? Fish may not have external ears, but they don't need them, given their body tissue is equal density with water and, thus, permeable to motion waves. But fish do have inner ears. The inner ear of a fish functions similarly to mammals, with a fluid cavity surrounding tiny hairs, moved by tiny bones that sway pursuant to water/wave displacement. The hairs are connected to nerves, which inform the brain of sound that passes through, enabling the hairs to balance the fish in three-dimensional space. But even more extraordinary is the external sensory equipment fish possess called "the lateral line," a faculty that functions like a sixth sense.

The lateral line is an amazing biological mechanism that allows fish to detect multiple forms of vibration through minute receptors lining the horizontal (lateral) body of a fish. These receptors, similar to tiny hairs within protective gel sacs imbedded in the skin, pick up the most sensitive motion. The lateral line is connected to nerves that transmit information to the brain, telling fish not only of the size of the water displacement, but also the direction, so that a trout can be alerted to the presence of prey or danger without even first seeing it. If you've seen the Discovery Channel, you've probably seen giant schools of brilliantly-colored fish demonstrate uncanny synchronization by maneuvering on a dime, whirling in unison as they collectively change direction; you've seen the lateral line at work.

In our earlier vignette of the Eleven Point River, we saw a number of things: a creeping angler-assassin, a beguiling water flow that seduced him to near-disaster, a boulder manipulating the current's route, and a glassy stream surface that served as a natural periscope for its subsurface residents. Ultimately, what we didn't see—fish fluttering about for cover—speaks loudest to their undeniable design for such an environment. Such a picture provides a remarkable witness to the design of trout and how they are able to use the water in which they live for maximum survival efficiency through the incredible engineering of their lateral line. I don't think the trout thought of that on its own. A trite answer is to attribute this stellar programming to "natural selection," which is to say, the trout we see today are there because they adapted to survive by using this lateral line. But is that really the case? We'll address natural selection in greater detail later, but for now, two brief points are warranted.

First, natural selection can act only, contingently, on information already *provided to it.* Therefore, natural selection can't select fish with lateral lines unless the blueprint within the DNA is *already* there to create trout with lateral lines. Therefore, to say natural selection causes the design of the lateral line commits the post-hoc logical fallacy of assigning a causal relationship to two successive, but unrelated, events and, to a lesser degree, begs the question (assumes its truth rather than proving it). That misunderstanding is like a consumer walking into a fly shop that selects only green-colored waders for their floor inventory and concluding the fly shop causes waders to be green. As an aside, I've also found the appeal to natural selection curious, given that ontologically, natural selection has no being, yet it's often ascribed personal, purposive motives—qualities appropriately attributed to a Transcendent Designer.

Second, this discussion moves us right up to the point of divergence between evolution and design. One fundamental distinction is in order before we go any further: the difference between macroevolution—referring to how the first life form of an animal came to exist (or to chemical evolution, as a subset that explains how the first cell originated)—and microevolution, referring to changes within already-existing life forms. The latter we don't deny: rainbow trout and golden trout had a common ancestor, much like a dog and coyote.

Microevolution, with its corresponding speciation, is real; but macroevolution, such as a dog becoming an alligator, has not ever been demonstrated. We will see that evidence of systematic intelligence found in DNA, epigenetics, and the statistically impossible means of the necessary protein arrangements essential to build life discredits macroevolution. And, as we have already seen in chapter two, logic necessitates a Creator as nothing comes from nothing. The design and inarguable intelligence seen in the life found in the spring continues to guide us to the truth from its Designer.

We would be remiss to not address one final "convenience" that makes water amenable to the sustenance of trout. Water is one of nature's most reliable solvents, whose physics permit copious compounds and elements to dissolve within it that, in turn, imbue the fish with nourishment. The most vital of these is oxygen, which is concentrated much more scarcely in water than in air. Humans need oxygen, too, but all they have to do is breathe it directly out of the air as the atmosphere is full of it. But in order for fish to breathe and, therefore, survive, a sophisticated device is needed to extract the soluble oxygen from the water. It is here that we see the brilliant engineering of the fish's gill system come into play.

If you have children and have completed step one of parental due diligence by taking them into the outdoors to view fish, or even to an aquarium, you've likely been asked, "But how do fish breathe underwater?" If you were like me as a child, a simple answer to the tune of "because they have gills" isn't sufficient. Why? Because gills are a foreign concept, an organ we have no familiarity in using. What are gills, and how do they work? For years, I never understood how these gills enabled fish to breathe underwater. I just knew that they did.

Simplistically, gills are rows of cartilage that can be exposed by the fish through opening and closing the gill slit on the side of its body, typically behind the head. They are the epicenter, where oxygen exchange takes place. The gills are essentially plates (gill filaments) lined orderly on top of each other, like an extendable sieve that marshals the flow of water. The retractable quality of gills is possible because each is adjoined to what is essentially a hinge bone. The surface of each gill is lined with tiny, raised spurs that look like "breathing teeth," which are called lamellae. These lamellae protrude outward on the top and bottom of the gill plate and contain numerous small blood vessels that are lined with precise, linear directional flow. The blood vessels run as close as possible to the lamellae surface, exposing them to the water that flows through the gills. As you might imagine, these lamellae are extremely fine, as one study indicated that a trout weighing one pound possessed twenty-three lamellae per millimeter.[61]

But why would the minuscule size of these lamellae be important to fish? Think about it: the more lamellae a fish has means the more points of contact it has with the water that carries oxygen. And here is where the genius of the lamellae design reveals itself. Rather than exposing blood vessels to the water, where a fish would bleed to death, the surface of the lamellae is covered by a thin mucus membrane that allows oxygen to pass in but prevents blood from flowing out. A cross-current pattern further designs the outstretched lamellae for exposure "against the grain" of water flow, so that, as water passes over the lamellae in one direction, the blood vessels exposed to this water current are flowing in the opposite direction.

Picture it somewhat like a cheese grater: such a design doesn't function as well if the cheese and the grater are moving in the same direction. Likewise, the cross-flow design of these lamellae work harmoniously, so that, as water passes over the blood vessels, the counter-flow facilitates a steady stream of oxygen, which is sifted from the water by diffusion through the cell membranes on the surface of the lamellae and transported directly into the fish's blood. Even more remarkable than this system of underwater oxygen exchange is the fact that rainbow trout have been observed to increase or decrease the number of lamellae used to collect oxygen commensurate with the oxygen levels in the water. That is, in low-oxygen water, fish deploy more lamellae, and in high-oxygen water, they deploy fewer.[62] Can a blind process think up this ingenious design of gills or how to measure oxygen in the water for optimal lamellae utilization?

As the preceding three examples of neutral buoyancy, lateral lines, and intricacy of gills demonstrate, trout appear to be "made" for the water. But the all-too-fortuitous features of a rainbow trout, the treasure of the stream, don't end there. Even your first glance at a rainbow trout, partaking of the sight of its raw, figurine shape, speaks to its design. How so?

In the year 2000, I was surprised by the long-awaited release of the new album *Kid A* by the band Radiohead, who had not released an album since their epic release *OK Computer* in 1997. In *OK Computer*, which I consider one of the greatest albums of all time and ahead of its time, the pervading theme laments a society desensitized to human needs by turning to a cold, synthetic lifestyle, which deems technology superior to human relations. The message of disconnectedness wrought by a digital world deeply resonates with me and many people today. But a line from Radiohead's first single from *Kid A,* called "Optimistic," curiously stated, "The big fish eat the little ones/ The big fish eat the little ones/ Not my problem give me some."[63] This newfound lyrical apathy to the plight within the organic world surprised me. However, the fact that big trout eat the little ones doesn't surprise me, as their sleek physique, ballistic head, shard-shredding mouth, and quick mobility speak "predator" to the world in which they reign.

The rainbow trout is known as a rover predator. Its torpedo-like shape affords an aerodynamic design to cruise through the water like a racehorse. The larger rainbow trout get, the more they graduate to larger prey, where their slender build allows them to swim with the utmost agility and speed to overcome and ambush prey—like drifting insects, bottom-dwelling crustaceans, and smaller fish. Many fish that are not as nimble, and so more likely to become prey, are designed with thicker scales to give them a layer of armor protection. However, heavier scales come at a cost—carrying the extra mass slows the fish down, making it more of a defender, versus a predator of other fish that lurks on the offensive. Trout, as roving predators, were not designed with heavy scales but, rather, have very fine, light-weight scales that help them glide through the water swiftly when on the attack. Even the rainbow's tail (caudal) fin is fork-shaped to enable greater swim velocity. Can such purposive design really come by accident?

Rainbow trout are uniquely beautiful fish with their svelte design and coloration, but they are also individually unique. Trout are like snowflakes: each one has different spot patterns and markings, even siblings hatched from the same nest (redd). Not only are trout individually unique in their spotting and design, but according to James Civiello, Hatcheries System Manager for the Missouri Department of Conservation, trout are able to change their coloration. Trout contain melanophore cells in their skin, which are basically receptor cells that adapt the trout's skin color to its environment. For example, the melanophore cells may darken or lighten a fish's skin based on the degree of sunlight a trout is exposed to. Civiello noted that trout become darker when living in more densely populated quarters. He recounted an experiment he did in a fish hatchery, where he added five light-green rainbow trout to a hatchery tank with 3,500 other dark-green rainbows. The more dark rainbows he subsequently added, the darker the original five fish got, evidencing how their melanophore cells adapted.[64] The process where skin cells change color to adapt to the environment is called crypsis. Is it reasonable to believe that this background-matching feature just "happened" by random, undirected means?

Population density does not act as the only agent to influence trout coloration. A fish's diet can also significantly impact its color. Civiello noted that trout, such as those in the Eleven Point River, are more likely to have a ruby red appearance due to their diet of amphipods (freshwater shrimp called scuds) and isopods (exoskeleton insects).[65] Conversely, fish raised in hatcheries reared on commercial food pellets are more likely to appear more opaque silver/violet in color. Dr. Gary Grossman has noted that red, orange, and yellow colors in a fish are most heavily produced by compounds called carotenoids, which do not occur naturally within fish but must be acquired through diet, specifically found in crustaceans and amphipods.[66]

A third way that trout can change their coloration is that which was briefly hit on at the beginning of this chapter, given males will change to a brighter hue in order to impress or attract a mate. This phenomenon is really not much different than hyper-hormone teenagers, who may dress more provocatively or flamboyantly for attention. When male trout *are* mature enough to spawn and fertilize eggs that the female trout lays, they must first get "picked" by a female to fertilize her eggs. Why the need for a competition? Because a female trout's eggs become permanently infertile if not fertilized by a male's sperm (milt) within thirty seconds of the eggs' release. Likewise, a male's milt is dormant if released outside of water and, once it is released within the life-supporting water, becomes impotent after twenty-to-thirty seconds when the sperms cells die. So, there is a brief, thirty-second window, where fertilization between a male and female must occur and when, obviously, a male and female trout must be near one another.

So how does a female trout pick a male? Sometimes, by the most aggressive male that runs others off from the female. But often, "the ladies" are stimulated visually by the most vividly colored male. So, in order to "get picked," male trout will undergo a seasonal color change called sexual dichromatism, whereby their colors become brighter in order to increase their chances of getting noticed by a female. Sexual dichromatism comes as a catch-twenty-two for some fish, because higher visibility for mating can also mean higher visibility to attract predators. This is seldom an issue for trout, who are typically at the top of the food chain within the water but can draw unwanted attention from herons and other birds of prey.

Dichromatism is not the only change that occurs to some male rainbow trout during the spawning season. Dimorphism refers to a seasonal change in body shape, but it also occurs during the spawning season. Dimorphism is most clearly seen in male rainbows (and many salmon species) by the enlarged "hook snout" that juts out from the bottom jaw. These hook jaws are called kypes and, essentially, have no purpose other than to aid a male trout in biting another would-be suitor to a female it is trying to impress. Typical men, right? Though not fully, the kype recedes after the spawning season, only to grow back during the next spawn even larger as it extends beyond the foundation of the previous kype. Thus, older males can often be distinguished by their larger kypes to better bite off the competition. An impressive design!

The intricate design features displayed by trout do not just end at the spawn. The fruit of the spawn, "alevin," also exhibit imaginative features too elaborately equipped to be attributed to some arbitrary happenstance. When fertilized eggs hatch within the underwater gravel beds (redds), the infants that emerge are called alevin. Given their size, the alevin would be an easy meal for most any species of life within the stream if they were to swim away from the concealed protection of the redd. Thus, alevin are conveniently born with an attached yolk sac that provides them with ample food and nutrients for their first fifteen days of life, while they abide under the gravel in the safe confines of the redd. After fifteen to twenty days, when their yolk sac has been absorbed and their mouths and digestive systems have matured to enable the intake of live food, the alevin emerge from the gravel as small, baby trout, called fry, that swim up the water column to age/size-appropriate food. Aided by the sensory equipment they come loaded with, the young fish can now begin feeding on zooplankton, small insects, and even algae.

Is it reasonable to believe that an indifferent, impersonal force thought up the extraordinary design of the alevin's yolk sac that enables its survival? In fact, if natural selection were to be attributed to this design feature, given we are told that it acts on random, adaptive changes over a long period of time, too much time, in fact, would elapse before this feature could be implemented for the fish's survival. Said another way, the fish would die from starvation or from predation long before the duration of mutations might produce this equipment.

The yolk sac screams design from the depths of the spring, as an ode to an intelligent Designer.

As trout mature from fry to adult fish, they do so with the aid of various innate sensory tools that guide them like an "invisible hand," to use an economics term. It behooves us to examine the sensory equipment and faculties of trout as further evidence of their inimitable design. The trout's sense of sight, smell, taste, and even inexplicable inorganic senses testify to its impossibility of chance engineering. These uncanny senses stand alongside internal systems reliant upon the joint existence of other systems like the circulatory system and thermal/floatation regulation that operate as if they were independently programmed to maximize life. And these programs are in place and operating in the earliest stages of the fry.

Consider how the sense of sight might be uniquely customized for this animal. We mentioned above that juvenile fry trout feed on commensurate prey, such as zooplankton that are very minute in size. That trout have color vision, similar to humans, and utilize rods and cones within their retinas for discerning light is impressive enough. But more impressive is the light spectrum trout are able to utilize for commensurate life stages that far exceeds the capability of human vision. Ultraviolet (UV) wavelengths, just beyond the violet spectrum, cannot be seen by humans—we see only the effects caused by the presence of UV rays via sunburn. Trout, on the other hand, possess UV-sensitive cones that are able to see UV light. However, this UV vision is only temporary and, according to recent research, is retained only up to the trout's infant (parr) stage.[67] After a trout grows beyond a few inches long, its UV-dedicated cones are mysteriously switched off. Why would this be? What point would it serve in the trout's betterment for its Programmer to shut off an advantageous trait?

Remember the saying, "Thank God for unanswered prayers"? It is akin to admitting our creaturely lack of foresight and perspective, where the providence of history teaches us that something we encountered that initially appeared detrimental turned out to be for our ultimate benefit. So it likely is with trout that lose their UV vision after the stage of life where they need to feed on tiny plankton. Why is this significant? Because while UV light does not significantly broaden a trout's visual spectrum, UV light does cast visual contrast on planktonic food targets, enabling the small trout to better see the food they need to thrive at an early age.[68] But as trout grow beyond this stage, their UV vision is providentially removed, for they begin to transition toward larger prey to facilitate their growth and caloric demands and thus no longer need to feed on plankton. Additionally, trout are more likely to school together in tighter quarters when they are still in the small parr stage, which yields greater safety in numbers. UV rays are believed to enhance reflective motion communication among schooling fish—another benefit most necessary for their early stage in life.[69] The inexplicable design of a trout's utilization of UV light commensurate with their life stage is incredible to comprehend. Is it rational to conclude that such improbable sophistication and intricate design just "happened" on its own?

The temporary utilization of UV light is not the only trick trout have up their sleeve to demonstrate their Transcendent design. Their additional visual furnishings make it all the more befuddling how such a "simple creature," relative to humans, can have superior visual senses, seemingly designed for their environment. Take, for example, the fact that trout are sensitive to polarized light, which assists them during dusk and dawn as their cones and rods are receding to adjust to increasing/decreasing light. A 2001 study noted that juvenile rainbow trout discerned prey at greater distances in polarized light.[70] Humans, on the other the hand, need the assistance of polarized sunglasses in order to see polarized wavelengths.

Any fly fisherman can tell stories of seeing a trout spot a quarter-inch fly on a size eighteen hook from fifty feet away, when humans have trouble seeing this fly well enough to tie it on their tippet line from three feet away. This is possible because the ovular shape of the trout's eye enables it to simultaneously focus in the front and to the side. It has near-perfect peripheral vision at all times to be on the look-out for both predators and prey. Better yet is the shape of the trout's pupil, which is similar to a raindrop lying on its side with the forward notch pointing at the trout's snout. This design feature, unlike the round human pupil, better allows the trout to inspect potential food located in front of it to discern whether it meets the brain's archived image standard of natural food (good to eat) or unnatural (avoid).

The final apparatus that distances the vision and design of trout from humans is their "third eye," which is called the pineal gland. A trout's pineal gland is located within a layer of the skull that is light-permeable and, thus, gives a trout detection of threats and shadows looming over-head, which explains why blind trout will evade overhead shadows.[71] It's inconceivable that such a simple animal could think up such exquisite design adaptations in order to be "selected" for continued survival.

Vision is not the only sense where trout display extraordinary design; their purposive senses of taste and smell also evoke wonder. Trout possess numerous taste buds in their mouths and gills designed to provide immediate discernment of edible versus inedible food. These taste receptors are directly connected to the brain by nerves that enable the trout to make a split-second decision for intake or rejection. To the fly fisherman, this adroit ability plays out during sight fishing, which demands lightning-quick precision to set the hook, due to how quickly a trout can suck in and spit out the counterfeit fly. The trout's fine-tuned taste buds are designed to respond to specific chains of amino acids, upon which all proteins and organic matter are made, to determine the authenticity of the food.[72] Said another way, this amino acid discernment comes at the smallest unit level, a pre-programmed design feature utilizing the utmost minutia of biotic detail. Amino acids, as we will hear more about later, are specifically constructed and arranged by the fish's DNA, which has been pre-programmed to produce this marvel.

But trout are not the only fish in the stream with remarkable taste perception. Even within the setting of our chapter on the Eleven Point

River, many catfish can be found who epitomize a fish designed to thrive within its environment. Unlike trout that possess taste buds only within internal cavities, catfish possess copious taste buds externally on their skin, fins, and barbels (whiskers). Fish, especially catfish, have more taste buds than humans. Dr. Gary Grossman has suggested that a twelve-inch catfish might have 680,000 taste buds on its body.[73] I would probably be a lot skinnier if I was designed this way—if I could just roll around in a pile of donuts to taste them instead of eating them, but I digress. But the remarkable feature where design meets environment is when you consider that catfish are typically found in lower light environments, often on the bottom of rivers with muddy or murky water. Fish can't see prey as well in these types of environments, so to determine whether a blurry object is prey or a submerged leaf, the catfish can reach out and taste the object with its barbels before consuming it. Bottom-dwelling suckers, similarly, have up to fifty-seven taste buds in a 1.3-millimeter exterior lip surface area.[74] The design enabling external taste is quite a convenient feature that would appear custom-made for such an environment as the dark bottoms of rivers and streams.

While the trout's sense of taste is impressive, its acute sense of smell might be even more impressive. Like its sense of taste, a trout's sense of smell (olfactory cells) diagnoses and searches scents pursuant to their amino acid compounds down to the molecular level.[75] Trout have two types of olfactory cells: those that identify potential food and those that identify environmental objects, such as other fish, foreign chemicals, etc. Thus, it has been postulated that trout can even smell the fisherman/woman's cologne, perfume, or aftershave as it wafts above the water.[76]

The odyssey of salmon to swim thousands of miles from the ocean to return to the natal stream where they hatched has been a well-documented enigma. Perhaps the most integral equipment to make this voyage possible is the salmon's sense of smell. It is believed that young salmon are "imprinted" with the odor of their birth streams while they are young. This imprinted smell is retained through the fish's life after it migrates to the ocean. Additionally, research has shown that salmon not only capture the smell of their home stream—perhaps retained within the salmon's skin mucus—but they also record the smell of tributary streams they traveled as they made their way to the ocean.[77]

When salmon make their way back to spawn in their home stream using their homing device—their innate sense of smell—their imprinted olfactory cues respond to scent concentrations, per Gary Grossman, "as faint as parts-per-million."[78] The salmon are further guided by thyroid hormone surges when encountering water that matches the imprinted odor, currents, salinity, et al. of the home/tributary stream.[79] While further research is needed, some scientists believe the salmon might also be sensitive to, and aided by, directional responses to the earth's electromagnetic field. Salmonid have pit organs embedded in their skin, which permit them to perceive electric fields. It's hard to imagine an organism randomly acquiring the ability to perceive inorganic forces. Regardless of navigation by organic or inorganic means, the elaborate homing sense of the salmon begs the necessity of a designer to orchestrate such an endeavor.

Genius is shown in creativity. Salmonids convey their creativity in using their sense of smell as not just a tool for procreation. In fact, Alaskan rainbow trout take full advantage of the return of sockeye salmon into the Bristol Bay tributaries. Using their sense of smell, rainbows are known to navigate different tributaries, following sockeye, to locate species-specific sockeye eggs that they feast upon.[80] Scent is not only used by some species for propagation and feeding, but also in a defensive sense. Some fish release so-called "fear scents" when their upper layer of skin is broken. Other fish in the vicinity detect the compounds in these fear scents and engage in predator-avoidance behaviors.[81]

Clearly, trout display innovative systems of design, manifested through senses, such as sight, sound, taste, smell, and touch. But what about those innate abilities that don't appear to be driven by sense perception? Instinct, if you will. While beyond the scope of this chapter, we would be remiss to ignore just a couple of instinctive traits of trout that warrant explanation beyond fortuitous, random chance. For instance, consider how, when food supplies often dwindle for trout during the colder winter months, the trout's inner programming slows the trout's metabolism, reducing its caloric demands and enabling it to survive on less.[82] Or consider how rainbow trout "know" how to better optimize cardiac output when sensing they are anemic.[83] Try to fathom how rainbow trout even "know" to respond to changes in water pressure, pH, salinity, and temperature to maintain neutral buoyancy equilibrium by surfacing to gulp the precise amount of air to regulate their swim bladders. We could continue on and on, but you get the picture. The rainbow trout we saw in the opening scene of this chapter is unambiguously a design marvel that points to an unequalled Designer. But are there other organisms present in this opening scene that show the handiwork of this Designer?

DESIGN FEATURES OF THE SUPPORTING CAST

The necessity for a supernatural Designer can be seen by peering into the spring and brooding over the multi-faceted mechanisms of the rainbow trout. There are simply too many synchronized functions in place, interdependent on other functions aligned simultaneously, to come about by unguided, undesigned means. In the same way, the intelligent assortment of letters required to write this book and the functional message those letters convey when precisely arranged, could not have come about by the random entering of characters on my keyboard. Yet, there are even "simpler" forms of life that can be found within our earlier vignette of the Eleven Point River (or any spring) that bear testimony to an ultimate Designer.

Recall within our opening scene, the fly used to hook that beautiful rainbow trout: the brown harvester midge. The harvester is tied to imitate one of the four primary insects universal to most streams that are an integral food source for trout: midges, caddisflies, mayflies, and stoneflies. The insects are bountiful in streams and progress through methodic life cycles. Midges and caddisflies hatch from eggs on the stream floor as larvae, transform into a pupae stage, and then make their way to the stream's surface. Upon emergence as an adult, these two flies dry their wings on the water surface before flying off to mate. Mayflies and stoneflies don't have a pupae or larva stage, but rather have a nymph stage that precedes their surface emergence. Trout voraciously feed on these insects at all stages and at all locations in the stream, from larvae on the bottom; to nymphs and pupae floating to the surface; to adults on the surface, readying to take flight; to adults a little later who have crashed to the surface after mating.

"Big deal," you might think. How does a simple, little insect, a quarter-to-half-inch long, point to a Designer? Let me answer by illustration: when I fish a midge pupae imitation, the brown harvester, I will often tie in a tiny glass bead on top of it. The reason being? Well, when midges begin their mad dash to the surface of the water, they, like most species of mayfly nymphs, struggle mightily to reach the surface. Keep in mind, they need to get there as soon as possible, for trout, with their piercing vision, gobble them up as they flail toward the top. But the remarkable thing is, their Designer has not left them without an aid. As the midge emerges from its cocoon casing, a gas bubble is released. This gas bubble provides a free and quick ride to the surface of the water. So, as trout are lurking, this simple, little bug has been designed with a means of escape, ushering it to the surface to avoid capture, where it can take flight, mate, and provide more offspring to the food chain. It's the great equalizer, like in *Star Wars: Episode Four*, when the forlorn R2-D2 and C-3PO escape the imminent capture of the foreboding Darth Vader by fumbling into an escape pod. The paradox of design is how this little air bubble, which impedes the trout from eating it, later benefits the trout with a greater propagation of midge flies. This extremely tiny insect shows a remarkable complexity that comes not from chance but from an intelligent Designer.

Like the midge, the mayfly also utilizes a gas bubble for transportation to the water's surface as it emerges from a nymph to a dun (emerging adult). Moreover, as pointed out in *Hatches*, the classic book on mayflies by Al Caucci and Bob Nastasi, somehow, mayfly duns emerge with their wings pre-folded "like a neatly folded tent."[84] It is awfully fortuitous that the newly-formed wings of this seemingly simply insect buoy it to the surface in aerodynamic efficiency, where their unfolding and quick drying is expedited for a quick getaway without being devoured. Not to be outdone, caddisflies have been called "the construction engineers of the aquatic world," particularly while in their larval stage.[85] One particular species, *Hydropsychidae*, showcase their apt design by anchoring themselves to rocks on the stream bed and constructing silk nets to catch food fragments flowing by.[86] Could such a resourceful design be invented by such a simple insect that allows it to catch prey while remaining concealed from predators?

Similar "defensive design" features can be found in another stream favorite, the sculpin. A favorite fish of children to both watch and catch, sculpin are the little, cranky-looking critters that scurry around the stream floor in capricious little bursts. The reason they move in such an awkward way, always on the stream floor, is that they lack a swim bladder. As you might imagine, the lack of a swim bladder comes as a severe impediment to mobility. It renders them virtually sedentary, seldom traveling beyond 150 lineal feet per year in the stream, but does deter the sculpin from entering deeper water, prevalent with predator trout they can't evade.[87]

To counteract their limited mobility, the sculpin has been designed with an uncanny ability to change its color to match its environment. This chameleon quality makes sculpin hard to spot—not only for trout, but also by my kids who love to prowl the stream edges for them. Sculpin blend in with the gravel stream bed seamlessly, giving them a defensive design that allows them continual participation in the stream ecoverse. Is it reasonable to conclude that this rare ability to camouflage itself resulted from millions of years of undirected, selective forces acting on the sculpin? By the time required for this unguided feature to be developed, would not the sculpin have been eradicated and made extinct by their lack of this very mechanism that affords its survival? Or how and why would those that did survive know that they even needed this adaptive camouflage feature? Would it not be more reasonable to consider that the sculpin was simply designed this way?

Likewise, consider that as brilliant as the physical camouflaging ability is, the sculpin shows perhaps greater evidence of design from non-physical, intuitive means. It is known that water temperature can influence rates of metabolism, energy conservation, and digestion in fish. How intelligent, then, that after feeding on the bottom, Bear Lake sculpin "know" to move to a location warmer by approximately ten degrees Celsius. Research has shown that this migration allows the sculpin to clear its stomach for the next day's feeding, which results in a growth increase of 300 percent over those who stay in the colder water.[88] I seriously doubt these sculpin studied their biological makeup to "know" of the advantages of moving to warmer water after feeding. Once again, something in their programming must be directing such an intelligible process. And if they are programmed to this very astute function, there *must* be a Programmer.

We've spent a great deal of time in the water, with some, perhaps, seeing for the first time the design brimming within the life-giving stream. But is there anything *outside* the confines of the water? As I survey the picture of the Eleven Point River, I might see a simple earthworm, plodding and burrowing near the bank. This "simple" animal, with five hearts and a binary axis brain, provides an invaluable function by plowing the soil and ingesting enormous amounts of dirt and organic matter, which oxygenates and enriches the earth to facilitate the growth of vegetation. In fact, earthworms are said to turn ninety percent of the leaves falling from orchard trees into soil, dragging and processing them underground. A one-acre plot can have as many as three million earthworms that transport about eighteen tons of soil per year.[89]

From the ground fertilized by these worms, we might see some beautiful flowers, orchids perhaps, growing along the bank of the stream. Some species of orchids demonstrate a stroke of design genius, with multiple parts relying on simultaneous functionality to ensure their pollination. One such example is the bucket orchid, a flower that secretes nectar onto its surface to seduce male bees. The bees land on this surface to gather nectar, which attracts females, but they often slip on this surface and slide into a "pollination chamber." The only way out is to crawl through a tunnel that affixes pollen sacs to the bee's back, so that it will pollinate the next orchid upon which it lands.[90] Or instead of flowers, perhaps you see dandelions, a simple weed, lining the bank. The late John Gerstner pointed to the dandelion's shrewd design of placing its seeds atop the plant in a lightweight, parachute structure, disbursed by a light breeze to further spread and proliferate. Whether orchid or dandelion, those are both quite ingenious plans—plans that did not come about by chance. As this chapter has demonstrated, no matter where we turn within the spring, nature screams design. The question is, from where did this design come?

ORIGINS OF DESIGN

For many, the preceding evidences in this chapter for design will be chalked up to evolutionary development brought about by natural selection—that is, the unguided, random directing of natural causes that "pick" biological nuances that are most advantageous to certain species. We live in an age where this philosophy is indoctrinated into the masses and, as dogma, tolerates no challenges. Therefore, in spite of the massive odds against new life forms and new body parts occurring by chance, the philosophy of neo-Darwin evolution implicitly assumes natural selection's truth, while myopically considering alternative views with an academic hubris that tacitly, and often overtly, implies the ignorance of anyone who thinks differently. But that doesn't have to be the case.

Consider, as noted earlier, that chance has no being. Ironically, the way "chance" is often described—as something that acts upon or even orchestrates the design of organisms—can curiously sound like the attributes of a purposeful, Divine Designer. Second, in order for natural selection to function, it must have new information to act upon. Herein lies the problem that we will address, the issue of macroevolution—how we get the first life forms. That is the question for which the neo-Darwinian view has no answer. Natural selection assumes, or begs the question, that the organisms it acts upon have the information they need to evolve themselves. As we will see, natural selection—that source to which many would attribute the elaborate design found in the various life forms of this chapter—is impotent to act on a design without a Designer.

Suppose you're having a tough day fishing. You've tried different spots and different flies, to no avail. Frustrated and ready to quit, you stroll along the bank, looking for one last potential hot spot. Suddenly, as you walk through a riffle in the stream with low water and lots of rocks, you are stonewalled. Dead in your tracks, you stop to read a compilation of rocks that have washed up onto the surface of a boulder's flat stump, just above the water level. The rocks are arranged in such a way to make out words. They read, "Caddis hatch here at eleven a.m."

Wow, what are the odds? Figuring you just won nature's lottery, you wait for half an hour, dress your line and tie on an elk-hair caddis to imitate the hatch of real caddisflies foretold by this rock prophesy, and sure enough, you absolutely slay the fish. Now, as you reflect on what happened, would you attribute this most fortunate tip from the compilation of rocks to chance? No rational person would. But rationally speaking, the odds of this happening are greater than the odds of life originating by random, unguided means.

In the illustration above with the "random" configuration of rocks, there are two important qualities that are represented in the most fundamental compounds necessary for life. One, there is an improbable event (the water washing up rocks in a way that arranged them into letters). Two, the improbable event conveys information (the letters in which the rocks were randomly arranged made words that expressed meaning). This demonstrates intelligence. In the same manner, the most elementary building blocks of organisms, DNA, and proteins, by their improbable sequencing that communicates intelligent information, also display the marks of irrefutable intelligence. Now, hang in there with me, as the following treatise is complex, but drives home a compelling, if not statistically and biologically inarguable, case.

While the technical intricacies of biophysics are beyond the scope of this book, the reader should know that DNA functions much like a computer. It uses digital code in a highly specific sequence that must all fit together in order to form instructions on how to make specific amino acids, that are then arranged to form proteins, which are the building blocks of life. Along the spine of each DNA molecule are receptors, called nucleotide bases, that store genetic information in the form of one of four letters—A, C, D, and T. The specific arrangement of these letters in an *organized,* collective DNA strand make up our genes, which, on average, contain about 1,000 of these bases, each with a one-in-four chance of the correct "code" or letter being in place necessary to code for distinct proteins.[91] However, three nucleotide bases are required in order to produce one specific amino acid, which is then assembled with the other different amino acids and strung together to make a chain that forms a protein. Thus, with every gene containing 1,000 bases, the average protein contains 300 amino acids.

Consider further that there are twenty different amino acids. There is a one-in-twenty chance of having the right amino acid in place (improbable event) for each chain in an amino acid strand. Only when the strand is properly arranged can it perform a function of protein construction (intelligence), which then creates enzymes and other biological foundations of life forms, such as body parts, organs, etc. But this improbable event of one-in-twenty must be precisely replicated 300 times for the average protein to form. The odds for randomly arriving at this precise combination are impossible. Therefore, evolution cannot account for the first life forms by the chance arrangement of ancient amino acids. Or, in the example used by Dr. Steven Meyer, even a modest protein of 150 amino acids necessary for a rudimentary creature would have 10^{195} possible combinations, the improbability further driven home considering there are only 10^{80} elementary particles extant in the cosmos.[92]

The improbable precision required for the design of amino acids and the arrangement of proteins to produce a trout should rule out random, unguided chance accumulation of organic compounds. The proteins that make up the trout and its organs, fins, etc., perform three vital operations: specific amino acid sequencing dictates fold and function; folded chains form shapes; and shapes then perform protein functions.[93] Moreover, not every amino acid sequence that is produced is functional. In fact, the number of amino acid sequences that can fold into a functional protein are dwarfed by the number of sequences that cannot. Douglas Axe, Ph.D., from the California Institute of Technology and research fellow at the University of Cambridge, set out to determine the ratio of foldable amino acid folds to those that are unable to fold into three-dimensional structures through the technological advancement of site-directed mutations.

Axe's research indicated that for every fold, there are 10^{74} non-folding sequences, or one in 10^{74} odds of randomly selecting a folding sequence. Even then, a folding sequence doesn't make it a functional sequence. Using our earlier example of a very simple chain of 150 amino acid sites, Axe found that the ratio of finding a foldable and functional sequence by chance is one in 10^{77}.[94] If this math isn't hard enough to overcome, Dr. Meyer urges us to consider the further odds of random assortment of compounds necessary for life to originate; each site connection in the 150-site chain (149 connections) must be a peptide bond as non-peptide bonds cannot form proteins, so there is a one-in-two chance for a peptide bond at each side (add an additional 10^{45} odds), and, furthermore, each bond must be a "left-handed" bond (called an optical isomer) to construct a protein.[95] If you do the math (10^{77} plus 10^{45} plus 10^{45}), the resulting number of 10^{167} squashes like a bug the idea that the necessary building blocks for life could randomly evolve by chance arrangement. It simply becomes a statistical impossibility.

But what about random mutation within the DNA strand or mutations that might change some of the amino acid sites within a strand that forms a protein? Could that not account for new life forms? To that, we look at the example of pages of this book—just as we understand the meaning of a passage, in spite of a typo, an anomalous mutation or substitution of an amino acid within a chain does not destroy the overall meaning, or function, because the sequence of the rest of the chain has been specifically arranged to provide meaning. That said, it does not hold that an accumulation of changes does not impair functionality. In fact, Axe determined in other experiments that to change one type of folded protein structure into a completely newfangled protein requires a myriad of changes across many sites—changes that to produce a novel fold ultimately result in a loss of functionality.[96] Thus, the degree of mutations required for transformation into a unique protein cannot be done without compromising the structural integrity of the fold, resulting in fatal loss of function.

The impediment of multi-volume mutations not only plays out at the molecular level, but also on a larger, cellular level. The moment a trout embryo is fertilized, and cell division begins, millions of intelligent instructions and signals begin to be deployed, turning specific genes on and off at key moments of development. These activated/deactivated genes tell the cell what its role and place in the fish might be. A cell might divide with instructions to build a stomach; another might be a digestive enzyme for the stomach; and another cell might divide and begin construction as a swim bladder connected to the stomach.

As common sense might indicate, the earlier in the construction process that one step randomly "changes" a key component, the more disastrous that change affects the project as a whole. This is akin to the calamity of a beautiful stream being polluted upstream at its headwaters, which has devastating impacts, not just at its point of entry, but for all the branches, forks, and life within the downstream watershed.

However, the further downstream the pollution's point of entry occurs, the less the detrimental impact is as a whole. The same applies to an animal's so-called "head-to-tail axis": the earlier in the development a change occurs, the more lethal the change is to the production of the animal. The later a change occurs, the more innocuous on the surface level and the more tangential the change becomes. Such was the conclusion reached by T.H. Morgan, Nusslein-Volhard, and Wieschaus, who found that mutations to early-stage fruit flies—such as nascent stage, body-forming proteins—aborted production of the animal.[97]

Another analogy would be the assembly of a complex machine. One "simple" but complex machine that has aided in the writing of this book is a Keurig coffeemaker. Ponder for a moment, if the size of the water-holding tank on the coffeemaker would "randomly" change to a larger size, what downstream ramifications would occur. First, the water tank would not be able to fit on the foundation that holds it. Second, the water intake valve would no longer be precisely aligned, so water would both leak out and not be taken up to be warmed. Third, the water intake conduit hose would need to be made longer to accommodate this change. Fourth, even if we imagined the two previous maleficent changes hadn't occurred, the water-fill sensor would be impacted, given it was designed to detect water volume of one specific quantity, while now the tank has a volume of a different quantity.

You could go on and on with other implications: changes in cup sizes, strain on motor, etc., but you get the picture of how early-stage changes are not only detrimental, but calamitous, and cannot be tolerated by the machine in order to survive. Later stage design nuances, however, are more tolerable, and might result in cosmetic changes, such as machine color or adaptions of convenience—like three, rather than two, cup size options. Such is why microevolution—from dog to coyote, for example—occurs, while macroevolution—such as jellyfish to dog—fails. The functionality of the machine is not predicated on the late-stage design features.

It is for those reasons that geneticists and scientists like John F. McDonald, Paul Nelson, Søren Løvtrup, et al. conclude that early-stage mutations are not only detrimental, but also *cannot* produce the new body parts and new life that neo-Darwinian macroevolution requires. While that fact cuts hard, perhaps the death knell to the neo-Darwinian paradigm—if empirical science is not subordinated to fanciful theory—is that there is no scientifically-substantiated evidence of animals ever being shown to tolerate early-stage mutations in a viable manner.[98] Ultimately, scientific findings conclude that early-acting mutations invariably result in loss of function, catastrophic loss of body parts, whereas new body plans require changes coordinated with mind-numbing precision, which are not shown to occur naturally or in harmony at a macro level. Conversely, tolerable, late-acting changes do not occur early enough in the animal's "head-to-tail axis" to affect significant body plan changes. This explains why only microevolution occurs in a species. Therefore, because no advantageous change results from mutations, natural selection has nothing advantageous to select.

Certainly, then, neither mutation nor natural selection possess the design capability to create the new information necessary for life. New cells necessary to create new life require the joint operation of varying proteins fabricated and arranged into place to perform their function. It requires the full assembly of many proteins and systems "hitting the ground running" and acting in concert from inception for an organism to arise. The odds of one, random protein strain arising was shown earlier to be statistically impossible. The odds of producing multiple proteins that work in tandem coordination at the micro-level are inconceivable.

A perfect example is the amazing clotting system designed for animals. Trout are known to have blood with extremely high viscosity. It would be easy, without elaborate clotting systems in place, for trout to bleed to death in the water. However, research as early as the 1950s has shown that trout have been designed with a more rapid-response blood clotting system than humans.[99] Consider the network of coordinated systems that must be in place from the onset to keep an organism from bleeding to death and, as result, becoming extinct if such systems relied upon a long period of random evolution. Michael Behe summarizes the complexity and necessary precision of clotting:

> When an animal is cut a protein called Hageman factor sticks to the surface of cells near the wound. Bound Hageman factor is then cleaved by a protein called HMK to yield activated Hageman factor. Immediately the activated Hageman factor converts another protein, called prekallikrein, to its active form, kallikrein. Kallikrein helps HMK speed up the conversion of more Hageman factor to its active form. Activated Hageman factor and HMK then together transform another protein, called PTA, to its active form. Activated PTA in turn, together with the activated form of another protein called convertin, switch a protein called Christmas factor to its active form. Activated Christmas factor, together with antihemophilic factor (which is itself activated by thrombin in a manner similar to that of proaccelerin) changes Stuart factor to its active form. Stuart factor, working with accelerin, converts prothrombin to thrombin. Finally, thrombin cuts fibrinogen to give fibrin, which aggregates with other fibrin molecules to form the meshwork clot . . .
>
> Blood clotting requires extreme precision. When a pressurized blood circulation system is punctured, a clot must form quickly or the animal will bleed to death. On the other hand, if blood congeals at the wrong time or place, then the clot may block circulation as it does in heart attacks and strokes. Furthermore, a clot has to stop bleeding all along the length of the cut, sealing it completely. Yet blood clotting must be confined to the cut or the entire blood system of the animal might solidify, killing it. Consequently, clotting requires this enormously complex system so that the clot forms only when and only where it is required. Blood clotting is the ultimate Rube Goldberg machine.[100]

Such sophistication comes hardly by chance. The specification required for a trout's blood to clot reflects design features that could not be adaptive, lest the trout die before its circulatory system could adapt. But what about the adaptations we *can* observe? Does this point to new information utilized by natural selection? Could this be new information or prior information newly presented? Different expression or different genes?

Examples abound of observable changes within the offspring of a species that are paraded as "evidence" for evolution. However, as in every case, new information has not been produced (especially within one generation). Rather, what is typically misconstrued and publicized as observed evolution, often due to the infusion of evolutionary semantics, is the different *expression* of previously existing genetic information.

Take, for example, an article appearing in the May/June 2016 issue of *American Angler* magazine, with the headline, "Hatchery Fish Genetically Change Over Time." The article highlighted research conducted at the University of Oregon that examined the differences between wild and hatchery-raised steelhead and how quickly their genetic differences advance. One line from the article announced, " . . . after one generation of hatchery culture, the offspring of wild fish and first-generation hatchery fish differed by more than 700 genes . . . " Near the article's conclusion, one of the lead professors of the research team was quoted as saying, "However, the large amount of change we observed at the DNA level was really amazing."[101]

That would be truly amazing, indeed, if that was the full story. It sounds like copious amounts of new DNA were created in one short generation. However, like anything, we need to read the fine print. And when turning the fine print, which in this case is the abstract for the full research article, we see what was not included in the magazine article: "Remarkably, we find that there were 723 genes *differentially expressed* between the two groups of offspring."[102] And with those two words, "differentially expressed," the key to unlocking this mystery is provided. As it turns out, there was no new information created at all. Rather, existing genetic information passed on by two parents was differently expressed in the offspring.

The above article speaks to the emerging science of epigenetics, the field that Jonathan Wells, Ph.D. from the University of California-Berkley in Developmental Biology, says will be the "unraveling" of the neo-Darwinian model.[103] Epigenetics refers to the science of information "above" genes, as the prefix *epi* means "above." Epigenetics looks at those sources of information that direct and turn genes on and off (their expression) at precise times to best sustain the creature for optimal survival. While environmental factors don't change the information or sequences encoded within DNA, the way genes are expressed can change by reacting to their environment as an adaptation for survival.

Ponder, if you will, the example Marc Ambler gives of Dutch people starved by a Nazi blockade during World War Two. Health records have been preserved that demonstrate the impact on children who were conceived during this period of mass starvation. Those records demonstrated that babies in utero during the final months of gestation, when their mothers were exposed to starvation and bleak nutrition, were found to be below-average weight at birth and for the rest of their life, while they, as well as their own children, were less likely than the rest of the population to be obese.[104] Conversely, those children who were in utero during the first months of gestation and whose mothers were liberated and able to eat a normal diet during the final stages of gestation, were found to have normal birth weights and to suffer from obesity later in life.[105] Studies such as this on people from World War Two and on animals point to epigenetics' role, something "above" the genes that responds to environmental stimuli to turn on/ off information that is already present.

Other examples in scientific research include that of bison bones found buried in a Canadian gold mine that indicate an entire population that was able to adapt quickly—too quickly for the Darwinian model—to climate changes. Scientists have also conducted research on mice, whereby manipulating nutrition was able to influence specific genes. When one gene was turned on, the mice took on a yellow color and became more obese; but when turned off, the same sibling mouse could be made normal to thin and brownish in color.[106] Science has discovered that genetic information previously cast aside as junk DNA has turned out to be anything but junk. Rather, it exists as a prewritten code, waiting to spring into action like a 911 operator responding to stressed situations. New information is not created; rather, latent information *already present* acts to switch on or off those genes that produce biological functions. Thus, when 723 new genes are said to be expressed, we see the role of epigenetics deploying preexisting resources in the next generation of fish to best adapt to their environment. Far different from macroevolution's "something out of nothing," epigenetics empirically explains *micro*evolution.

Epigenetics play a far greater role than merely controlling the activation of certain genes. They are also responsible for coordinating and directing proteins, thus arranging them into the precise locations for functional systems to acclimatize. Akin to our example of the Keurig machine, making the precise and complex pieces of machinery that fit together in harmony is not sufficient to have a functional coffee machine. Someone must be present to arrange those pieces in the right order. Similarly, epigenetics order protein arrangements, three-dimensional cell structures, membrane ion channels, and the like to make the production of the parts meaningful. Something beyond DNA is at work in development of life—behind the genes. The question is, Who?

With this trip to the spring, you've once again taken in the beautiful craftsmanship of a Grand Designer. We've moved in this chapter from the theoretical and ethereally theological to the up-close physical and juggernaut force that the natural world has to offer. You've felt the power of the stream as it numbs your limbs, and you've clutched the prince of the spring himself, the rainbow trout. Truth in this chapter became real, like grasping and clasping a gelatinous-skinned trout with both hands, as you feel the life pulsating from it.

This trip has not come without its travails, as the entry to the Eleven Point River clearly depicted. But the beauty of discovering truth is worth the struggle to lay hold of it. I realize that for some, the worldview this chapter presented might have been received as powerfully as being swept off your feet in a frigid mountain stream. And that's okay—my intention was not to change your mind wholesale, but to get your feet wet. But as this trip continues, as that water sloshes around in your waders, consider and see that a Divine Designer for the symbiotic life in the stream is not just necessary, it is empirically rational. Chance, on the other hand, has no being, has no power, and thus, is an irrational hope. It is my hope that the next time you venture out to the spring with your kids, family, and friends, you look at things differently. May you see the variety of flies that dance around you, the dandelions that sway on the bank, or that rainbow trout, arrayed with visual treasure, as organic lessons conveyed by the theology of the spring—lessons taught from creatures with fortuitous designs far more precise than chance could ever yield. Go and see for yourself.

Reflection Questions

1. How would you explain the distinction between macroevolution and microevolution? Can you give examples of either being observed in nature?

2. Theistic evolution is the belief that God created the first primordial life forms and, from that, used evolution to bring about the assortment of species we find today. If we grant that efficiency is a mark of intelligence, how then does the concept of theistic evolution logically fall short? (Hint: If God is truly God, would He need to use the equivalent of a "biological slot machine" to bring about the variety of species He ordained to create?)

3. Earlier in this book, I noted that "chance has no being." In this chapter, a similar premise was applied to "natural selection." Can something that has no being act purposely, let alone intelligently? Why do you think that a secular concept like "natural

selection" is sometimes described very similarly with attributes of a personal deity, as pointed out in this chapter?

4. Anchor tenants of the spring, such as trout, mayflies, sculpin, worms, and even plants, were highlighted within this chapter. These creatures, which at first glance from the bank might appear inconspicuously banal, were shown, upon closer examination, to be extraordinarily sophisticated in their design. What other animals can you think of that, by either sheer beauty or intentional design, reflect the irrefutable marks of a Designer?

5. If matter is innately intelligent, why, then, wouldn't it just emerge from that theoretical point of singularity in its most grandiose manifestation? Why wouldn't it come to life, hitting the ground running in optimal form from its nascent stage? Why waste its time, spinning its wheels in the alleged primordial morass? If efficiency is a mark of intelligence, does matter fail on that account?

6. How does the fact that human DNA operates by digital code influence your view on the origin of life? Is it possible to have digital code without a Designer?

With technological advancement often comes less exposure to nature and, with that, each generation commensurately becomes more prone to miss the wondrous ingenuity found in nature. For generations, people have been captivated by the unexplainable intelligence demonstrated by the most minute animals. As we conclude this chapter with an excerpt from Proverbs 30:24-28, consider the gifts of wisdom bestowed on the sundry animals of the passage, and how they point to a unifying intellect governing the created order.

> Four things on earth are small, but they are exceedingly wise: the ants are a people not strong, yet they provide their food in the summer; the rock badgers are a people not mighty, yet they make their homes in the cliffs; the locusts have no king, yet all of them march in rank; the lizard you can take in your hands, yet it is in kings' palaces.

Part Two

THE CREATOR'S IMMANENCE
FOUND IN THE SPRING

CHAPTER FOUR

REFLECTIONS OF THREE IN ONE: THE TRINITY IN THE SPRING

In those days Jesus came from Nazareth of Galilee and was baptized by John in the Jordan. And when he came up out of the water, immediately he saw the heavens being torn open and the Spirit descending on him like a dove. And a voice came from heaven, "You are my beloved Son; with you I am well pleased."

—Mark 1:9-11

I FELT LIKE A STEALTH ghost had just crept up on me. One minute earlier, I was dug into a sharp bend in the stream—an ideal staging area to present my fly. One minute earlier, I was casting upstream toward the spring—the very nexus of it all. One minute earlier, the spring was in plain view, its headwaters bequeathing a svelte, natural float for my fly. One minute earlier, I was calm, relaxed, and acutely focused within the predictable cohesion of the stream environs.

But a minute later, mystery arrived. Paradoxically, I didn't initially sense its presence visually. Rather, what I can liken only to a pre-storm silence alerted me. It was as if whatever had arrived was able to mute the ambient soliloquy of nature by the unveiling of the unknown. The placid sounds of birds singing, water flowing, and frogs crooning was instantaneously muzzled. Paralyzed by the feeling of a beady-eyed stranger watching me, I was afraid to turn and confront this presence—apprehensive of even making eye contact.

Suddenly, a soothing warmth replaced the crisp, cool stiffness of fresh, spring air. My soul was awakened at this celestial dawn. Some supernatural power was monkeying with the natural thermostat of the spring but, without saying a word, was dispelling the fear invoked by such an interruption. My hands, just moments earlier cold and shriveled, were now sweaty.

Then, the grand finale appeared on the stage of the stream: fog. It descended out of nowhere, yet appeared to arise out of the stream itself. Ushered in by a wake of warm air, this small cloud swath languidly strolled toward me, amorphously altering shape, while gracefully unfurling itself. No longer timid, I just stood there, hypnotically wanting to feel it pass over me. Completely swallowed up, I naively stretched out my free hand in a feeble attempt to embrace this hallowed wonder. My attempt, subtly arrogant in thinking I could hold on to the company of this enigmatic fog, seemed to expedite its fleeting departure.

As the cloud passed, the dense, warm air that felt so calming dissipated. Standing alone again in the chilly air that was present before the fog came, I watched the fog wisp away downstream, to suddenly vanish just as abruptly as it arrived, denying the next fisherman the aura I had been so graciously granted. I felt special. After such an exquisite moment in the stream, I wasn't the least bit surprised to catch a rainbow trout on my next cast. Perhaps the ethereal moment left me ablaze with a heavy dose of romanticism, but I look back on it as if God treated me to a glimpse of hitting the reset button on creation. Everything was good. Everything necessary to avail the moment was in place: the spring above me, the stream before me, and the fog that had hovered and passed. Yes, God is still actively sustaining His creation.

THE ANALOGY OF THE TRINITY

You waded into the shallow run of the stream when you began this book. But now you will be challenged to move away from the safety of the bank and the security of the shallow ripples and to wade out into the deep. If you can accept exhilarating challenges like fly fishing the

Gunnison River in Colorado, which requires a hike down the plummeting Gunnison Gorge, the challenge of probing the stream's inner sanctum with all your cognitive faculties should excite you. The more you immerse yourself in the spring as a whole, the better feel you get to confront its ethereal mystery. The better feel you get to exist.

The Holy Trinity—I would venture to guess that there is not a more confusing and misunderstood doctrine of the Christian faith. With the exception of perhaps end-times discussions, there is not a topic that can get more contentious and befuddling. The doctrine of the Trinity and the failure to grasp intricacies within this doctrine have led to ecumenical church councils, splits in the early church, heretical splinter groups, and entirely new religions altogether. Nearly all of the discord results from a failure to properly grasp the reality of the Trinity—what it is and what it isn't, how the Trinity functions internally within its three subsistences (notice I didn't say "Persons," but more on that later), and how the Trinity applies Its work to impact us. Given what is at stake, it behooves us—now that we have deduced from the spring and the natural order that God *does* exist—to get it right in showing *how* He exists. A discourse on the Trinity and how the spring speaks to and illustrates the Trinity by way of analogy is, thus, in order.

I must disclose up front, given this book's central thrust of demonstrating how general revelation through the spring bears witness to theological truths, that a substantive discourse of the Trinity cannot be developed by natural theology. The Holy Trinity is revealed only through special revelation via sacred Scripture. However, the general revelation of the spring serves as an analogy or a natural "type" that points to and buttresses our understanding of the Trinity as revealed in Scripture.

Before we launch into a detailed treatise on the Trinity, it would serve us well to preemptively address a few underlying items of basic importance. If we eliminate misunderstanding upfront at the springhead, so to speak, we'll cut a clear channel to flow downstream in orthodox belief. But the dangers are real—like that faced by a dear friend I took fishing one morning, who was unaware of the dangers of stepping out into the deep without solid footing. Thinking he was well-versed with the streambed, he stepped out into a pool much deeper than he had surmised. His step never landed. His other foot struggled to anchor in the loose gravel that gave way, ushering him into the death hole. As his waders filled with water, he struggled futilely to regain his footing. Certain drowning was averted only by my latching onto his remaining unsubmerged hand, pulling him to safety.

So, too, is our teaching on the Trinity: the waters we are about to enter are deep but require us to approach only after establishing a solid foundation that won't give way to the abyss of doctrinal error that drowns so many others. Dig in, and hang with me—the foundation we are about to build will preserve you for a lifetime.

The first presupposition germane to our discussion is the concept of "analogy" itself—a term most have heard and used. An analogy simply compares two different things to draw upon common traits to better understand one of the things being compared. Analogies work best when applied to things we can know in a tangible and comprehensive way. For example, my wife may tell me that as she lined up to run her first half-marathon, she felt the anxiety of a child leaving for her first day of kindergarten. I knew exactly what she meant, even though I never ran a half-marathon, because I remembered the nervous excitement of leaving for my first day of kindergarten: the fear of the unknown, the removal of my maternal comfort zone, the trepidation of being exposed to a group of strangers for a prolonged time in a vulnerable way, and, yet, with it came with the excitement of beginning a new phase and ascending new horizons. Her analogy was made clear because I could personally relate to and directly grasp both concepts.

Consider a more salient fly fishing example often overheard at my local fly fishing club. When we gather to tie flies, someone might be affably dubbed "Frank Sawyer" aloud after demonstrating savvy in tying a particular fly. Frank Sawyer was an Englishman, renowned for inventing numerous fly patterns still used today—the pheasant tail perhaps the most notable. Obviously, everyone knows the individual who excelled in tying a certain fly is not *the* late Frank Sawyer. Rather, by using analogy, the tier's excellence of a completed fly is communicated.

But God is not Frank Sawyer. And God is not like our first day of kindergarten. By His nature of being God and by virtue of Him being perfect, infinite, and eternal, we could never have anything remotely close to an exhaustive knowledge of God. We could know nothing of this Supreme Being beyond what He has willfully chosen to reveal to us. Consider how many of the ways we describe God illustrate what He is not—such as infinite (not finite), omnipresent (not limited to space), eternal (not limited to time), immutable (does not change), etc. The only thing we see clearly is that God is altogether not like us. Our imperfections are altogether different and diametrically set us apart from a perfect Being that self-exists.

Given our differences with the being of God—so vast that we could never plumb one percent of His depths—we can see why any analogy made of God will be innately flawed. Because we cannot truly grasp concepts like infinity and eternality, our analogies will invariably come up deficient. In some ways, comparing the perfect Being to one of the objects of His creation sounds downright contemptible, as if to make them equals. So, should we abandon any attempt to better understand God by use of analogy?

I would contend, like many classical theologians before me, that we must disclose upfront that any analogy developed with our minds to help others better understand God, however noble the intent, is a very imperfect analogy. That said, as God is the Author of language, there *must* be some meaningful way for human language to be used so that some degree of discussion and communication about God can take place. However dissonant God and humanity are, some similarity must exist between our being and God's Being for a basis of discussion to even be possible. The philosophical concept called "the analogy of being" makes the same point: that we would be utterly incapable of communicating about God if there was not some locus of commonality.

Medieval theologian Thomas Aquinas facilitated the understanding of how human language can be meaningful in talking about God by distinguishing different ways in which humanity uses words. One way was identifying language used *univocally*. Univocal use of a word takes place when the same word is applied to two different objects but is relative in its meaning. For example, when hiking a nature trail at Ha Ha Tonka State Park near Camdenton, Missouri, with my wife, I can turn to her and tell her she is beautiful. Then, as the trail winds down to the spring, which emerges from the base of a 300-plus-foot dolomite formation like an aqua grin, I can gaze into the spring and call it beautiful in the same breath. In this case, the word "beautiful" functions univocally to indicate both objects are aesthetically pleasing. Implicit, however, is the understanding that applying the word beautiful to my wife—with her facial symmetry, dashing smile, and her flowing and shimmering onyx hair—is not exactly the same meaning as when I call the inanimate spring beautiful.

However, language linking creaturely objects like my wife and the spring disintegrates when applied to the Transcendent Being Who created them. The moral perfection and eternal nature required of a wholly-other Being alone necessitates a communication chasm that limited minds cannot bridge or comprehend. Therefore, some type of accommodation must be applied in order for meaningful conversation to be possible.

Aquinas again provided a solution in what he called the *analogical* use of language that made God-talk meaningful. In a sense, every word we use is dependent on analogy so that when we read or use words, the composite letters or sounds convey a common idea between the sender and receiver. The words and letters represent something common enough to both speaker/sender and receiver/listener to permit understanding. In analogical language, there is enough of a likeness between the things being compared to make communication possible, albeit by an imperfect likeness. Or, as Kyle Claunch describes it, "[Things are] corresponding to one another in an accommodated way."[107] Our language, when used of God, can never be exactly the same or exactly different in how it applies to Him; it requires an accommodation.

For example, we can use the word "pure" in an analogical sense to use the water of the spring as an analogy for God. When we call God pure, we mean that He is without blemish in His goodness and moral perfection. There is not the slightest hint of any element in His Being that would be a detraction from His holy character. But when we call the water in the spring pure, we mean that the water occurs as undefiled and consumable as any liquid we find in nature could be. It has emerged from a domain free of human intervention and direct contamination of additives, contaminants, etc. Relatively speaking, when we compare fresh spring water with any other fresh water source—such as stagnant pond water, lake water, river water, etc.—it is *pure* because, in relation to these other bodies of water, the spring water is overwhelmingly fresh and unadulterated. Therefore, spring water is as clear as any you'll find. However, there might be pollutants you can't see that have seeped into the groundwater and are now present in the spring. And some dirt and debris does not get fully filtered out of water moving through an aquifer that emerges at a spring. In fact, contrary to popular belief, most geologists advise against drinking water fresh out of a spring. So, while the spring's degree of purity falls infinitely short of God's degree of purity, the word "pure" in the analogical sense makes a meaningful analogy between God and the spring. Ultimately, we understand that God alone has *pure* Being.

You may be asking at this point, "Well, this makes good sense, but why spend time distinguishing between types of language?" To answer, I would note that there are some people who believe that our language and our being differ so greatly from God that we should abandon any attempt to relate Him to others. On the other hand, there are people who make no distinction and use language that demotes God to a being like us—a nice, fluffy, cosmic Santa Claus, if you will. I would submit that language, specifically analogical language, enables us to talk about God in a meaningful way. In fact, the Bible commands us to do so (Jn. 17:3; Col. 2:2-3; Rom. 15:18-19). Analogies are the means of accommodation that permit us to share the awe and wonder of the Ultimate Being.

There has been no shortage of analogies offered up to try to explain the Holy Trinity. Ancient Trinitarian analogies reveal their age by utilizing primitive elements such as earth, wind, and fire; sun, moon, and earth; the sun, its light, and its energy; a tree root, trunk, and leaves; states of matter, such as solid, liquid, and gas, etc. Other attempts have been made using every-day, tangible commodities, such as an egg: the white, the yolk, and the shell. Augustine was fond of a very abstract, trifold analogy using the mind: first is pure knowing of itself; next is memory, knowledge, and the willing of their use; and the last is the cognitive activity that unites them.[108]

While analogies provide assistance in helping to understand a very nebulous subject like the Trinity, they are not without blatant weaknesses. It has been my experience, and it is the chief thesis of this chapter, that there is no better analogy to explain the Holy Trinity than a freshwater spring. While the spring has not been a widely used analogy for the Trinity, it was an analogy used by the early church father Tertullian, who interestingly enough, was also the first writer known to use the term "Trinity."[109] Within the spring, we delineate the unity of the essence of the spring: the spring orifice itself, the stream that flows therefrom, and the fog that arises from the stream. Like the Trinity, the deductions are conveyed through three entities: God, nature as His medium, and a human audience. We will develop this analogy and its limitations, in the pages to come.**

** One objection that might be raised with this analogy is that it is modalistic (a doctrine I later strongly repudiate) and simply a variation of the old water/ice/steam analogy, which is said to fail because the water molecules in the fog hovering above the stream surface are not the same molecules flowing as water through the spring orifice. While I readily preface that all analogies are imperfect—the spring analogy included—I would counter by noting that when we speak of the shared Divine essence of

Laying aside the analogy for a moment, the second presupposition we must address to prevent any misunderstanding of the Trinity is the word "Trinity" itself. Some opponents of the historically orthodox view of the Trinity are quick to note that the word "Trinity" is not found in the Bible at all. This would be a true statement. However, words like "omniscient," "monotheism," and "incarnation" don't appear in the Bible, either. Nonetheless, we tacitly hold to the unwavering belief in such propositions because the principle of each is clearly demonstrated in Scripture. The principle of the Trinity appears consistently throughout the metanarrative of Scripture, but readers expressly meet the Persons of the Trinity gathered in tri-unity in passages, such as Mark 1:10-11; Matthew 28:19; Ephesians 2:18; et al. Whereas the whole of the New Testament implies the Trinity, parts of it expressly present Its Members. It is not unlike when we enter the area of a natural spring. From a distance, we see stretches of stream channel, or we see the mist hovering through a path on the mountainside. We know they don't exist in isolation. We know they testify to the tri-unity of the spring.

The aforementioned point of the Persons and unity of the Trinity underscores our need for another presupposition: the Trinity is fully monotheistic. At first blush, this sounds like a paradox because the prefix "tri" implies the number three. Thus, some make the mistake of thinking the Trinity professes a belief in tri-theism—that is, three distinct gods. However, the God of the Bible, manifested by the Trinity, is monotheistic, which is only one God. Logically, there must be only one Divine, self-existent Being Who has the power of being in Itself, as affirmed by Jesus in John 5:26, "For as the Father has life in himself, so he has granted the Son also to have life in himself."

---

the Trinity, we likewise don't tend to segregate each compartmentalized unit of Divine essence from the shared whole. Much like when speaking of the water comprising the spring, we are speaking of it collectively, not as millions of distinct H_2O molecules acting in discordance. Moreover, to implicitly separate the Divine essence into individual units so as to attack the spring analogy vis-a-vis different water molecules places the critic on tenuous ground that potentially impairs the doctrine of simplicity, which will be discussed in this chapter.

The over-arching corpus of the biblical record bears witness to monotheistic belief. The Jewish prayer called the *sh'ma* (shema), passed down from generation to generation, is recorded early in Scripture and reads, "Hear, O Israel: The LORD our God, the LORD is one" (Deut. 6:4). The prophet Isaiah declared in Isaiah 43:10b, "Before me no god was formed, nor shall there be any after me." Jesus later admonished His listeners in John 5:44, "How can you believe, when you receive glory from one another and do not seek the glory that comes from the only God?" And the apostle Paul instructed followers in Corinth that, " . . . we know that 'an idol has no real existence,' and that 'there is no God but one'" (1 Cor. 8:4).

Naturally, in order to be God, God must exist as a Being that is wholly transcendent over any creature or created thing. His very substance must be a Divine substance, not an assortment of finite material or rare elemental compounds. In theological terms, God's unalloyed, Divine essence makes Him a simple Being, which does not mean He is a simpleton, rudimentary, or non-complex. Rather, God's simplicity speaks to His indivisibility. God is simple because He is complete, whole, and perfect. His Divine essence cannot be divided, apportioned, or separated from the homogeny of His Being. That which is infinite, that which is immutable, and that which is omnipotent cannot be divisible or compartmentalized. It cannot be removed from the whole or intermingled with any admixture that is not purely Divine. God's Being *must* be simple—a Divine composite, not one composed of parts with varying essences. God, then, must be monotheistic.

The Divine Being that is God exists as three Persons. The first Person of the Trinity is known as God the Father. The second Person of the Trinity is known as God the Son, or Jesus, per the name given at His earthly incarnation. And the third Person of the Trinity is God the Holy Spirit. The Three form the Divine Godhead, all possessing the same Divine essence, but in three separate, eternal Persons with unique functions to affect the shared Divine will.

I am reluctant to use the word "Persons" in our discussion of the Trinity because that word tends to cause grave misunderstandings. Our inherent limitations as creatures shape our minds to project subjective biases when we try to envision Divine concepts and new ideas. We contextualize things in a manner that is familiar to us. So, when we hear of God manifested as three Persons, we visualize three finite people, standing next to each other. Three totally different, autonomous people, with different DNA, different backgrounds, and different characteristics. The "Persons" of the Trinity are not that way at all—They share the same Divine essence that is indivisible in each Person so that each is one hundred percent Divine, not thirty-three percent Divine. All are equally God. Their wills, Their nature, and Their Divine attributes are all fully God, united in one Divine essence.

When describing the subsistence of the Trinity, we are careful to use words like "distinct" and "personal consciousnesses" to guard against the theological error that exists on the opposite continuum of the aforementioned tri-theism, and that is the error of modalism. Modalism claims that there is one God Who takes on three different modes—much like a stage actor who wears multiple masks. At one time, God is Jesus, the second Person of the Trinity, and the next moment, He morphs into God the Father. Then, after a quick costume change, He dons the part of Holy Spirit. Not only does such a teaching malign the majesty of God, turning Him into an impetuous schizophrenic, but it egregiously ignores key teachings of the Bible, where the Persons of the Trinity verbally address one another (Gen. 1:26; Jn. 12:28), or events in the biblical text when all three Persons of the Trinity are present in the same place, conducting different actions—such as the baptism of Jesus in Matthew 3:16-17. God the Father cannot be the Son, and the Son cannot be the Father in the same place, in the same time, and in the same relationship—just like a drop of fog condensation cannot simultaneously be the water pouring through the spring orifice or flowing down the stream channel.

A better word than "Person" that more properly conveys the intended meaning is the word "subsistence." The word *subsist* literally means to "exist under." While logic and natural theology has earlier demonstrated there can be only one Divine Being, from the simple essence of that Divine Being subsists three personal Consciousnesses. These three distinct and equally Divine subsistences of the Trinity, united through the Divine essence, have eternally existed in co-relationship to One Another.

Sacred Scripture teaches this co-relationship through a clear differentiation of the subsistences of the Trinity without a distinction in essence. The Bible clearly delineates that each Person has a unique role that He carries out in accordance with the consonant Divine will. Theologian Dr. James White wisely cautions that we should be careful to understand that "difference in function does not indicate inferiority in nature."[110] Just because God the Father sends God the Son into the world for the redemption of His people, the Son is no less Divine than the Father. Moreover, just because Jesus sends the Holy Spirit into the world to apply our redemption does not mean the Holy Spirit is any less eternal, any less omnipotent, or any less Divine.

The distinct Persons of the Trinity can be applied via analogy of the spring in the following way: The spring orifice is always the spring; the stream channels are always the stream; the effusive moisture, whether fog or transparent vapor moving about the air, is always the spring moisture. However, they are all connected and consist of the same essence, which in this case is the water. Their molecular essence is always in contact with one another. They are all corporately and equally "the spring," even though they have three different subsistences or manifestations.

To further develop the spring analogy, the unifying material that binds all three subsistences of the spring together—the essence—is the water molecules themselves. The essence/water molecules, as manifested in any one of the three subsistences, are each as "co-eternal" as the molecules in another subsistence. Those H_2O molecules emerging from the spring (the first subsistence), those homogenous molecules flowing as water through the stream channel (second subsistence), and the water condensing from the stream surface into a fog (the third subsistence) all existed as water molecules within the perpetual hydrological cycle that feeds into the confluence of the aquifer (beyond this "ecoverse") before they ever exited the spring orifice. Thus, several doctrines become clearer when viewed through the lens of the spring. The spring speaks to the doctrine of simplicity in that water is its sole, indivisible component. But more importantly, the spring demonstrates, like the Trinity, how its essence—water—is the necessity for its being (a spring) and by which its subsistences "eternally" exist. Remove the essence from this picture, and you have none of the three subsistences. Worse, you have no spring.

THE PERSONS OF THE TRINITY AND THEIR REFLECTION IN THE SPRING

Having established a general knowledge of the three subsistences of the Trinity—that is, Their identities as Father, Son, and Holy Spirit—we can now develop a deeper understanding of their unique hypostatic roles. "Hypostatic," when used as a theological term, is a Greek word meaning "the ultimate reality that comprises a 'Person' of the Trinity." The spring, again, comes to our aid as a useful analogy to better grasp not only the uniqueness of each Member of the Trinity, but also how Their unity subsists through the Divine essence. By eternally existing via the same Divine essence, each subsistence is able to operate as an outflow of the shared Divine will. By understanding no division exists within the Divine essence—which, in our analogy, is the water that flows through the spring, forms the stream channels, and is taken up as moisture disseminated through the airspace of the surrounding spring ecosystem—we are able to more intimately embrace the triune God.

God the Father

Our discussion begins with the first Person of the Trinity, God the Father. He is always ascribed Deity throughout the Bible and by nearly every world religion that subscribes to monotheism. Simply put, God the Father is the Fountainhead of all of reality. While the Divine essence is eternal, the Persons of the Trinity proceed from the Father, Who is not preceded in order from anyone or anything. As all that is the reality of a spring system flows from the spring as its origin, so is God the Father the source of all that is.

I would contend that there is none who has yielded a better formulaic treatment of the Trinity than John Calvin. Calvin's contributions to Trinitarian understanding were both practical and vanguard. Despite being nearly 500 years old, Calvin's teachings on the Trinity continue to distill an esoteric subject in a remarkably understandable way. He stood in the current of thousands of years of tradition and, in vanguard fashion, corrected some feeble misconstructions of the Trinity. It is no mistake that I lean on his prodigious work, overlaid within the vignette of the spring. Calvin is a choice resource to frame the outflow of the Persons of the Trinity from the Father, akin to the outflow of a spring, writing:

> This distinction is, that to the Father is attributed the beginning of action, the fountain and source of all things; to the Son, wisdom, counsel, and arrangement in action, while the energy and efficacy of action is assigned to the Spirit. Moreover, though the eternity of the Father is also the eternity of the Son and Spirit, since God never could be without His own wisdom and energy; and though in eternity there can be no room for first or last, still the distinction of order is not unmeaning or superfluous, the Father being considered first, next the Son from Him, and then the Spirit from both. For the mind of every man naturally inclines to consider, first, God, secondly, the wisdom emerging from Him, and lastly, the energy by which He executes the purposes of His counsel."[111]

Just as the essence of the spring is eternal, relative to the hydrological water cycle perpetually outflowing from the spring, God is the Fountainhead of all physical and metaphysical reality, including the

Persons of the Son and Spirit within the Godhead. Everything that exists does so because He is the self-existent One Who brought it into being. While we won't rehash all of the attributes of God as concluded in the previous chapter, it does help us to understand them in context to the first Person of the Trinity and how His name alone speaks to His eternal Being.

In the previous chapter, we pointed out that the holy name of God is *Yahweh*, or *Jehovah* in the Hebrew. The name aptly befits God, as it uses the noun form of the verb "to be," denoting God as the "I AM," the eternal being that "just is." But in terms of how He is referred to within the context of the Trinity, the modifier "Father," as revealed by God to refer to the first Person of the Trinity, can be applied in various ways.

First, as the Author of the created order, the term "Father" describes His paternal role as the Designer of the universe, as one might be the father of their garden planted in the backyard. A second use of the term can be used to describe Him in relation to the spiritual children that He calls to Himself. He is their spiritual Father to whom they owe their spiritual lives and eternal existence. A third use of the term "Father" communicates inner relations within the Trinity Itself, as metaphysically God the Father precedes and (in unity) relates to God the Son in a paternal ordering, which we will find is not just a temporary arrangement to affect the redemption of God's people.[112]

It would not be a mistake to consider God the Father the "Power Source" of all that is. It *would* be a mistake, however, to picture God as a physical thing, like a power plant or a mystic sage with a white beard. The Bible expressly teaches that God is a Spirit when Jesus is talking about God the Father in John 4:24. We should be careful not to equate the Being of God as a wispy apparition confined to a shape or form. God exists on an entirely higher plane of being, and because He is not material, He has no limitations of space or time.

If there is no place God cannot be and nothing that exists that He cannot know, then God cannot change because there is nothing to change into. There is nothing greater for Him to become, as He is beyond space and time. The essence of the spring speaks to God's unchanging nature—what we call God's immutability. The water that flows out of the spring has been moving through the deep recesses of the earth, within the stable climate of an aquifer. The aquifer is impervious to the summer heat or the winter cold; and as the water supplier on the "other side" of the spring, it maintains its inventory at a constant temperature. Therefore, like God Himself, Who is unchanging, the essence of an Ozark spring perpetually flows forth at a reliable, year-round temperature of fifty-six degrees, virtually without deviation. The analogy breaks down in times of flooding or heavy rain that can enter the aquifer near its source and alter the usually-consistent outflow temperature to a range of fifty-six to fifty-nine degrees.[113] On the other hand, God and the Divine essence are impervious to external conditions. He declares, "I the LORD do not change" (Mal. 3:6a).

If God is to be regarded as anything, He should be regarded as holy. By "holy," we are using the word in an analogical sense, meaning beyond "pure" or simply "sacred." God is holy in the truest etymology of the word, which, in Hebrew, came to mean "cut apart"—such as rending a garment to use a better selection of material for something else or to wholly separate something from that which does not compare to it. God is so holy in His being, so perfect in His majesty, that every attribute we know about Him is a cut above the created world. That is why His love is a holy love; His justice is a holy justice; His mercy is a holy mercy; and His knowledge is a holy knowledge. The attributes supersede the categories we see and experience as unholy humans. God's attributes are an outflow of His holy character. It is for that reason that those who have personal encounters with the holy God in the Bible—Moses, Isaiah, Job, Habakkuk, Peter, et al.—come away shaken, terrified at the power, awe, different-ness of this Divine Stranger, a cut apart in His unmatched Being. It is as God asked Isaiah, "Who is like me?" (Isa. 44:7a).

The truth is there is none like God because there is none holy. There is none who has being in himself, as each of the Members of the Trinity possess in full harmony. But it is God the Father in Whom this harmony is grounded, and He proceeds as the Source of all that is.

One Divine property and role that is unique to God the Father is that He eternally decrees all that will happen. While certainly difficult to visualize, within the biblical account, we always see Divine decrees originating from God the Father and carried out by the other two Members of the Trinity. Logically, there must be a willing of all that will come to be, and it must be in harmony with all the Persons of the Trinity, given they are all Divine. The shared Divine will flow through the shared Divine essence, like water through a stream.

Such a *relational* order within the Trinity speaks to another unique property of God the Father: He does not proceed from anyone. We must be extremely careful here because when we talk about procession, we are not saying one Person of the Trinity "creates" another. All Persons of the Trinity exist eternally. However, we are referring to order in which the Persons relate to One Another and exact the Divine decree. Just like the spring precedes the stream, God the Father precedes God the Son in His hypostatic identity, initiating eternal plans. God's not being ordered, or *begotten*—a word that causes misunderstanding, which we will address shortly—speaks to His hypostatic Person. The unique property that is essential to His Person is His non-begotten-ness, that is, His being first in the order of the flow of all that is, in which He is manifested and acts first amongst the other two Persons of the Trinity. Bruce Ware makes the case that God the Father's property as Father necessarily entails eternal authority (not greater/lesser *value*) within the Godhead, noting of interactions between Persons, "This relationship marked by the Father's authority and the Son's submission is never, never reversed."[114]

What, then, are some of the decrees unique to God the Father? First, He initiated the creation of the universe. This not only includes all physical things—past, present, and future—but also metaphysical and intangible things like time, logic, the laws of physics the universe obeys, universal moral laws existing as an expression of His holy character, etc. All of the cosmos came into being because God decreed it to happen. When God saw fit to enact His eternal decree, He merely had to utter the words, "Let there be light," and, as the Bible records in Genesis 1:3, "there was light." God asserted His Divine primacy to Job, asking, "Where were you when I laid the foundation of the earth . . . Who determined its measurements?" (Job 38:4-5a).

God the Father not only decreed the initiation of the created order, but He decrees everything that comes to pass *within* the created order. While this, at first blush, might seem like a staggering statement, it is irrational that the being that is truly God could have anything occur outside of His control. Not only would this strip Him of the essential property of omnipotence by limiting His authority and capability, it would ultimately strip him of being God. As incomprehensible as it sounds, the hairs on our head (Matt. 10:30) are known and decreed by God. He causes big things like springs to gush forth (Ps. 104:10), and He causes the smallest of things—such as a sparrow dying—which, according to Jesus, cannot happen apart from the will of God the Father (Matt. 10:29). In conducting the flow of the universe, God uses means and secondary causes, even evil (Acts 2:23), to bring everything He decrees to come to pass. The directing of means and causes to accomplish His will is known as the "doctrine of providence."

If the spring itself had divine consciousness, it would be analogous to the spring orifice spewing out a piece of impermeable chert rock from deep within its aquifer. The propulsive emission of the spring shoots this rock out and entrusts it into the arms of the stream, which carries it to a precise spot some 700-plus feet downstream that needs reinforced flooring to prevent losing seepage. The spring orifice, like God the Father, causes this chert to come into the stream "ecoverse," where stream members, such as the current, along with secondary causes carry out the will for this rock's placement in the stream "ecoverse."

God the Father not only decrees everything that happens in the created order, He also enacts the plan of redemption and the ultimate election of His people. As the eternal plan to redeem His prized creation, God the Father decreed to send God the Son into the created order as their Savior (Isa. 53:10; Jn. 3:17, 7:28; Heb. 10:7-9). Before time or creation even existed, God the Father decreed—out of His love and holy mercy—those He would redeem through union with the second Person of the Trinity, Jesus, and the impartation of spiritual life through the third Person of the Trinity, the Holy Spirit (Eph. 1:3-5; 2 Thess. 2:13; 2 Tim. 1:9). God the Father, by eternal decree, grants the spiritual birth of people. All human beings are born physically alive but spiritually dead (Eph. 2:1-5)—eschewing the light of the holy for unholy, unspiritual desires to be their own god. Spiritually dead people cannot understand spiritual truths (1 Cor. 2:14) that incline and inform them toward reconciliation with God (Jn. 3:3-5). During His incarnation, Jesus Himself taught not only that no one could believe in Him unless the Father first decreed and drew them to Him (Jn. 6:44, 65), but also that belief itself is a gift from the Father (Jn. 6:29) and that every single person the Father decrees to believe in Christ will come to Him (Jn. 6:37). The coming to, or desire for, Christ—a spiritual act—comes by way of God the Father decreeing individuals be granted spiritual life.

Finally, God the Father acts as the Divine Ruler. He exudes and presents the holy standard by which all moral beings will be judged. Early twentieth century theologian Louis Berkhof put it well: "[It is God the Father's] work of representing the Trinity in the Counsel of Redemption, as the holy and righteous Being, whose right was violated."[115] He mediates His eternal edicts, His law, and His control over all that is, in harmony with the other two Persons of the Trinity in holiness. He stands in, as the other two co-equal Persons are decreed to be sent out, as the holy Ruler and Sovereign Monarch over the universe. In relation to the spring, God the Father is represented as the spring pool, the first subsistence of the spring, from which essence (water) flows the other two subsistences, and therefrom exists all that is the holistic "spring system."

God the Son

We know Him as a personal Being, most commonly called by His incarnation name, Jesus Christ. Unsurprisingly then, the term, "God the Son," or "second Person of the Trinity," can, at times, sound cold and impersonal. A common misnomer is that "Jesus Christ" is His full name. It is not. Jesus—or the variant Hebrew name, *Joshua*—was His name, the root meaning of which is "rescuer" or, in a redemptive application, "Jehovah is salvation."[116] "Christ" stands as Jesus' Divine, eschatological title. Like each member of the Trinity, God the Son exists eternally with a distinct personality, yet comprised of the same Divine essence, whereby all Persons of the Trinity subsist in Divine harmony.

The name "Jesus" is not even the first name used for the second Person of the Trinity in the chronology of the New Testament. For this, we turn to the unparalleled brilliance of the prologue to the Gospel of John, whose flow of truth connects back with the very beginning of the Bible, bearing witness to the self-existence, work, and eternal being of the second Person of the Trinity. Before doing so, peering into the stream, representing God the Son, will be clearer if we first examine how early Greek philosophy facilitated its comprehension.

The Greek philosopher Plato, who preceded the writing of the New Testament, believed, among other things, in the superiority of the immaterial realm over that of the material/physical world. The "forms," as they were called, were like perfect ideas of all things that exist in the material world as flawed imitations. The dilemma faced by Plato and later derivative Platonists was just how the immaterial forms received existence in the physical world. Simplistically put, the answer the Platonist philosophers developed was that the medium connecting the physical with the non-physical was what they called the *Logos*, which is the Greek word translated in English as "word." But *logos* meant more than merely "word" to the philosophers. It signified the intangible, but real, meta-physical reasoning and rational order that permeates the physical world—a kind of mental discourse played out from God's mind.[117] In time, Greek philosophy came to regard the Logos as the impersonal intermediary that the ultimate form/god, who was transcendently aloof, utilized to create and coordinate the cosmos.

Eventually, the Jewish philosopher Philo came along in the early first century and attempted to meld Greek philosophy with Jewish theology, positing that the Logos was a distinct entity through which the cosmos was created and governed. Imagine God willing a thought, and the thought itself visibly springing into action to become a reality. My thoughts are me, just like your thoughts are you. They are essential to make us who we are. We cannot exist in our full being without our thoughts. But our thoughts, alone, as segmented from the rest of our being, are just a part of what is collectively "us." While our thoughts and ideas are distinct from our brains, thoughts cannot exist wholly separated from the rational source that expresses them. Such is the unity and distinction of the Logos, which unifies God's ideas with material acts. Philo's work was developed more fully by Justin Martyr in the second century, but the groundwork was being laid to connect the metaphysical "inner discourse" of God to a personal Being, Who manifested that discourse. The manifestation of this Being was vaguely understood as the actualization of the private, Divine discourse into physical and metaphysical reality. But to the Jews, the Person and nature of this Being was still a mystery.[118]

The apostle John, under the inspiration of the third Person of the Trinity (more on that later), gave the answer to this mystery with the Logos being none other than the second Person of the Trinity Himself—the pre-incarnate Jesus Christ. John's Gospel begins, "In the beginning was the Word, and the Word was with God, And the Word was God." In the original Greek, the word translated "word" is *Logos*.

This passage used categories that not only would have been understood by the Greco-Roman world, but also would have enlightened them by filling in missing pieces their own epistemology could not provide. The passage would have, likewise, resonated with John's Jewish audience by offering a link to the beginning of the Old Testament Hebrew Bible. John fluidly accomplished this by introducing the Logos as Divinely God, yet distinct from God the Father, eternally present with Him during God's own inner rational discourse. Given the Greek language can be much more expressive than the English translation, this simple verse packs much greater meaning when we understand that the word translated "with" in the Greek means an intimate relationship as used elsewhere to convey a close "face-to-face relationship."[119]

Moreover, the simple verb "was," translated from the Greek, indicates a continuous action from the past, something without a point of origin.[120] This speaks to the Logos being eternal. Calvin revered John's masterful precision, noting how after distinguishing the unique person of the Logos, he "calls us back to the one essence" by emphasizing "the Word was God."[121]

The prologue from John is also significant in that it carries forward direction allusions to the Genesis creation account, where God spoke, and the creating was done. John 1:2-4 reads, "He was in the beginning with God. All things were made through him, and without him was not any thing made that was made. In him was life, and the life was the light of men."

Correspondingly, if we reach back to the opening verses of the Bible in the book of Genesis, we see that God was not alone at creation. Case in point, Genesis 1:3 reads, "And God said, 'Let there be light,' and there was light." John Calvin offered a deft comment concerning the presence of God the Son, while God the Father spoke creation into existence: "It were certainly most absurd to imagine that it is only a fleeting and evanescent voice, which is sent out into the air, and comes forth beyond God." Calvin bolsters the case for the eternality of the Logos and His participation in creation by explaining, "Since at the very moment when God said, 'Let there be light,' the energy of the Word was immediately exerted, it must have existed long before."[122] Genesis 1:26 also speaks to the personal plurality of God at creation with the conversational declaration, "Let us make man in Our image."

John takes the development of the Logos one step further in chapter one, verse fourteen, adding, "And the Word became flesh and dwelt among us . . . " God's Word and creative thought has now appeared as a real human being in Jesus Christ. John then fully submerges us in the stream, declaring the Logos became man, Jesus Christ—truly God and truly man—in order to consummate the eternal plan of redemption. In his theological genius, John used a term that squared biblically with Old Testament teaching, yet was also applicable and understood by his present Greek audience and beyond—even to us today.

The spring, too, helps us understand how the second Person of the Trinity exists eternally as and within God but with distinct properties of the Son. It sounds confusing to fathom that God the Son is eternal in His essence, eternal in His person, and yet eternally proceeds from the Father. Calvin comes to our aid again, plainly articulating, "His essence is without beginning, while his person has its beginning in God."

The picture delineated earlier of the Logos as the rational discourse emanating from God the Father may help our understanding. Envision within that illustration the first and second Persons concentrically co-existing in symbiotic procession, as thoughts visibly springing into action (Son) after emerging from the mind that wills them (Father). God, as an eternal Being, thinks thoughts that are eternal. Thus, those thoughts can reside distinctively/hypostatically "within God," flow from God, and be God, in essence.

The spring and stream support that analogy. The spring is the origin of all the area that forms the spring system: the spring orifice pool, the stream channels, the fog and moisture that proceeds from it, and the immediate land/airspace nourished by the moisture. (For our illustration, if the spring system existed in a closed vacuum, that isolated "universe" could be called, coining a new word, the spring's "ecoverse.") The spring and stream, as demonstrated earlier, are two separate subsistences of the spring, yet they could not exist in isolation.

The spring is unique and differentiated from the stream channel. But if there were ever a point where they were segmented from each other, we would cease to have a fresh water spring. It would simply be a pool or a pond. Imagine the picture of an azure blue spring pool that keeps collecting water from an orifice, but doesn't have any outflow. It would be irrational and impossible to have a spring that perpetually generates essence but has no outflow and never gains volume.

Next, imagine a stream channel, segregated perhaps only by a few feet from this spring pool, flowing onward without a confluence point that feeds it. It is inconceivable and irrational. But a picture of the two juxtaposed to one another points to the fact that you can't have a corporeal spring unless all the parts are "eternally" in place together. If they aren't "eternal" and in place together from the onset, you can't have what is defined as a spring. (Note: This illustration does depict one weakness of the analogy: the third subsistence of the spring, the fog. The fog and/or invisible moisture is not a necessary subsistence in order to have "a spring," as the third Person of the Trinity *is* essential for the existence of the tri-personal Trinity. The necessity of a Divine Person for all of the created order is a different plane of existence than the appearance of fog necessarily accompanying a stream. However, scientifically it could be argued that a spring and watershed necessitate the water vapor that carries moisture into the surrounding ecosystem.)

While the spring's subsistences must be in place together from its relative eternity, a logical order amongst them is a necessity. The spring pool necessarily is the first subsistence of the spring system, from which flows the stream in a harmonious fashion. The water that emerges perpetually from the spring orifice, that shared divine essence in our spring analogy, is already "the stream." The stream is eternally/perpetually an outflow of the spring, just as the Person of the Son is eternally an outflow of the Father. There is never a time when the stream is not there, just as there is never a time in the existence of the spring that the orifice is not there. Once the water flows through the orifice, those collective water molecules bonded together representing the shared, inseparable essence are immediately "the stream" as they flow from the spring. This is perhaps what Calvin meant when he said, "That logos, who was God, was with the Father, and has his own distinct and peculiar glory with the Father . . . certainly could not be an external or figurative splendor, but must necessarily have been a hypostasis which dwelled inherently in God Himself."[123]

Understanding now that the second person of the Trinity created everything out of the will of the first Person, just as the stream is the subsistence of the spring that encompasses all that flows from the formative power of the spring, we would be remiss to examine His other functions. His roles, like his titles, are profound and reflect nuances at different times of redemptive history. One name enduring throughout, as His place in the Triune order would indicate, is His being referred to as the "Son," both before the incarnation (Jn. 1:14; Gal. 4:4), during the incarnation (Lk. 10:22; Jn. 17:1), and after the incarnation (1 Cor. 15:28; Matt. 20:23). It would be a mistake, however, to confuse (as we often do, given the limitations of the English language) the meaning of "Son" by reducing it as being any less Divine than God the Father or Holy Spirit.

Existing eternally as the Son does carry distinct properties not shared by the other Persons of the Trinity. Namely, according to Bruce Ware, "The Son's unique property, necessary to Him as Son yet not possessed by the Father, is that He is eternally begotten of the Father, begotten not made." Confusion over this word "begotten" has plagued the church for centuries, as false implications arose that the Son was a created being. This errant conclusion can be attributed to differences in the Greek and later derivative languages, seen as the word "begotten" in English indicates something produced or created. Debate continues today over implications of this word.

But as B.B. Warfield and other scholars have explained, the word often translated "begotten" in the Greek is *monogenes*, meaning "unique" or "one and only."[124] In fact, the same Greek word in John 1:14, translated by many Bible translations as "begotten," is also applied to God the Father, the unique "One and only" first Person of the Trinity, a couple of verses later in John 1:18. Thus, when Jesus is described as "begotten" in John 1:14, John is not saying He was born and created by the Father, but rather that God the Son exists as the unique One,

Whose incommunicable property is the uniqueness of His identity as the eternal Son, which resides in and eternally flows from the Father. The Son's inimitable identity is incapable of being shared with any other being, akin to the unique subsistence that encompasses every spatial area consumed by the stream, bringing life to all it reaches, yet emanating from the spring. While this doctrine was affirmed by early church creeds and church fathers like Augustine, the spring motif offers timeless symbolic affirmation.

Fortunately, the second Person of the Trinity didn't just stop at creation. Not only did God the Son create the universe, but He also sustains it second by second. Hebrews 1:3b proclaims, "he upholds the universe by the word of his power." Congruent with that truth the apostle Paul declared, "For by him all things were created, in heaven and on earth, visible and invisible . . . all things were created through him and for him. And he is before all things, and in him all things hold together" (Col. 1:16-17). Jonathan Edwards affirmed this reality, noting:

> It is evident that the same Word, the same Son of God, that made the world, also upholds it in being, and governs it. This is evident, in part, unto reason. For upholding the world in being, and creating it, are not properly distinct works; since it is manifest, that upholding the world in being is the same with a continued creation; and consequently, that creating the world is but the beginning of upholding it.[125]

What reality could best sustain the spring's ecoverse than the stream itself? All that the spring encompasses is continuously filled by the stream, akin to the truth of Ephesians 4:10 that proclaims God the Son "fills all things." Every part of the universe has been filled with His Divine blueprint. Amazingly, His sustaining power did not cease during the incarnation, when He lived as a man, for He still commanded every molecule and every scientific law to obedience.

Early church father Athanasius noted, "Existing in a human body, to which He Himself gives life, He is still the source of life to all the universe, present in every part of it, yet outside the whole . . . His body was for Him not a limitation, but an instrument, so that He was both in it and in all things, and outside all things, resting in the Father alone."[126] Likewise, the subsistence of the stream sustains its ecoverse—its branches transport vital nutrients to other parts of its interdependent system. The stream runs great lengths to nourish its resident plants and animals, like a mother spooning medicine to her blanched children. It traverses hills, acting as a natural thermostat, providing consistent, stable airflow and moisture. Its arms and depths provide diverse neighborhoods for the life teeming within its bounds.

The life swelling within God the Son is possible because as the ultimate reality, He Himself is life. John 1:4 plainly reveals that "in him was life," and later, in John 10:10, he builds on this to show this life the Son gives is abundant, more fully understood as eternal. Jesus states in John 14:6 that He "is the Life." God the Son unequivocally affirms His and God the Father's logically necessary self-existence by noting in John 5:26 that They both have life in Themselves.

Analogically, just as the stream has life in itself (relatively speaking in the sense of perpetual flow of essence that requires the stream to always "be"), the stream is the life for the ecoverse. The life that lives in the closed universe of its waters could not exist without the stream. Its perpetual flow replenishes and balances the oxygen necessary for existence. Look no further than the tragic flooding that occurred around the winter of 2015 in Lake Taneycomo in Branson, Missouri, haven to some of the best brown trout in the United States. It resulted in water stagnation, low oxygen levels, and the ultimate death of hundreds of fish. However, the stream is not only the sustainer of life within its banks, but it also sustains life residing outside its banks. There, the flora and fauna alike flourish from its logistical hydration, airflow, and watershed topography. The stream is the constant, reliable sustenance enabling its inhabitants to survive.

God the Son is Truth. He is Truth in Himself as the outward manifestation of the ultimate reality. In Him, there is no lie or contradiction

(Heb. 6:18). All that God wills, all that He says, all that He reveals, all the acts He performs are revelations of truth executed and dispensed by Jesus Christ, His Word, and truth. In the stream, all of its unfettered reliability concerning laws of chemistry, physics, and biology—all the reality of the stream—are consistent expressions of truth. The stream is the truth for all its tenants who cannot operate contrary to it. The life abiding within it is dependent to live and adapt to the calculus and physical demonstrations of the stream. And it is only by Jesus Christ, the One who sustains and fills all things, that the stream exists.

The plethora of roles and titles ascribed to God the Son vastly exceed the scope of this book. Entire books have been devoted to examining the person of Jesus. So, in closing, we shall focus on two final roles He fulfills as the second Person of the Trinity. The first is the crossover and interrelated role as the "Messiah," the "true Israel," "Lamb of God," "Redeemer," "our Reconciliation," "our Righteousness," or simply, "Savior." These titles speak to God the Son's redemptive role as the One promised in the Garden of Eden to right the devastation wrought by the fall of the first man. The holiness of an infinite, perfect God demands that He cannot compromise His holy character to tolerate that which is imperfect, unholy, and rebellious. His holiness also deems a transgression against an infinite Being as an act of cosmic treason, which warrants an infinite punishment. Thus, the just penalty laid down at the Garden for cosmic treason against God, what we call sin, is death. And thus, death passed to all men and women because all have sinned (Rom. 5:12), resulting in humanity's utterly hopeless predicament: universal, infinite separation from God.

It was then, at the incarnation, that God the Son's redemptive titles came into view. Jesus was born of a virgin so as not to be tainted with the original sin innately present within every human being. As God the Son, Jesus was truly God and became truly man, with a human nature and an eternal, Divine nature united in one Person. He lived a life of complete righteousness that exclusively affords one eternal peace and standing with God. As our Redeemer, Jesus consummated the eternal plan of redemption by "The Great Exchange." Jesus died a sacrificial death as our Substitute on the cross—the execution device used to crucify Him—where God the Father removed the sins from all people He would redeem and placed/punished them on Jesus, the only Person capable of bearing an eternal punishment per His eternal Divine nature. The Father then took the only human holiness to ever exist—Jesus' perfect righteousness—and imputed it to the people He would redeem. Thus, as our Savior, our Redeemer, our Reconciliation, God's holiness was not compromised. There is no analogy from the stream befitting of that.

Finally, in a role inconceivable to some, the second Person of the Trinity acts as the Divine Judge. The very Jesus that took on human flesh at the incarnation to redeem His prized creation will also return to exact Divine justice (Jn. 5:27, 16:11). Now, the idea of final judgment is antithetical to the modern libertine mind that seeks autonomy and resists accountability to anyone. However, it is a myopic view to reject what we previously covered—that there must be a Creator to account for us. Ultimately, we have been made "from him and through him and to him" (Rom. 11:36); we are not our own (1 Cor. 6:19); and we are His inheritance (Eph. 1:18; 1 Cor. 15:23). When we are humble enough to admit our very existence is owed to God, the idea of a final judgment, when the harmony of created order will be restored by God the Son and handed back over to God the Father (1 Cor. 15:24), is not at all inconsistent. We can then confess both God the Son and the subsistence of the stream as the life-givers and judges to which the life within them is owed.

God the Holy Spirit

There is nothing as resuscitating when the trout stop striking than being out in the stream and having a patch of chilled air inexplicably engulf you. Without a hint of wind, a fog evasively breezes in, wrapping you in its bosom as if the Holy Spirit Himself breathed upon you. This scene, like the one beginning this chapter, often appears at dusk, as if to peacefully grant closure to the day, while letting the observer know that the Sustainer of the spring will preserve its beauty until the next day. This motif points its audience to the beginning—when the Divine Spirit hovered over nascent creation, ordering the lifeless morass into beauty. What is more lamentable than those who never get out into the habitation of the spring to experience its fog are those who never experience the third Person of the Trinity: God the Holy Spirit. While less is written of Him than the other two Persons of the Trinity, His role and His Divinity are no less worthy.

Analogically, in the theology of the spring, the third Person of the Trinity, God the Holy Spirit, is represented by the fog that is sporadically manifested within the stream. Unlike the spring and the stream, which are always present and visible, the fog is not always visible to the spring's spectators, even though it is always present, just like God the Holy Spirit. It is not just the visible fog or mist that is seen, but also the moisture-charged air emanating from the outworking of the stream that encompasses the watershed. The water carried about the ecoverse by this fog and vapor is the same substance of the spring, moving through the air in a wave of nourishment and bringing those it reaches into a direct connection with the stream.

God the Holy Spirit, like God the Father and God the Son, subsists from the Divine essence but uniquely manifests Himself so that His Person is distinct. The fog or mist of the stream captures this word picture well. Its patchy effulgence sporadically morphs about the spring's ecoverse, like a mini-supernova of moisture, serving as the intermediary between the spring and the immediate physical world it supports. The mist represents a middle ground, an intermediary point of bifurcation between liquid and land. It is not fully saturated like the water flowing through the stream, though being comprised of the same condensed essence, and it is not vacuous air, either.

The Holy Spirit could be likened to an Intermediary between the first two Persons of the Trinity and the created order, as well as the Intermediary between those physical humans He indwells and their spiritual union with God the Son (Eph. 2:18). The Holy Spirit has been called a spiritual amphibian of sorts, co-existing with the God the Father and God the Son in heavenly places before the created order, and yet also forming the physical earth and forming the spiritual life within each of God's elect He indwells. In the pages that follow, we will delineate His unique role in the Godhead and see how His analogous Person functions within the spring.

The first thing we must establish is that God the Holy Spirit is a Person who exhibits personal characteristics; He is not an impersonal force or energy. The Greek translation for Holy Spirit, *pneuma,* literally means "to breathe" in its root form. The Holy Spirit is referred to by Jesus with personal pronouns (Jn. 15:26, 16:14). Jesus also likens the Holy Spirit to a Defense Counselor, a very personal role, using the legal term *parakletos* (where we get the term "Paraclete"), which means "One who comes alongside those set apart" [people regenerated by the Holy Spirit].[127]

The Holy Spirit can talk (Acts 8:29; 10:19-20), something not done by a dispassionate force. The Holy Spirit can also be grieved and insulted (Eph. 4:30; Matt. 12:31-32), reactions possible only for a person. Scripture also ascribes deity to Him; thus, sinning against the Holy Spirit is considered sinning against God (Acts 5:3-4). Furthermore, salvation, that can come only from God, is attributed to a work of the Holy Spirit (Titus 3:5; Rom. 8:11). Therefore, we can safely conclude that the third Person of the Trinity is every bit God and every bit a Person, just as the fog floating down the stream corridor is every bit spring and every bit fog subsistence, consisting of the same essence of water molecules sifted from the subsistence that is the stream.

God the Holy Spirit does not appear downstream as a secondary character in the Bible. He appears as early as the second verse of the entire book, performing one of five prominent, Divine roles that are unique to His Person, namely bearing witness to the work of God. In Genesis chapter one, immediately after God the Father begins His work of creating the cosmos through God the Son as the creative agent, we read in the second part of verse two, "And the Spirit of God was hovering over the face of the waters." These waters and the earth were not yet ordered and arranged to suit the apex of the creation to come. The only thing that stirred was a brand new, physical reality that had been brought into existence, and its Creator was hovering above to display His Authorship. The same verb used in Genesis 1:2 is later used in Deuteronomy 32:11 to describe an eagle fluttering above its nest of younglings, bearing witness to all of nature in its regal place of guardianship and author of the life within the nest.

Throughout the Old Testament, we see the Holy Spirit fulfill His role as proclaiming the presence of God, often in the form of a cloud or fog. His presence with the Hebrews during the Exodus in the form of a cloud not only bore witness to God's presence in leading them out of Egypt, eventually to camp at the twelve springs of Elim (Ex. 13:21; 15:27), but also to His presence as their Protector. His protective presence was demonstrated, literally, as a cloud moving to stand in the way of the pursuing Egyptians, blocking an attack on the rear flank of the Hebrew exiles (Ex. 14:19). The presence of God with His people on that occasion indelibly testified to His promise to protect and preserve them for generations to come. Before God delivered His law to His people at Mount Sinai, He first descended from the mountain to Moses in a cloud (Ex. 19:9). During Israel's sojourn in the wilderness, the presence of God was manifested at the tent of meeting as a cloud that would descend and rest upon the tent's entrance. The cloud signified the presence of the Holy One, causing all the people to rise in worship (Ex. 33:9-10). Throughout the wilderness wanderings, whenever the cloud of God would depart from the tabernacle, the people would pack up, knowing it was time to leave, knowing the futility of abiding outside the presence of God (Ex. 40:36-38; Num. 9:15-23).

God the Holy Spirit did not function as a witness to the presence and sovereignty of God in the Old Testament alone. In one of the clearest passages demonstrating the distinct Persons of the Trinity, converging in time and space to declare their tri-mutual glorification at the baptism of Jesus, we see God the Holy Spirit in the likeness of a dove, simultaneously acting alongside God the Father and God the Son. His benediction came fluttering down, hovering and descending upon the baptismal waters to rest on God the Son, proclaiming Triune glory at the Son's mission and declaring where life could ultimately be found (Matt. 3:13-17).

I cannot help equating the presence of God and the presence of life signified by the Holy Spirit with scenes from my childhood. I remember waking up at the dark, pre-dawn hours to embark on a trip to Bennett Springs State Park. Tired and restless after a couple of hours of riding in the car, infusions of excitement would come with the scant rays of sunlight that intermittently scraped over the verdant ridgelines, only to be lost again when the car plunged down the next hill. This cycle repeated itself as we traveled up hills and down hills where the light was always overcome again by the pre-dawn darkness. But I always knew the tease was about to end when we would wind our way down one particular Ozark ridge. As we descended, we could see the fog rising from the stream along the contour of the jagged valley below. The fog, like the Holy Spirit, bore witness to the presence of life. To a little boy, its draw was irresistible.

For the early American pioneers, the sight of the fog lifting from the stream was no less cause for exuberance. Imagine, if you can remove yourself from modern comforts, traveling across uncharted terrain by wagon or horse. The pioneers were unable to move by night; and, if travelling by day (depending upon the time of year), the heat of the sun could be grueling on both people and animals. While worrying about heat, profuse sweating, and exhaustion, they also bore the mental anguish of moving across unknown regions and not knowing where the next source of water would be. Consider going days without water, only to come across a stagnant pond or mud puddle riddled with cholera, E. coli, or other bacteria that was bound to cause sickness. But then, consider the delight of a traveler, after wandering over hills and valleys with no water in sight, to crest the top of a hill and see the fog of the stream below, bearing witness to the replenishment and sustenance of life itself. That fog and mist could not proclaim a greater message, a message of a new hope. A new ordering of life.

The task of ordering is another seamless function of God the Holy Spirit, a seamless outflow of the Divine will through the harmonious Persons of the Trinity to bring things to their completion. In addition to witnessing the presence of God, the Holy Spirit is seen ordering the created world from a mass of matter into a fully synchronized universe, programmed to perfection. The raw dirt and land created by God the Son was not yet fit for the Godhead's final purposes of being subdued by humanity. It took a work of God the Holy Spirit to arrange the waters into oceans and rivers, and the land into continents, forests, and grasslands. God the Holy Spirit hovered about, energizing the created world and setting things into motion. Calvin put it aptly: "It is obvious that the eternal Spirit always existed in God, seeing He cherished and sustained the confused materials of heaven and earth before they possessed order or beauty."[128]

In Genesis chapter two, after the earth, sun, plants, and animals have been created, we read where God sent a mist (or *spring* in some translations) over the land to nourish it. The mist fed small bushes and plants and prepared the soil like a heap of clay to be molded into the first human being (Gen. 2:6). Once the dirt had been ordered and prepared, God formed a human body from it. In a remarkable play on words, we are told in Genesis 2:7 that God breathed His holy breath, or Holy Spirit, into the man, *"pneuma-ing His holy pneuma"* if you will, giving the first human life by the creative ordering and life-giving power of God the Holy Spirit.

The Holy Spirit continues to bring order to the created world within the lives of believers. It is the Spirit that indwells believers and brings order to their spiritual lives by guiding them in how to pray, what to speak, and how to live in the ways of truth (Matt. 10:20; Rom. 8:26-27; Jn. 16:13). The Holy Spirit equips believers with talents and gifts, making order of their lives for the use of ministry (1 Cor. 12:9-11; Ex. 28:3). Even the Bible itself, God's special revelation, was brought to completion by the ordering of the Holy Spirit, supernaturally inspiring its authors and bringing to mind the recollection of what to write (Jn. 14:26; 2 Pet. 1:21). By His ordering, the Holy Spirit brings that which He acts upon to completion—the universe, our spiritual lives, and even God's revealed Word—a symbol of how He Himself completes the Trinity.

A third primary function of the third person of the Trinity is that He is the Life-giver. Given the congruity from which persons and functions flow from the Trinity, it is not surprising to see some apparent overlap of roles. Overlap in the work of the Holy Spirit can be seen in how He is ordering that to which He gives life all in one fell swoop. But the overwhelming context where we find the Holy Spirit imparting life is by granting spiritual life to spiritually dead people by way of regeneration.

Regeneration is a big word that is synonymous with what we call being "born again." It is the supernatural act by which God, out of His eternal decree and by His eternal grace, gives spiritual life to people, all of whom, as noted earlier, are naturally born with physical life but with no hint of spiritual life. In our natural state, the disposition of our hearts is enslaved to sin and completely hostile toward God, Whom we consider our enemy (Rom. 8:7-8; Eph. 2:1-3). As noted earlier, because we have no spiritual life in us, we do not even have the ability to understand spiritual things (1 Cor. 2:14).

Chapter six will provide a composite treatment of regeneration. Suffice it to say, for now, the Holy Spirit's initial work in our lives, the new birth, fashions itself instantaneously to the core of our being. He overcomes us, not only to radically purify and change the disposition of our hearts with a new desire for Christ that we lacked just moments before, but He also indwells us, making us alive as entirely new spiritual creatures able to understand spiritual truth (Eph. 2:5; Titus 2:5; 2 Cor. 5:17; 1 Pet. 1:3). Like the wind that comes upon us while fishing in the stream, we neither see it come nor do we see where it goes, but the evidence that it was here is clear by the ripples in the water, the swaying of the grass on the bank, and the changed inclination of our hearts. And like the wind, we have no control over where it goes or what it does, just as the Holy Spirit comes and goes, giving eternal life to whom God the Father has ordained (Jn. 17:2). The necessity of regeneration by the Holy Spirit for salvation is made clear by Jesus when He said that "unless one is born again [by the Spirit] he cannot see the kingdom of God" (Jn. 3:3).

Analogically, like the Holy Spirit, the mist of the spring also comes and goes, giving and sustaining life to the physical world it touches. Like the mist that came onto the land to prepare the dirt to form the first man, the mist and the fog of the spring run ashore from the stream to breathe a vital infusion of nourishment to the plant life that adorns its ecoverse. To most, the fog of the spring might not seem like a big deal, just a nice mystical touch to the spring motif. However, research has demonstrated that fog and mist provide very fortifying benefits to the foliage in the immediate environment they encompass. For example, researchers have determined that fog is ten times more concentrated than rain, which can explain how plants are nourished in places like the Smoky Mountains, where eighty percent of the sulfur and nitrogen comes from fog.[129] The Redwood Forest of California is another example where studies have shown that trees utilize fog water for sustenance in lieu of dry soil.[130] Moreover, fog climates have been shown to reduce the transpiration of plants—that is, the loss of moisture.[131]

The fog not only enriches the soil and the vegetation growing from it, but the stream water itself is also enriched from it. A study conducted on the east side of Maui, Hawaii, determined that stream water is enhanced by fog. Specifically, the study found "isotopic values of mountain streams and springs to be unexpectedly enriched in heavier isotopes for their altitude . . . The best explanation for the observed isotopic composition was that fog drip contributed substantially to stream water and shallow groundwater."[132]

Naturally, while the Holy Spirit quickens us with new spiritual life by His regenerating work, we continue to exist physically. And because we continue to exist physically, we still are fraught with the inclinations of the natural-born man or woman before the Holy Spirit gave us spiritual life and, with it, a desire for concomitant righteousness. While we will wage this internal war with the sin that lies within us until the day we die, it is another role of the Holy Spirit—and a fruit, or evidence, of our new birth—to help quench this sin as we are sanctified. As our Sanctifier, the Holy Spirit indwells us in order to help make us holy, conforming us to the image of Jesus (Rom. 8:29). We are instructed to "walk by the Spirit" to mortify the desires of the flesh—that is, our pre-regenerate nature that is adversarial toward our Creator (Gal. 5:16).

But how do we "walk" with the Spirit? As our Sanctifier, the Holy Spirit convicts us of our sin and righteousness (Jn. 16:8). When the Holy Spirit, God Himself, takes up residence within us at regeneration, He doesn't lie idle until we die. He actively works within us, convicting us of sin—those things that don't honor Him—and, conversely, steering us toward those righteous things that do give Him honor. The things that once gave us no hesitation to do—lying or gossip or sexual impurity— now begin to bother us as we walk with Him, relying on His guidance in our lives on a daily basis. He guides us to the truth of the righteousness we need—the righteousness of Christ not inherent within us. This internal pruning of our souls, with new desires budding like blossoms on a fruit tree, transforms our lives towards Christ-likeness. R.C. Sproul, as he does so brilliantly with such brevity, shrewdly said, "It is the task of the Holy Spirit, Who is sent by the Father and the Son, to apply the work of Christ to our lives."[133] As we walk with Him, with each step, the work of Christ is applied to us, sanctifying us.

The Holy Spirit also sanctifies us by empowering us to discern spiritual truth. In order to guide us in all truth (Jn. 16:13), we must first have an ability to understand it. I doubt there's a person in the world who's never encountered a text from the Bible which he can't understand. Or perhaps you have read a particular passage thirty times before, and then, all of a sudden, the light of understanding turns on during the thirty-first time you read it. That is the work of the Holy Spirit, our Helper and Illuminator, Who shines light onto the truth so that we can understand it. We should categorically note that the Holy Spirit does not reveal new knowledge, but, rather, He enlightens us with understanding of the timeless truth He has already specially revealed in Scripture.

Illumination is biblically explained in 1 Corinthians 2:10, where the apostle Paul, writing under the inspiration of the Holy Spirit, explains, "These things God has revealed to us through the Spirit. For the Spirit searches everything, even the depths of God." To be sure, Paul is not saying the Spirit is not Divine or not omniscient in having to search through the Father's infinite database of knowledge.[134] Rather, the word search is on our behalf and refers to the ability to see truth we missed, gifting us with understanding of what was previously not discerned. Theologian J.I. Packer summed up the sanctification of illumination well: "The Spirit, however, opens and unveils our minds and attunes our hearts so that we understand (Eph. 1:17-18; 3:18-19; 2 Cor. 3:14-16; 4:6). As by inspiration He provided scripture truth for us, so now by illumination He interprets it to us."[135]

The fog, as the third subsistence of the stream, has no sanctifying power. Those objects that the fog of the spring encapsulates are amoral, which, by nature, cannot be made more or less holy by another amoral subject. Only God Himself has the Authority to consecrate an impersonal, amoral object as holy, as He did with the ground, where He first appeared to Moses at Mount Horeb (Ex. 3:5). This is another limitation of the analogy of the spring to the Trinity. However, one could figuratively argue that all things enveloped by the fog, as an extension of the spring, are "sanctified" in the sense that they are in the presence of the spring, that integral reality which sustains its constituent ecoverse.

Finally, the Third Person of the Trinity acts as our Comforter. When Jesus prepared His disciples with the news of His departure in John 14:16-17, He promised to send the Holy Spirit to be their "Comforter," Who would always dwell within them. His indwelling continues to provide comfort, not unlike the comfort He provided Israel in the Old Testament, dwelling in the camp as they sojourned to the Promised Land. The very word translated in the Bible as "comforter" comes from two Latin words—*cum forte,* meaning "with strength." The phrase has its etymology as a legal term, as in a defense attorney or counselor that comes to the aid of one who is accused by giving them strength, comfort, and voice. This would have been especially meaningful to the early church that met underground and risked execution for their beliefs during a time of rampant persecution by the Roman Empire. The Comforter was within them. *Their* Advocate was the very Spirit of the Divine King.

It is the Divine King that both makes peace with us and leaves His peace within us—a peace the world that doesn't know Him cannot understand. When Jesus said He would always be with us (Matt. 28:20), He wasn't speaking in rhetorical platitudes. He was speaking truthfully, as the Spirit of Jesus abides in all believers. This undoubtedly resonated with the apostle John, who comforted later believers by writing, "he who is in you is greater than he who is in the world" (1 Jn. 4:4b). What greater comfort could there be than that?

I would be remiss to not apply the comfort given to us by God the Holy Spirit to the comfort delivered by the fog of the spring. Like the revelation of the holiness of God, it can frighten us with its mystical aura and, at the same time, comfort us, redirecting our thoughts by illuminating the things of life that really matter. As the warm air of the fog enraptures us and the wispy strands of mist hover about, we are soothed. Little things—like the next fish we catch, or last night's ballgame, or even the promotion at work—don't seem to matter as much. Our thoughts are held captive to a greater reality, the ultimate reality that the fog bears witness to.

No analogy of a perfect God can be a perfect analogy. God, in His holy essence and in His altogether-different plane of existence, makes perfect analogies impossible. But that is not to say that His creation, and those jewels of it that we find near-perfect, cannot speak meaningfully about Him. God, like the spring, is one Divine essence in three distinct Persons/Subsistences. Some people get lost in that paradox of the Trinity, never to return. Some people lose themselves in the beguilement of the spring, never seeing that to which it points. But it is in the theology of the spring where the paradox is reconciled, the Creator is found, and, by one essence and three Persons, the living water subsists.

Reflection Questions

1. Several examples were provided of analogies of the Trinity found in the natural world. What are some analogies of the Trinity that you have heard? How have those analogies been flawed or beneficial to your understanding of the Trinity?

2. Why is it necessary that God exist as a Spirit, a non-physical Being? How can you use this truth when someone asks, "If God is real, why can't I see Him?"

3. Would the appearance of a stream fog or mountain mist give you comfort? Would a visible manifestation of the presence of God comfort or frighten you?

4. How would you explain the distinct persons of the Trinity to someone who believes in modalism? How would you explain that God is not tri-theistic?

5. Just as you can tell the presence of the wind in a certain location by the effects on what it leaves behind (grass swaying, leaves rustling, disordered hair, etc.), what are some evidences of the Holy Spirit coming into someone's life?

6. What are some examples of analogical language that you use every day about your job? Your spouse? Your closest friend?

7. I wrote, "In a sense, every word we use is dependent on analogy." What do you think is meant by that?

CHAPTER FIVE

LIVING WATER: DRAWING AND SUSTAINING THEOLOGICAL AND PHYSIOLOGICAL LIFE

The God who made the world and everything in it, being Lord of heaven and earth, does not live in temples made by man, nor is he served by human hands, as though he needed anything, since he himself gives to all mankind life and breath and everything. And he made from one man every nation of mankind to live on all the face of the earth, having determined allotted periods and the boundaries of their dwelling place, that they should seek God, and perhaps feel their way toward him and find him. Yet he is actually not far from each one of us, for "In him we live and move and have our being"; as even some of your own poets have said, "For we are indeed his offspring."

—Acts 17:24-28

I SHOULD HAVE KNOWN BETTER, that it could only end in frustration. I've watched this movie too many times to not know how it ends. It was my fault for being so naïve during a family reunion to think I could slip in a few minutes of fishing on the Blue Ribbon stretch of the Current River. Don't get me wrong—the idea of fishing during a lull in the reunion was not all naïve. My family understands that if I am within any certain radius of a stream, I invariably get drawn in, rod in tow. But I *was* naïve, thinking I could get in some fly fishing while having one of my boys with me.

I have a son—one who will remain nameless—who possesses the incorrigible gift of finding the most creative ways of landing himself in the water EVERY time I take him fishing. No exaggeration—it's as if the outing cannot qualify as an official fishing trip, unless he gets lured near the bank and falls in. I usually tell him to go upstream if he is going to pull this stunt and to do it by the guy who is catching all the fish so that he might scare some of them downstream to me. On this particular day, his talent was on display again. The groggy kid, bored at the family reunion, became instantly rejuvenated upon bodily contact with the stream. But, as mild a nuisance as it may be, I always try to tell myself it's much better than if he was sitting at home on a couch. It's just part of being a boy, or a human, I figure.

What is it about the magnetism of water and children? It's as if water has some kind of innate, life-giving power that acts as a natural defibrillator when kids get near it. They spring to life from their slumber, despite its cold temperature, depth, or appearance. A body of water could be covered with green pond scum, with a surface temperature of fifty-six degrees, but they wouldn't mind. Kids are seemingly immune to cold water. It's as if they undergo some physiological change and morph into cold-blooded creatures that have no problem tolerating frigid water temperatures. Unlike myself, the older I get, the warmer the water has to be before I'll get in. But kids are just drawn to water with little reservation, as it stimulates life within them.

The sad thing is, I know plenty of adults who live on the opposite end of the continuum. They won't get too close to a church for fear that they might fall in and actually become a part of it. Afraid they might lose themselves in its waters or have to give up something that binds them to the routine flow of life—call it comfort—they remain held in the passive bondage of merely existing. The irony is that losing themselves, or their current grip on life, is often the opening act of a metamorphosis toward truly living.

Whether they realize it or not, adults, too, feel an attraction to water, though its allure is often more overlooked, perhaps due to their transition into a role of provider. Life-giving water is simply viewed in practical terms of what is needed to nourish and clean ourselves. It has become a mundane attraction by necessity, one portion of a busy daily routine. But the element of intrigue is still present, like some beguiling mystery that draws us to it, and not just for the obvious reason of the life sustenance it provides by hydrating our cells. It goes beneath the surface, literally, as we are attracted to the unknown, the uncommon. We know there is life beneath the surface, but what it is and how it survives in this hidden world—one in which we could not survive beyond three minutes without an air tank—is what fascinates us. Such is one reason why I love fly fishing. I'm like a surgeon doing exploratory surgery on nature, and my fly rod is the scalpel that punctures the shroud of the unseen domain, a key unlocking a portal to another world. And the spring is where it all takes place. It becomes a sort of organic temple, that threshold where the natural gives way to the supernatural, and, through it, a greater sense of God and being alive in Him is imbued.

"Have you been born yet, and are you alive?"[136] This rhetorical question, simple in construction, was posed by rock and roll legend Jim Morrison. The front man of the band The Doors, he offered up this probing question on the posthumously released album, *An American Prayer*. As straight-forward as this provocative question is phrased, it was, in many ways, prophetic, being addressed to a generation making rapid technological advancements toward the tuned-out existence of plugging into a television ("TV death," as Morrison called it) or a computer to occupy every free moment. Fast-forward forty years, and it has become all too common to exist but not live.

Though a man with incredible intellect (he had a 149 genius IQ), Morrison's life was a constant struggle to assimilate truth and meaning, and, as most know, he lived out this quest on the stage of rebellion. From his early college days, Morrison embraced the teachings of atheist and nihilist philosopher Friedrich Nietzsche, who declared that life is nothing more than "a will to power."[137] But all one must do is turn to the copious biographies written about Jim Morrison to see that his life was anything but happy and tranquil. In many ways, he was torn between seeking his own will to power and seeking the joy and peace that comes with the ultimate truth. This internal tension is reflected in some of his poetry, where he equates "heartache with the loss of God."[138] Within minutes of proclaiming "cancel my subscription to the resurrection," he ends a song rather apocalyptically by shrieking, "Save us, Jesus!"[139] In many ways, it is an artistic microcosm of the life of a sensitive non-believer, up to the very end.

At this point, you might be asking what Jim Morrison has to do with theology or springs. That's a fair question. Morrison is relevant for two reasons, the first being similar to the opening text of Scripture for this chapter from the book of Acts. The apostle Paul quotes Stoic and Epicurean poets and philosophers popular in his day when he proclaims, "In him we live, and move, and have our being." Paul, ever so shrewdly, never compromised the truth, but used the common truth of the world to funnel the secular toward more specific truth about God. (The fact that this dialog was taking place at a location known as Mars Hill should be telling, as Mars was the Greek god of war, thus, metaphorically framing the picture as spiritual warfare that was taking place between the spokesman of the Creator God and the spokespeople of temporal culture.)

Paul resonated with some of his audience by engaging in discourse that began with general, local truths. His discourse was palatable to Greek thought because to them, the three great mysteries of philosophy and science were questions of life, motion, and being—deep questions to which Paul was able to provide cogent answers. Paul proceeds to leverage these general truths as the pivot for what logic requires: that one absolute, exclusive God brought all people into being, and they exist only by His providence. His corollary teaching in Athens is similar to his instruction to the church at Ephesus, that this God "fills all things" (Eph. 4:10).

While I would never encourage anyone to emulate Jim Morrison, there are some common questions he or other secular pop culture figures pose that turn a conversation back to the ultimate Truth. One could even say that the anti-theist Nietzsche, whose life ended in an insane asylum, got it half-right with his theory of the meaning of life being a "will to power." The Bible and nature teach that man, in his natural state, hates God (Rom. 8:7), cannot understand spiritual things (1 Cor. 2:14), and lives "in the passions of [the] flesh" (Eph. 2:3). Fallen man naturally lives for himself, which is essentially a will to power, and, conversely, the very definition of sin, as defined by the Westminster shorter catechism, is "any want of conformity unto, or transgression of, the law of God."[140]

Now, I'm under no delusion that when Morrison asks, "Have you been born yet, and are you alive?" that he means it in the ultimate sense of the phrase, that is, spiritual birth. But the question he puts before us is a legitimate one. Have you been born yet, and are you alive? Are you mindlessly going through the motions, existing each day with doleful indifference in a slate-shaded world with no hope, meaning, or purpose? Are you the fount of your own hope, joy, or purpose, which inevitably sputters in flow commensurate with the capricious will and impotency of its source (you)? Or are you alive with the perpetual flow of what Jesus called "living water" (Jn. 7:37-38)? Water that springs forth and never dries up. Water that infinitely fills. Water that unceasingly satisfies. Water that colors life anew with previously unseen iridescent hues. Water that springs forth in eternal deluge, an ever-flowing adhesive between you and its eternal source. It is in this spring that we drown our natural-born proclivities of self-reliance to live, move, and have our being in the supernatural waters of eternal life.

Rest assured that the new spiritual life engendered by the new birth (for which a spring, in my opinion, provides the best natural iconography, bridging the natural and supernatural, in depicting how this life is drawn and sustained), is not synonymous with a temporal quick-fix or a better way to an easier life. But spiritual birth does carry, as a byproduct, an enhanced sensitivity to better enhance the physical, emotional, and spiritual dimensions of life. In the same way that we recapture the wonder of life by visiting the spring itself, greater meaning and joy in life do come from unplugging and taking a closer look at the spiritual living waters offered by our Creator.

But springs are not just wonder, but also a means of provision, both spiritually and physically. They are chronicled within the Bible as fountainheads, yielding physical and spiritual nourishment. We will examine in the current and succeeding chapter how God uses the "living water" of springs to not only provide for physical human needs, but also to offer a renewed sense of truly being alive—transforming people from the walking dead of cultic busyness to those awakened in supernatural joy within the created order. Specifically, we will examine how springs occupy a unique place in God's life-infusing metanarrative: how they draw and sustain life theologically and physically (through the remainder of this chapter), yet also psychologically and spiritually (chapter six). By expositing these facets of life in bite-sized pieces, we will provide a composite picture of the spring's means of life-transfusion and, ultimately, how it points to the Creator through the abundant life it pours forth.

THE SPRING'S DRAWING AND SUSTAINING THEOLOGICAL LIFE

We start with a biblical/theological exposition because, while we have shown in the preceding chapters the mediate living discourses within the spring that generally speak to the necessity of God's existence, Scripture is His immediate, special revelation to us. The scriptural account is the final authority on all things, is inspired by God Himself, and is the foundation we must lay before moving on to supplemental means of God using springs to draw and sustain life. There is no paucity of biblical data to inform us of the significance springs have played in the progressive redemption of God's created order. For the sake of brevity, we will set forth seven windows within the Bible that are emblematic of God's providence in using springs to affect His Divine, life-giving plan.

Genesis 2:6

The first mention of springs in the Bible, appearing in the second chapter of the first book, is a contested one. The text reads, "And a *mist* was going up from the land and was watering the whole face of the ground" (emphasis mine). Some Bible translators use the word "spring" in place of the word "mist." Others use "mist," but add a footnote, indicating the word "spring" is also acceptable. So, which one is it?

"Mist" gets support from the fact that the Hebrew word *ed* in the text is translated elsewhere in the Bible as "mist" and is commonly used in Hebrew to connote the idea of mist. However, the word "spring" gets support from the fact that use of the word in other ancient languages denoted a flowing spring. Furthermore, the surrounding context in Genesis two lends support to the translation of "spring." One contextual example is verse ten, which tells us that a river flowed out of Eden (humanity's first domicile—a garden sanctuary) and, after watering the garden, branched off into four different rivers, flowing into four distinct lands. In order to provide sufficient water supply for four rivers while obeying the law of water which always flows downhill, context suggests that Eden was situated with a profuse fountainhead at an elevation higher than its surrounding lands. Such a topographical clue is consistent with where we would expect to find a spring that is the source of downstream diffluence. (Note: For additional insight, Meredith Kline, author of *Because it Had Not Rained*, and Mark Futato, author of *Because It Had Rained* have offered journal articles with equally interesting takes on this term.)

My personal opinion is that Genesis 2:6 could mean both "mist" and "spring." Have you ever camped near a spring? If you have, you would recall waking up to a cool temperature and a wet ground. The spring serves as a natural barometer to ensure a dew point is met nearly every morning, given the spring's moisture and the cool air the spring infuses into the surrounding watershed. Mist and fog are regular participants in this phenomenon; thus, a spring in Eden would produce concomitant mist and dew to hydrate and enrich the lush garden foliage.

Regardless, scriptural and linguistic evidence have consistently affirmed for 3,500-plus years that springs sustained the first human life. Springs not only provided the essential nourishment to humanity and their garden sanctuary, but also actually preceded the first human life. Springs are given a place of preeminence in the biblical narrative by being presented in the opening pages of Scripture with an integral role of providing consistent nourishment.

Genesis 16:7

Just one chapter removed from Abraham cutting a covenant with God and being declared righteous before God on account of his faith, we find the bondservant of Abraham's wife pregnant and on the run with Abraham's child. Abraham was a former pagan, whom God called to Himself. Through his lineage would flow God's covenantal promise to establish a people for Himself and, in that, a history of redemption, where, ultimately, the promised Savior would arise. But Abraham, being eighty-six years old, gave up on God's promise that he would have a son with his wife, Sarah. In an act of doubt, Abraham and Sarah took matters into their own hands by having Abraham impregnate their bondservant, Hagar, in order to ensure a line of offspring. Naturally, this dynamic created tension amongst the family, so Hagar fled without permission.

We are told in Genesis 16:7 that either an angel or "manifestation" of God found her *by a spring of water in the wilderness, the spring on the way to Shur"* (emphasis mine). That Hagar is found at a spring—a place of peace and refreshment in a wilderness of danger—is not insignificant. Also of note is that this is the first place in the Bible where an angel of God appears and intervenes in order to convict a fugitive of her need to repent and return. In His grace, God sought Hagar out at the spring, surrounded by wilderness, to reveal Himself and His will to her. Through this motif, God uses a spring as a nexus of grace—a symbolic backdrop where He reveals Himself to us in the midst of a wilderness chaos and convicts us of our need to follow Him.

Genesis 24:10-27

The next step in fulfillment of God's covenantal promise, finding a wife for Abraham's son, Isaac, takes place with a spring as its core setting. Abraham knows that if Isaac intermarries amongst the surrounding Canaanite people, their heathen culture will corrupt him and steer him away from the worship of the true God. So, he commissions his servant to travel back to his homeland to find a suitable wife for Isaac. Abraham's emissary travels to the Mesopotamian city of Nahor, where he stops on the outskirts of the city to pray that God would reveal the right woman to him. A spring, which served as the town's water supply, was right where Abraham's servant stopped to pray. Before the servant could complete his prayer, we are told in verses fifteen and sixteen that a beautiful young woman named Rebekah appeared.

Not only does the text introduce Rebekah, who is integral to covenant fulfillment, at the spring, but it goes out of its way to inform us that she was attractive and that she was a virgin. Later, her hospitality with the spring water only reaffirms, along with her purity, that she was the person God had providentially revealed to Abraham's servant. Thus, the spring not only buttresses an element of revelation in the fulfillment of God's covenantal promise, but the spring also forges a physical sign of purity, pointing to the purity required of a suitable wife for Isaac. The purity personified by the spring is drawn upon later in Song of Solomon 4:12, where the purity of the bride-to-be is compared to a "locked spring." Doubtless, people across many millennia and milieus since have come away from encounters with the spring with similar senses of revelation and purity.

Genesis 26:19, Deuteronomy 8:7, and Exodus 15:27

These three passages lay out the progressive reliance and anticipation of natural springs as means of survival for the Hebrews as they wandered and settled into the Promised Land. This reliance on springs goes back to the second patriarch, Isaac, who settled in the land of Gerar and was forced to move from spring to spring because of hostile local people. We are told in Genesis 26:19-20 that after Isaac's servants found a well of spring water through their excavation to secure a source of water, the local herdsmen claimed it for themselves. Isaac displayed a knack for turning the other cheek, as he moved on to tap water from another spring, only to have locals once again quarrel with him over it (v. 21). Isaac moved around Gerar, relying on spring wells for survival, until the point where God appeared to Him in Beersheba (vs. 23-25) to reaffirm his promised blessing. Isaac responded by building an altar to God and tapping a spring well at the location, which soon after served as the site for a peace covenant with the local king, Abimelech, who saw God's blessing.

Centuries after Isaac, Moses relied on springs as he led the Jews out of Egypt in the progressive fulfillment of God's promise. Moses' role was to lead the people to the Promised Land, one described in Deuteronomy 8:7-8 as " . . . a good land, a land of brooks of water, of fountains and springs, flowing out in the valleys and hills, a land of wheat and barley, of vines and fig trees and pomegranates, a land of olive trees and honey." While chronological placement in a text does not necessarily imply a hierarchy, the preceding passage that served as an emblem of hope and anticipation for the Hebrew deliverance contains a natural development from the most essential resources of the land to the derivative "luxury" goods that are dependent upon them. Thus, springs and brooks find primary placement in the list, upon which the subsequent enjoyment of figs, barley, or even honey is predicated.

But in order to even reach the Promised Land, the Hebrews needed water to survive the sojourn. With the constant worry about finding water at the next stopping point, the people were prone to getting weary and losing hope during their forty-year flight. So, one can understand their frustration and despair when they found water unfit to drink in Marah, only to have God intervene, through Moses, to heal the water in Exodus 15:25. After this act of deliverance and trust, we find in Exodus 15:27 that God, through Moses, leads His people to Elim, a desert oasis with twelve springs and seventy palm trees. Elim and its springs were sufficient to nourish the encampment of hundreds of thousands of people and, as a temporary type of replenishment and quickening, point to the living water of the Promised Land and of the ultimate promise of springs of living water bestowing eternal life.

Exodus 17:6

In what is perhaps the most ethereal picture of Divine provision in the annals of humanity, we find the supernatural interjecting within the natural to impose God's sovereign blessing. Moses' striking of the rock exudes countless binary strands of hope: Providence with mystery, destiny with good fortune, the natural converging with the supernatural, and typology with temporal provision prefiguring eternal restoration. The archetype of Exodus 17:6 has been borrowed for centuries by the destitute of humanity, clinging to the hope that only a Divine intervention can provide. From those afflicted of a pandemic bubonic plague, to people across continents conquered by brutal regimes, to emancipated slaves of America in the late 1800s, the metaphor of Divine provision, rooted in Exodus 17:6, has often sustained the downtrodden.

In this text, we find Moses leading a haggard and bitter group of people, who are on the brink of mutiny due to their dehydration. God supernaturally guides Moses to a natural solution: a rock. Moses is instructed to strike the rock with his staff in front of the elders of Israel. Moses complied, and upon doing so, a natural spring opened up on top of what was likely a natural karst outlet, and water flowed forth en masse. And the people, and even all their livestock, were supplied with enough water to drink.

This picture that romanticizes Divine provision is significant on multiple accounts. First, it shows how the supernatural can act in perfect harmony with the natural to affect the Divine purpose. While it is possible the sub-surface water was "created" by God as this miracle occurred, it makes sense to believe, knowing the topography of Israel being situated on karst formations (not unlike the Salem plateau within the Ozark lands of the Midwest), that the spring was already present. God merely orchestrated the puncturing of the spring orifice by Moses, thereby bridging a supernatural work to a natural process, realizing the epitome of Divine provision.

But secondly, the striking of the rock and the spring that flowed forth point to something even bigger—Jesus Himself. Centuries later, He would be struck in front of the elders and elites in order to make provision for His people. And out of the Rock that is Christ would flow waters of life, offering eternal, not temporal, nourishment. Therefore, the theme of the spring's provision in Exodus 17:6 is one of eternal significance.

2 Samuel 5:8

For millennia, the holy city of Jerusalem has been an epicenter from which religious life has flowed. Christianity, Judaism, and Islam all hallow the ancient city. However, before Jerusalem—considered holy to different groups for a host of different reasons—would morph into the nucleus of Abrahamic religions, it was inhabited by a group of pagans called the Jebusites. The Jebusites had fiercely fended off the Jews from their initial conquest into the Promised Land, and dislodging these holdouts from their heavily fortified city would require something beyond a typical military campaign. It took the rise of King David and the help of a spring for the Jews to finally capture Jerusalem and unite the Promised Land.

How could the tranquil setting of a spring—a common ingredient in God's unfolding plan of redemption and the locus of life-giving themes of revelation, provision, and deliverance—maintain these virtues through a means of military force? Our text of Second Samuel 5:8 indicates that it was a spring (the Gihon spring, Jerusalem's primary water source) and its underground tunnels that granted David's men access into the city. The Jebusites taunted David, believing the city was so well-fortified that even "the blind and lame will ward [David] off" (2 Sam. 5:6). But David sought a military invasion based on surprise, not head-to-head force, which would have certainly racked up mass casualties.

Scripture tells us in Second Samuel 5:8 that David commanded his troops, "Whoever would strike the Jebusites, let him get up the water shaft to attack 'the lame and the blind . . .'" The spring's *tsinnors*, Hebrew for water caverns, were God's provision of subterranean arteries into the heart of Jerusalem. He revealed to David where access to these spring channels could be found outside the city. And it was by the spring's shafts that deliverance of Jerusalem was granted to David. Thus, in a stroke of irony, it was through the tunnels emanating from the Gihon spring—a source of life for Jerusalem's inhabitants—that the Jews discreetly entered and took Jerusalem, ending the life of the Jebusite reign and establishing a new capital for spiritual life that proceeds to this day.

The Gihon spring narrative does not end with its bequeathing of Jerusalem. The spring reemerges in Second Chronicles chapter thirty-two, when King Hezekiah preempts the Assyrian invasion, led by Sennacherib, from sacking Jerusalem by redirecting the water flow of the Gihon. Hezekiah commissioned the digging of an underground tunnel that diverted water from outside the city to flow into the western side of Jerusalem—not only to provide for residents on the other end of Jerusalem, but also to deny the enemy access to a much-needed resource. Archeology has uncovered Hezekiah's underground tunnel, which spans nearly a third of a mile, ending in what is thought to be the pool of Siloam.[141] In the New Testament, the pool of Siloam reemerges as an accessory to one of Jesus' healing miracles. He instructed a man born blind to wash in the pool of Siloam to be healed

(Jn. 9:7). Once he received his sight, he pointed to Jesus as the source of his healing, but ultimately, in a greater object metaphor, Jesus opens our eyes from spiritual blindness to spiritual life. And like Hezekiah's tunnel, both the pool of Siloam and the shaft leading to the Jebusite conquest have been validated through archeological discovery.[142]

Proverbs 25:26

Our final spring passage requires little discourse to convey how the spring draws and sustains life in a theological sense. However, it will provide us with a sort of conduit toward a greater exposition in the final section of chapter six that reveals how the spring draws and sustains spiritual life. The text reads, "Like a muddied spring or a polluted fountain is a righteous man who gives way before the wicked."

There is, perhaps, no crime against nature more pernicious, and no act more wicked, than the polluting of a spring. Pollution of springs is a holistic act of violence—one that is not self-contained to the spring or only impacts an isolated spring channel. The poisoning of the spring doesn't dissipate downstream. A polluted spring or groundwater source can be cost-prohibitive, if not impossible, to cure. You can't shut down one branch of stream to treat a polluted spring. Compromising the spring's purity results in a perpetual effect, one that perpetually brings forth contaminants that fills all of the spring, all of its stream channels, and all the entire watershed. Water, meant to draw and sustain life with its quality of liquid profusion, turns those virtues on their heads to become the never-ending marauder of death.

Like a contaminated spring, so is the natural condition of our human hearts. Theologians and philosophers often refer to the heart as the hub of moral will, the nexus from which flows the exercising of our moral faculties. And like a polluted spring, our natural hearts are irreparably polluted hearts. They are wicked and deceitful to the core and incapable of any human clean-up efforts (Jer. 17:9). According to Jesus, the only thing that flows forth from our hearts, in our natural condition, is evil; for example, that evil which comes out of our mouths proceeds from a corrupted heart (Matt. 15:18-19). Invariably, our hearts, like a polluted spring, need Divine intervention to be cleansed and replaced with springs of living water.

We have examined just seven theological perspectives of the spring drawing and sustaining life. The Bible contains many more aspects of the spring that exceed the scope of our study. However, we have clearly seen the indispensable ways God has used springs to not only grant the means to physical life, but also to provide revelation, purity, provision, and deliverance. Said another way, God's operative Providence—that which ordains the flourishing of life against unlikely odds, according to His purpose—has been revealed with a grander awareness through the lens of a spring setting. God uses the spring's mediums to embed a sense of purpose and abundance in life that precludes His subjects from merely "existing." Next, we will explore how springs have drawn and sustained physical life through the history of civilization.

THE SPRING'S DRAWING AND SUSTAINING PHYSIOLOGICAL LIFE IN HISTORY

The cohesion of atoms within a water molecule is symbolic of humankind's attraction for water. Humanity's biological design demands a human/hydro communion if we are to survive. It comes as no surprise, then, that springs have been deemed nothing less than salubrious provisions as long as humanity has existed. You might picture ancient cultures hopelessly in the throes of drought, scavenging through dusty landscapes. Their fortunes turn in an instant, granted new life by the sudden resurgence of fresh, cold water erupting miraculously from the ground beneath them. Consider primitive, pastoral people groups, those forced to rely on less than six inches of rain per year, leading their flock to a once-dry wadi now brimming with water. To them, it is Divine deliverance that replenishes a herd—a herd that is their source for food and drink—on the verge of dehydration. Or consider the American pioneer or the first Roman settlers to Britain—sick, starved, and dehydrated, traveling through uncharted territory. By accident, they stumble upon the lush foliage or mineral deposits emerging from hot springs thought to hold healing, medicinal qualities. By providence, they believe their physical salvation is at hand. Given these vignettes from the annals of history, it is little wonder why springs have forever straddled the fence between natural and supernatural lore in the minds of humanity.

To the people above, water was not some fungible good. It was a sacred endowment. Throughout history, humanity has survived because our ancestors knew the value of water, how to draw near it, and how to maximize it. Here, we see how springs draw and sustain physical life.

Secular and biblical archaeologists alike trace humanity's most primitive development in communal living to areas of the Fertile Crescent in Iraq between the Tigris and Euphrates Rivers (one of the same rivers explicitly identified in the Genesis account above). The earliest human settlements can be traced to this area of the earth, and it should be no surprise that these people gathered and flourished in an area nurtured by a sound water supply. Said another way, springs and rivers drew the first humans, and civilization itself, to its waters for propagation of life. These early societies have often been referred to as "hydraulic civilizations."

Water was life for our ancestors. Accessible water was the first priority for any community as it provided nourishment to drink, hydration for livestock, the means to grow crops, and, prior to the domestication of the camel, transportation.[143] Thus, he who controlled the rivers controlled much of civilization.

Call it natural instincts, but primitive people didn't survive by being dumb. Tour guides in Israel will recount that some of the most strident conflicts in the Holy Land have emanated from claims on land with superior water sources/supply. In order to survive, the earliest humans were forced to live alongside reliable water sources, such as rivers, like the Nile, Tigris, and Euphrates. Or, if certain societies were not located near a river with reliable effluence, they could survive near freshwater springs that dot much of Israel's topography. For example, near Jericho, Israel—one of the oldest settlements known—lies Elisha's Spring, which, to this day, flows twenty gallons per second and is still as capable of nourishing people, animals, and crops as it did thousands of years ago.[144] Cultural habitation ebbed and flowed around water, as human settlements would fan out commensurate with expansive water supplies and contract back in to a concentrated community around fixed water sources during times of drought.

But as settlements grew and demands for water commensurately increased, new problems arose which required new solutions. Humanity developed interesting ways to locate distant water. One example is how Australian Aborigines made up spiritual songs sung aloud for miles as they followed walking tracks, which led to water. The song lyrics, passed down from age-to-age, served a pneumonic purpose that ensured one was on the right path to water when a visual landmark corresponded with the lyric of the incantation. But the walking track songs also became a kind of societal salve as they were passed down, binding generations together.

Another more sophisticated advancement was mankind discovering the boom and bane that came with their ability to divert water systems. For example, Fred Pearce, in his book, *Keepers of the Spring*, noted records of the first water wars in Mesopotamia, where the King of Umma sought to raid his downstream neighbor, Girsu, and cut off their water supply. The King of Girsu is said to have saved his domain by digging a new canal to the Tigris, thus giving him command over downstream communities.[145]

Irrigation provided humanity the means to further access water that enabled cities to disperse beyond a consolidated water source. Soon, instead of people being drawn to the waters, the water was being drawn to the people. Much of the ability for early cultures to capture and manipulate waterways lay in their fortuitous location along what are called alluvial fans. Alluvial fans are basically where a stream or water flow departs a steeper gradient and enters a flatter grade, such as a plain. The water entering this more level terrain spreads out in a fan shape, where the water deposits sediment, such as sand and fine gravel, amenable for channeling. Early social irrigation efforts that manipulated seasonal floods were developed around such alluvial fans in places like the village of Choga Mami, which lies in eastern Iraq near the Gangir River—an area that receives around eight inches of water per year.[146]

In his book, *Elixir*, Brian Fagan demonstrates how communal mores of primitive people—those living in environments with too little rainfall to survive—have been shaped by irrigation efforts. Proper irrigation management emerges as the fine line between life and death during times of famine. Fagan chronicles the ingenuity of people like the indigenous Engaruka of Tanzania, who've learned how to meticulously maintain a continuous grade for feeder channels up to 1.8 miles long. These manmade channels must be fashioned with exquisite precision in order to deliver water to their fields and maintain their livelihood.[147] Social and familial ties within the Marakwet people of Kenya were cemented by irrigation channel construction, where the only guarantee to secure water for your fields was to assist in canal digging.[148] While lineage bestowed rights to existing furrows, only those who participated in communal maintenance and repair were guaranteed ongoing water. Or consider the Sonjo people of northern Tanzania, who survive today only by rigid irrigation efforts and the flow of water from springs considered sacred, and they do so by the decisions of an elder council that meets to allocate water usage amongst people, arbitrate disputes over water, and even assess fines for failure to participate in communal water projects.[149]

Hydraulic civilizations were not confined to small, local settlements. The brutal Assyrian empire was known to reshape entire landscapes with their irrigation efforts. Assyrian military commanders carried out the designs of water engineers by forcing slaves and conquered exiles to painstaking digging efforts. In approximately 700 BC, the ruthless King Sennacherib moved the Assyrian capital to Nineveh, across the Tigris River from Mosul in northern Iraq. The development of Nineveh was made possible only by way of a massive water diversion campaign. Sennacherib is said to have tapped into water sources from rivers thirty-one miles away to water gardens and irrigate a thousand grain fields to feed the city.[150] In addition to canals, Sennacherib utilized other technologies to build his city of splendor, such as the first known aqueduct, which would later be perfected in the Roman Empire and, through the use of *qanats*—a technology that likely originated in what is now modern-day Iran and came to the Assyrians by deported Persian slaves.

Qanats are basically tunnels dug into the side of a hillside of alluvial fans or locations where natural water seeps are known. Qanats maximize the laws of gravity by tunneling back into the hillside at a precise gradient until the underground spring or groundwater source is penetrated. The qanat, obviously extremely dangerous to dig, then functions as a sort of lifeline that provides a constant, year-round source of water that leads into a village or city. Even small qanat can provide as much as 114,000 gallons of water a day, while some qanats have been discovered that are fifty miles long.[151, 152]

Qanat technology spread westward as the Persian Empire rose between 600 to 400 BC. One must wonder if one positive byproduct of the Jewish exile was learning the art of qanat digging. The provision of qanats sustained life in post-exilic Israel by not only providing water to people who received little rainfall, but also by serving as hiding places for Jewish rebels resisting the Roman occupation. It is said that a monastery was built above one qanat near Jerusalem that once served as the hiding place of the Ark of the Covenant.[153] Qanats even infused life into the reaches of the Greco-Roman empires. The beautiful fountains found in the agora within the city of Corinth came from qanats. The digging of qanats also enabled arid, rocky places like Cyprus to sustain life and become impervious to drought. The people of Cyprus use qanats to this day and revere qanat diggers as a specialized occupation with "no higher calling."[154]

As the channels of time flowed on, civilization advanced further west into North America. To this point, the vicissitudes of civilization had seen springs and its waters bring people to it for life and, conversely, people bringing the springs and waters to them to propagate communal life. With the colonization of America, man's reliance upon water did not change. Yet the means by which the spring imparted abundant life to a developing country would take on entirely new channels that would forge the way for the cultural advances we know today.

First, springs provided the American pioneer with mental and physical health. Wandering through uncharted territory, one could never be sure when the next source of water could be found. Liquid water was not enough; it had to be healthy water. Many a sick, hot, and parched pioneer has left journal entries bordering on despair, with finally-discovered water noted as contaminated and looking like aged milk. Potential settlements were heavily weighed on whether or not the land and water were healthy. The discovery of good springs and streams not only secured healthy drinking water, but also plowable crop land, transportation, and sustenance for livestock. For this reason, Cynthia Thrall, a missionary back in the 1820s, condoned a prospective mission base because the land and water was "said to be healthy."[155]

Springs not only offered serendipitous watering holes to quench thirst, but also served as a means of drawing in and nurturing food sources. Mineral springs were a natural magnet for wild game—such as buffalo, deer, and elk—which, in turn, yielded sources of food for the settlers. Furthermore, the rich mineral content of spring waters facilitated livestock development. Hogs were reported to grow larger and faster when provided with briny water from salt springs.[156] Settlers and Native American Indians would utilize the water from salt springs to manufacture salt and other minerals that could, in turn, be used to feed livestock or be sold commercially. Nathan Boone, the son of legendary frontiersman Daniel Boone, established a rock furnace at a salt spring in Missouri, where he manufactured around thirty bushels of salt per day.[157]

In addition, the springs discovered in North America provided natural armistice. They were universally viewed as a place of peace and considered sacred ground to American Indians. It has been said that warring Indian tribes, no matter how hostile they might be, would lay down their arms and share a peace pipe at a spring. German-American botanist George Englemann wrote, "Even the raw natural man feels himself close to God and lays his tomahawk down in awe before he enters this place."[158] Therefore, missionaries considered springs ideal sanctuaries to evangelize Native Americans.

Peace of mind was not the only emollient exacted from the spring. As America transitioned into an industrial and commercial society in the nineteenth century, the age-old philosophy of the spring bringing physical peace to the body through healing came into prominence. Healing qualities have been associated with springs for thousands of years. Ancient Greeks built temples around/atop thermal springs in honor of Aesculapius to placate the "healing god" into suffusing healing agents into the water. Spring bathhouses, inscribed with the goddess of health, Hygieia, were erected around large, warm-water mineral springs to convey good health to worshippers.[159] And in Bath, England, a bathhouse was constructed around a hot spring in the middle of the first century AD, where people would travel across Europe in hopes of being healed.[160] Legend has it that the cure for leprosy was found there.[161]

With the long-reaching mystique of healing springs, it should be no surprise that the discovery of hot springs in America brought with it a renewed hope of healing physically, mentally, and financially, as hot springs resorts would soon become big business in places like Hot Springs, Arkansas. As early as the American Revolution, thermal springs were said to recharge and heal those afflicted from anything spanning from rheumatism to battle wounds. It has been said that George Washington sought refuge at Berkeley Springs, West Virginia, as a young colonel seeking to heal his rheumatism.[162] Hot springs developed as ad hoc infirmaries and hospitals during the Revolutionary War.[163] Thus, as settlers spread west, the discovery of thermal springs came to be seen as an emblem of hope for mind and body, where people came to heal fractured psyches, injured limbs, and chronic conditions.

But is there any truth to the healing claims of these waters? For instance, commenting on the first bathhouses developed at Hot Springs, Arkansas, in 1830, geologist George Featherstonhaught said, "These waters annually perform very admirable cures of chronic complaints . . . and thus seem providentially placed."[164] Matt Kaplan writes that there might be some truth in these claims, though not what we would expect. He notes what one can experientially conclude—that sitting in hot, humid settings can alleviate joint and muscle pain. But he approaches the matter more caustically, citing a 2013 study in the *Proceedings of the National Academy of Sciences*. In short, the study, extrapolating research done on mice, showed that cancerous tumors realized up to fifty percent slower growth for mice housed in warm and humid environments than mice in cool enclosures.[165] The study also found that mice kept in warmer conditions, such the ambiance of a thermal spring, possessed more cytotoxic T lymphocyte cells that are proficient at destroying cancer cells.[166] The reason is not attributed to any intrinsic power of the warm climate or the warm spring waters, but more likely to the fact that organisms in cooler environs must divert bodily resources from the immune system to sustain a constant body temperature. So, while not denying the providential healing prowess ascribed to these springs, their restorative effects may have more to do with curbing extant disease, rather than curing it.

With their redolent aromas, medicinal hot springs quickly enthralled the masses, morphing from physiological to social places of refuge. By the 1830s, Americans were making hot spring tours akin to modern day vacationing, where hot springs became hubs of fashion and social life. The Appalachian and Ohio Valley hot springs attracted diverse visitors from the common folk to President Andrew Jackson. By 1886, there were 634 warm/mineral water spas in the United States, demonstrating how springs had evolved as the loci of physiological, social, medical, and financial life, which all converged to meet physical human needs and develop civilization.[167]

Given the multifaceted ways springs have served as the nexus for abundant life, one could make the case that the word "spring" alone evokes a communal draw. Such a word, given its universal appeal, can and has been used to entice people to establish residence in places containing the word "spring." We want to live in a place that connotes such utopian tones. Case in point, based on my informal research from the website www.topix.com, there are twenty-seven cities in the United States named "Springfield." Furthermore, there are at least 536 cities in the United States that contain the word "spring" in their name.[168] But our last exemplar of the spring providing physical life takes place in a community devoid of the word "spring" in its name. This final stop is the small town of Eminence, in Shannon County, Missouri.

Eminence is the *de jure* gateway to the Ozark National Scenic Riverways. But in other ways, it's a portal to a living vignette of hydraulic harmony. Its residents are the kind of people to whom the breeze of nature can whisper arcane secrets about the land's treasures and who can perceive it with a comprehension as clear as the Jacks Fork River. These are simple people, but far from simple-minded. They are simple in a more theological sense—one that requires little to be complete. Natives of this corridor of scenic rivers come equipped with a wisdom that textbooks of mankind could never convey—an unpretentious savvy that doesn't grace the corridors of academia, but is all the more pragmatic given their stream-centric environment. If you didn't know better, you'd think this was the people who inspired the music for *The Joshua Tree* album by the band U2, as they traveled across the country meeting people who inspired the album's lyrics. Their identity has been forged by the two rivers—Current and Jack's Fork—that have cradled them for over 200 years. It is in these waters that provision has always been granted, and it is in these waters they trust.

Settlers did not inhabit the areas of southeast Missouri, where Eminence is found, until the early 1800s. Prior to that, the timber-rich and spring-laden land was inhabited by Native American tribes—such as the Osage, Delaware, and Shawnee—who found the terrain amenable for hunting, transportation, and yielding up any natural resources adept for survival. The ecosystem was a diverse menagerie of plant, aquatic, and animal life, with over 1,000 species of plants, 113 species of fish, and fifty-eight different mammals—including elk, buffalo, deer, turkey, black bear, and mountain lion.[169]

The first white pioneers are said to have used the bountiful pine trees to build their cabins near any of the hundreds of springs in the area. Like a church built over a sacred site, many springs had spring houses built over the top of them to provide natural refrigeration to preserve food and sustain life. The spring house, at the same time, served to protect their most natural resource: clean water. Throw in the river's bottom land, ideal for planting crops, and it's no wonder this area drew an onslaught of settlers throughout the nineteenth century.

One ideal location for settlement within the 80,790 acres that now comprise the Ozark National Scenic Riverways was a flat valley within some rugged Ozark hills, anchored by what is now called Alley Spring, which feeds the Jack's Fork River. Perhaps it was the abounding resources, or perhaps the picturesque Rockwellian setting with deep azure pools, giving birth to water flows flashing diamonds, or perhaps a combo of both that made Alley Spring, just outside of Eminence, the hydraulic hub of the Ozarks. But the earliest settlers were far from beautiful. On the contrary, they were tough people, who lived off the land and took what it would give them. They were known as a "wild and godless" people, who, early on, epitomized the prediction that "God would never cross the Mississippi."[170] Eventually, Protestant missionaries broke through, and churches began dotting the spring valley. Their efforts invigorated a hunger for literacy by promoting Bible-reading among the scattered cabins.[171]

However tough life might have been, Alley Spring offered a respite. It became the nave of physical and social sustenance, where the God-ordained means for abundant life were freely offered to residents. In

1868, the community, drawn together around the spring, built a grist mill, whose wheel was powered by the ever-surging spring water.[172] People would travel from miles around to grind their grain for food. As they gathered around the spring, it flourished into the heart of social life.[173] Soon, a blacksmith shop opened, and then a store, followed by a saw mill and a school. Social activities like dances, picnics, pie suppers, shooting matches, and a new game called baseball soon followed, bringing more people together, sculpting a new culture.

Alas, the consolidated camaraderie of Alley was not meant to last, as America was on the move with new plans. Westward expansion was calling American settlers, and with it came the demand for timber to complete railroads and build new towns. Alley Spring and Eminence, in their own way, were a microcosm of this transition, moving from an agrarian community, living off the rivers, to a timber economy, harvesting the near-endless supply of trees that lined the river corridors. God-given resources, like trees and the rivers that transported them, were rapaciously exploited for financial enterprise. Timber frenzy hit the area, as trees were cut, tied together into rafts as long as 1,000 feet, and floated down the river to the nearest railway.[174] Once again, the rivers provided life, but at what cost? Eventually, the logging efforts stripped the riverways of their verdant cover. One woman decried the scene, saying, "I hated what I saw."[175] Profits waned, but not until the rivers were left naked and ravaged.

Eventually, restoration efforts, led by state and federal forest services and residents, replenished the forest. But what viable options did the people have left to live and thrive here? Some unconventional endeavors arose that sought to tap into the life-giving springs along the Current River. One such pursuit was undertaken by Dr. C.H. Diehl in 1913, who, believing in the healing properties of spring water, built a hospital atop Welch Spring (which flows into the Current River within one hundred yards of the spring orifice) to treat patients with tuberculosis, asthma, emphysema, etc. The hospital hoped to draw people from the entire United States to the cool, allergen-free air that could circulate into their rooms, offering a natural healing respite. To Dr. Diehl's chagrin, the remote location failed to attract sufficient patients to maintain his vision. Eventually, Dr. Diehl died and, with him, Welch Hospital. However, you can still hike a half-mile trail today to visit the ruins of Welch Hospital, which rests on a hill overlooking the turquoise waters of Welch Spring like a permanent conservator.

Ultimately, the renewal of viable life within the Eminence community would arise through the ingenuity of men like Harvey Staples and others who turned to the unmatched beauty of their water for provision. Staples, like many other entrepreneurs in the area, found a way to bring people and water together and, through their union, secured meaning and a means of subsistence for the residents of Eminence. And the way they did it was through tourism—specifically, canoe and inner tube rental services. The trajectory of river tourism continues as an economic spring flow to this day. The waters have provided again, making Eminence one of the float-trip capitals of the Midwest. Every day of every summer, these waters perform a beguiling waltz. They parade their iridescent rivulets before torrents of visitors, captivating audiences and daring them to find greater scenes of pastoral harmony. Pine pillars rise again like guardians along the stream's crags as the current murmurs on in unbroken song. Revival fills these cool waters anew, drawing and sustaining new generations to this centrifuge of life.

The spring is more than just an icon of beauty. Spring waters have drawn people since the dawn of creation and sustained life the world-over. In this chapter, we have seen just two ways the spring's efficacious waters obey their Creator to draw and enliven humanity, both theologically and physiologically. Whether unfolding redemptive history or watering the seeds of human civilization, the spring has forever occupied a central motif in the created order. And it is the God who fills all things, including spring orifices, Who directs these waters in a confluence of purity, revelation, deliverance, and provision to bring us life. Dynamic progression issues from the spring's headwaters as they branch out downstream, molding more dimensions of life. People interacting with the elixir of spring waters come away changed. In the next chapter, we will continue our journey through the stream channels, beyond the theological and physiological life they bestow toward a fuller restoration of mankind through the psychological and spiritual life they embody as a natural archetype.

Reflection Questions

1. There are a multitude of biblical and extra-biblical references to the spring that I did not reference in this chapter. What are some other spiritual associations with springs you can recall? Have you visited any other communities whose life derives from springs?

2. Countless settlers and missionaries have recounted how Native Americans, regardless of how hostile they were to one another, deemed springs as sacred ground that mandated peaceful interactions. What does this say about the natural condition of mankind?

3. The "Prince of Preachers," Charles Spurgeon, once remarked, "The ferns and the rabbits, the streams and the trouts, the fir trees and the squirrels, the primroses and the violets, the farm-yard, the new-mown hay, and the fragrant hops—these are the best medicine for hypochondriacs, the surest tonics for the declining, the best refreshments for the weary."[176] Do you think his advice is applicable only for his nineteenth century audience, or does it have bearing today on the relationship between nature and our physical health?

4. Our culture seeks possessions that provide limited contentment and end up owning us but doesn't seek the spring and its gallery of beauty, that is not owned by any but offers unlimited joy to all. Do you agree with this statement? What are some ways the spring can free you of the trappings of modern culture and give you more abundant life?

5. Proverbs 21:1 reads, "The king's heart is a stream of water in the hand of the Lord; he turns it wherever he will." What does this

passage say about the ultimate control of both streams and those who seek to divert them? How does God show more power and authority in redirecting the stream of the heart than men who redirect the stream channels to manipulate water supply?

CHAPTER SIX

LIVING WATER: DRAWING AND INITIATING PSYCHOLOGICAL AND SPIRITUAL LIFE

Now there was a man of the Pharisees named Nicodemus, a ruler of the Jews. This man came to Jesus by night and said to him, "Rabbi, we know that you are a teacher come from God, for no one can do these signs that you do unless God is with him." Jesus answered him, "Truly, truly, I say to you, unless one is born again he cannot see the kingdom of God." Nicodemus said to him, "How can a man be born when he is old? Can he enter a second time into his mother's womb and be born?" Jesus answered, "Truly, truly, I say to you, unless one is born of water and the Spirit, he cannot enter the kingdom of God. That which is born of the flesh is flesh, and that which is born of the Spirit is spirit. Do not marvel that I said to you, 'You must be born again.' The wind blows where it wishes, and you hear its sound, but you do not know where it comes from or where it goes. So it is with everyone who is born of the Spirit."

—John 3:1-8

IT BEGAN AS A CRISP, if not unremarkable, October morning. I could see my breath in the autumn air, one of nature's signposts of consistency this time of year. Water cascaded at a relatively brisk pace for Lake Taneycomo, whose dark pools reflected the rust of the fall foliage. The water felt hurried. I could empathize with it—anxious to start fishing and yet hopeful that some fall magic would deliver me the action I craved: hooking into a big brown.

I love fishing in the fall. I was born in the fall. I got married in the fall. My first child was born in the fall. Needless to say, I love autumn. The autumnal ambiance entails a spirit of renewal within the spring and the surrounding watershed. Promise emits from the spring like fog atop its surface.

I mentioned the morning began unremarkably, which included the fishing. I managed to seduce a few rainbows, but the size and frequency of the fish I caught were no cause for boasting. The cool air joined forces with the chilly water to curb my reaction time. I opted to break for breakfast when the strikes lulled to a still.

Typically, fly fishing immediately after breakfast is a recipe for a lethargic response to strikes. A lethargic response leads to catching few fish. Catching few fish leads to frustration that you carry with you on the drive home. But the vexation that came upon me on the drive home that day was not due to frustration, but awe. As I returned to the waters of Taneycomo on that October day, little did I know that something extraordinary was about to transpire. I was about to recede into the middle ground between the natural and supra-natural. (I use the word *supra* intentionally, as *super* commonly means "superlative," while *supra* means "above." What was about to happen was above the normalcy you see in the natural world.) The stream was a fitting site to host this supra-natural event.

I will leave the second part of this story within the body of discourse within this chapter. Needless to say, something happened to me in the water that October day—something that I struggle to explain from the pit of my soul, yet, paradoxically, something that impressed upon the core of my being the majesty and precision by which the Creator of the universe controls the cosmos.

I've mentioned before that my favorite television show of all-time is Rod Serling's classic series, *The Twilight Zone*. I love the artistic vision and creativity that television was forced to rely upon during the era when shows and movies couldn't hide behind special effects. One episode, called "A Penny for Your Thoughts," reminds me of the supra-natural meeting that took place that October morning in the stream. The main character, Hector Pool (a banker, as I once was), begins his day like any other, buying a newspaper on his way to work. However, when Hector pays for the paper, he flips a coin that supra-naturally seems to land on its side, not heads or tails. From that point on, Hector is granted access beyond the limitations of the physical world, where he is able to hear the thoughts of others.

Throughout the episode, Hector's newfound ability to supersede the boundaries of the physical world plays out. He is able to snuff out a gambling and embezzlement scheme. He miraculously becomes more attentive to the desires and preferences of a female colleague he's longed to impress. He becomes attuned to his boss having an affair. But most importantly, in what saves his job, he "hears" a fellow employee make plans to steal and abscond with the bank's cash. Pool's new psychological sense wins the day, gaining him a promotion and the lady he sought. As Pool leaves the bank after work, he runs into the boy who sold him the newspaper and knocks over the coin that had landed on its side that morning. Once the coin falls, Pool's psychical abilities flee him. Yet he doesn't mind; he's happy to walk away from this intrusion on his psyche as a changed man.[177]

There are times when we walk away from the spring as changed people. Obviously, the spring has no animate ability to directly manipulate our senses. However, with its waters as a tonic of life and its ecoverse a type of garden sanctuary, the spring is used by God to stir the human psyche in mysterious and profound ways. It is little wonder, then, that the God of the universe uses the spring as the ultimate metaphor to draw people to Himself, and through His Divine sovereignty and grace, grants waters of life that flow for eternity. This chapter will more closely examine how the spring affects psychological and soteriological (salvation) life.

DRAWN TO ABUNDANT PSYCHOLOGICAL LIFE IN THE STREAM

Springs and watersheds employ diverse grounds for drawing people. As we saw in the previous chapter, some are drawn out of physical need, some by theological Providence, and others for recreation or restoration. Regardless of the myriad of causes, it's the spring's *effect* that is unique to all. Its waters offer an epiphanic balm, helping us discover lost connections to each other and to the Creator of this hydro-centric community. And at the end of the engagement, we find ourselves changed—not in a physical or tangible sense, but changed to the core of our psyche in a way we really can't fully grasp. In the following pages, we will explore individuals who have been reborn in a psychical sense by the elixir of the spring and its congenial ecosystems.

At the beginning of chapter five, we proposed that many adults unknowingly thirst for natural waters. Once we take the time to set foot in these streams, we remember our primal draw to them—how we love to swim through water, dive below it, ski atop it, float along it, fish within it, and basically subdue every facet of this water world that is so foreign to our natural land-faring environment. In fact, humanity is mandated in the second chapter of Genesis, after being created in the garden from which the four rivers flowed, to control, work, and watch over this terrestrial trust. Community originated within and under this directive. Therefore, given one of our most primordial instructions, it is no wonder this natural love of the land and streams is still present within us.

We don't have to reach back far over the corridors of time, or within the pages of this book, to find one such archetype that found life through the spring. Meet Luther Rowlett, who lived among the Ozark Scenic Riverways like no other. A folk legend of sorts, Luther was born and raised near Eminence, Missouri, living an eclectic life as a World War Two veteran, writer, and philosopher, but it was his symbiotic relationship with the streams that set the course of his life. In a certain sense, the rivers were his literal home and his livelihood.

Known for his trademark pith safari helmet and bib overalls, Rowlett was an amphibious character, who spent much of his days in the stream or sleeping on its banks. Sit in a local Eminence café, and you'd be hard-pressed to meet a local over the age of fifty who wasn't taught to swim by Luther. He existed for hanging out in populous swimming holes along the river to pour into kids the art of swimming so that they could get out and experience life in the stream.

If Luther wasn't donating countless hours to working with kids in the river, he was acting as the stream whisperer: the man the locals called on to rescue tipped canoers and recover their sunken valuables. Rowlett's remunerations—his means to purchase basic survival items, were indirectly provided by the stream. Upon being dispatched for a recovery, Luther would arrive on the scene and peer through a glass-bottomed pail like a snorkel, performing stream reconnaissance with the kind of acute senses only a person who is one with the river might possess. Luther would retrieve such items as coolers, wallets, and outboard motors. During the fall gigging season, locals cruise up and down the river to spear rough fish by light given from a generator. Luther once boldly plunged into the cold water to recover a generator from a wrecked boat. Remarkably, Luther retrieved lost wedding rings, bailing spouses out of the proverbial doghouse. The relieved beneficiaries of Luther's services gladly gave him hefty tips for his services.

Some locals claim that Luther didn't even have a permanent home. Former resident Carl Medley recalls Luther and his sister finding refuge in an old, abandoned cistern, where they would hang their heads for the night. When Luther wasn't in town, he would literally swim up and down the river from Eminence to Doniphan, a seventy-nine-mile trek, surveying his domain to help out where needed. When tired, he might hitch a ride up or down stream with the locals, all of whom knew him and considered it a privilege to catch up with him. When the weather got too cold, Luther would put his hitchhiking skills to use and catch rides to Florida, where he would live over the winter. But when the waters warmed, you could rest assured that Luther Rowlett heard the call of the Ozark streams, drawing him back to life in the spring.

Luther Rowlett's cognitive perception of reality was holistically shaped by the spring. Upon surrendering to the stream's providential call, Rowlett's life would be guided by a rare wilderness acuity imparted by the very waters that met his every need. This generous man, who lived so simply close to nature, was also known for his unabashed Christian faith that came from the ultimate Spring. His ambulant life of the stream, coupled with the preternatural sense he displayed, is reminiscent of another monastic theologian, who was psychically transformed by nature hundreds of years before Rowlett.

Francis of Assisi, born in the late twelfth century to a family of nobility, also chose to live simply and served God in a way that brought him closer to nature. Upon confronting the harsh evil of life while off to war, Francis walked away from the blessings he had and embarked on a life of eschewing worldly goods. Francis removed himself from worldly distractions and lived as an ascetic, relying solely upon God's provision made through the natural world. Often, Francis would become so malnourished by lack of food that his survival was in doubt. But in those dark hours when he was forced to crucify any self-reliance or material means, Francis focused solely on God and the natural world through which He worked and grew closer to God.

Legend has it that through his physical deprivation, Francis gained a supernatural perspicuity with the natural world. In one particular story that developed, Francis demonstrated such closeness with the stream that he could communicate with the animals within. The legend goes as follows:

> The stories of his relations with animals have brought joy to generation after generation for eight hundred years. By what instinct did they recognize in him the brother par excellence? We don't know, because we are almost completely ignorant about their affinities with the human race and especially about their rapture in the presence of the mystery of holiness

when it manifests itself in an exceptional man. The life of Francis of Assisi provides so many examples that we don't know which ones to choose. The wolf of Gubbio is a character apart, who will be treated in a little while, but let us stop for a moment by the lake of Rieti, where a fisherman offered Francis a tench [a type of Eurasian carp] that he called brother, advising it, as he always did in such cases, not to let itself get caught, and then releasing it back into the water next to the boat. Instead of disappearing, the tench began to wriggle joyously before the man of God. It would not go away without Francis's leave—and his blessing.[178]

Now, I don't include this story as a carte blanche endorsement of its full veracity, nor do I endorse all of Francis' theology, for that matter. But it does have something to say about how our yielded closeness with the spring, and nature in general, can sometimes grant us peeks beyond the veil of nature that defy natural explanations. The waters of the spring can be used by the God of the universe to endow our senses with a kind of salubrious sobriety, one that enables an almost transcendent participation within the immediate cosmos.***

Nature exhilarates people with this atypical, transcendent activation of the senses through different pursuits. The most exhilarating pursuit for me is fly fishing. There is nothing else like it, no other experience that makes me feel more alive. Fittingly, those atypical engagements always occur when I'm fly fishing, when I'm fully enveloped in the spring waters. With no advance notice, I get overtaken by these flickers of grace, whereby I temporarily develop a supra-natural sense

---

*** Let me be clear that with this word picture, I am in no way advocating experiential theology—the thought that theological truths are fluid and normative only in relation to my subjective experiences. Nor am I endorsing its heretical corollary cousin of extra-biblical revelation. God's normative truths have been specially revealed in an objective sense within the New Testament—a canon that has been permanently closed (Rev. 22:18-19).

of the stream's physics surrounding me. One of those flickers was the opening story of this chapter, a story I can now conclude.

These rare flashes of hyper-nature sensitivity are hard to explain. My wife can certainly vouch for them, as I will come home a different man, unable to quite articulate what happened. What I can't express in words, she can infer from behavior. Therefore, she could see that something happened to me out in the stream that October day at Lake Taneycomo. Allow me to try to explain.

My favorite method of fly fishing is called nymphing. Nymphing is a sub-surface technique that drifts a fly—one typically imitating an emerging hatch, pre-adult nymph (hence the name), or stream-dwelling creature (streamer)—through the strike zone, where the fish are located. Nymphing often relies on using a strike indicator (i.e., a cork or a "bobber"), not only to let you know when a fish strikes, but also to control the depth of your fly under the water. While most fly fishermen prefer the visual excitement that comes from fishing dry flies on top of the water and seeing a trout rise to take the fly (which is a majestic and stimulating technique that I also love), I prefer nymphing, which often relies on instinct over visual reaction. I returned from breakfast on that October morning on Lake Taneycomo and began nymphing.

Nymphing tries your mettle. It's hard. For starters, your strike indicator is small enough as it is. I typically use one smaller than a dime that provides maximum sensitivity to any touches of the sub-surface fly. Add to the indicator's diminutive size the difficulty seeing it when fishing flowing, choppy water—especially when the sun is out, shimmering off the crackling ripples. Finally, the fisherman must be fast enough to set the hook against the lightning-quick reaction of the fish. Trout can literally, within milliseconds, suck in a fly and spit it back out upon detecting it is not a legitimate food item. The window of opportunity for the fly fisherman is razor-thin. The fly fisherman must react to the indicator's slightest movement, such as a change in drift path or the slowing of the indicator flow, for example, to even stand a chance of setting the hook.

On most days, you will miss more strikes than you set when nymph fishing. But on those rare days when you least expect it, you get into a groove while nymphing and become an unstoppable force. That October day in Lake Taneycomo was one of those days. To use another nerdy Star Wars analogy, I became a Jedi of the spring, able to sense things ahead of time. Before the indicator ever deviated its course or slowed down, I overrode my physical senses and, with a quick twitch of the wrist, set the hook to find a trout at the end of my line. My mind would tell me to adjust drag or mend line before my eyes could see the need for adjustments. It was like Neo at the end of *The Matrix*, when he finally learns how to control the immediate physical dimension by effortlessly dodging bullets and using martial arts.

On those rare days, a fly rod in hand imbues its wielder with a spring consciousness. What comes upon you is not just a newly-acquired prescience, but a new awareness, where your physical sense perception blends into the surrounding cosmos. Your reception of the stream flows up from the grip of your fly rod, channels down through your line, and ends at your fly with an enhanced sense of sight, feel, and sound. I caught fish after fish on that October day, setting the hook before the indicator even responded to the fish's assault. It wasn't even fair. After becoming so enthralled, leaving the water and transitioning back into life outside of the stream felt strange because I was in a zone—one granted a glimpse of the metaphysical orchestration of the Holy God, Who upholds the spring. High-sticking my rod, I conducted my autumn harvester into the mouths of feckless rainbows. I could have littered the bank with scintillating fuschia flashed by twelve, thirteen, and even some fifteen-inch trout.

On occasions like this, I spend the entire drive home trying to digest what happened out in the water. I replay in my mind the "stream omniscience" I displayed, almost where I could have hooked fish with my eyes closed. I arrive home, walking around the house, quick-twitching my wrist, setting imaginary hooks as if my neurological system is still decompressing. I tell my wife, "Something happened in that stream today." Something met me on its turf and ushered me into it.

I came home, driven like Thomas to confess, "My Lord and my God" (Jn. 20:28)! You cannot come away unchanged. You cannot come away with a deeper imprint of the Holy.

Yet, what stirred us psychologically in the spring was not the Holy Himself. What happened was ordained by the Holy, by His grace, to grant a glimpse of the cosmos He commands. It was just a mere type, pointing to the incomparable holiness of God. It is like A.W. Tozer says:

> We cannot grasp the true meaning of the divine holiness by thinking of someone or something very pure and then raising the concept to the highest degree we are capable of. God's holiness is not simply the best we know, infinitely better. We know nothing like the divine holiness. It stands apart, unique, unapproachable, incomprehensible and unattainable. Only the Spirit of the Holy One can impart to the human spirit the knowledge of the holy.[179]

The spring is crafty in how it can adapt to and use varying circumstances to enact changes in the psyche of its guests. Many a young man and woman have taken refuge in the spring as a sort of cocoon, where a coming of age occurs, preparing and propelling them to the next epoch of life. It is the theology of the spring that moves us with an infusion of psychical life, transforming us just enough to shuck the hulls that encase us, moving upward in abundant life.

One such example is the rite of passage young people take when embarking on their first group camping trip. I have heard many stories, not unlike my own, of the first post-adolescent taste of independence made on a camping trip with friends. We've lived for years under our parent's roofs, dependent on their provisions, learning right and wrong, and maintaining proper boundaries. And yet, it's almost like we have to take a step back into the pure, primordial ecoverse of the spring to seize this mantle of full autonomy for ourselves.

For me, that coming of age trip was to Bennett Springs State Park with a group of seventeen-year-old guys over spring break my junior year of high school. For the first time in most of our lives, we were completely left alone for an extended period without supervision or sustenance from Mom and Dad. Left alone to get the tent up. Left alone to start and tend a fire. Left alone to catch, clean, and cook our own fish. Left alone to share stories around the campfire while listening to The Eagles' greatest hits. Left alone appeasing law enforcement and the sporadic checks by park rangers. Left alone for mischief—like Kevin falling into the stream, or Clay putting on camo fatigues and face paint and vanishing into the woods for hours. I'll never forget that trip, mostly because after being left alone at the spring, I came back believing, for the first time in my life, that I might be capable of making the next step as an autonomous adult.

The spring's channels offer symbolic, if not psychical, passage to the next stage of life. The arms of the stream are nature's way of unfolding the pages that usher in a new dawn. The spring was the very venue where nature gave its final blessing to my impending marriage. After our engagement, my first trip to meet her extended family involved a family float trip down the Jack's Fork River. I was told beforehand that our staying power as a couple would be flushed out during this canoe trip.

I laughed it off at the time, but there was more truth in that statement than I realized. The masks of a relationship come off on a float trip. It's hard to imagine any other marriage simulation that better pits opposite sexes, whose brains often work in opposite directions. We had to synchronize altering strokes in order to move in the same direction, communicate in quick bursts when the stream forked, and deal with the unpredictable adversity of the river running us into a patch of root wad. But we could also exhale and relax together when the water took us into a tranquil run. My then-fiancée and I survived the float trip, handling it well, more in love with one another than before. Yes, the couple that endures the float together, stays together. In many ways, the float trip down the stream is a microcosm of married life. This is why when I offer marital counseling to engaged couples, one of the things I recommend is that they first go on a float trip together. I'm kidding, of course, but not entirely.

Years later, in part due to that betrothing float trip, the spring offered an idyllic setting for another coming-of-age moment. It delivered in ways I never thought possible on that dreaded occasion of giving my oldest son "the Talk." There's no way to make this coming-of-age talk any less awkward, but I decided a day of fly fishing would provide the setting for some great object lessons on the pervasive topics of where babies come from, puberty, etc. Since it was spawning season, I could demonstrate the consistency of a God of order, Who ensures the propagation of trout that, like humans, require the sperm of the male fertilizing the eggs of females to bring about new life. After thoroughly scaring him into shock with the talk, I took him from the cabin down to the spring, where we began to unwind by fishing.

What ensued after the talk was quasi-mythical, if not landmark, in the boy's life. In what I can only take as an ode from God sanctioning the boy's transition, he proceeded, for the first time in his life, to out-fish me, his dad. I didn't *let* him beat me—pride is one vestige of the fallen flesh I still battle. He just put it on me, catching five trout before I had caught one. After having his psyche shaken to the core, the boy was ready to transition to the next phase in his life, to begin growing as a man, by breaking through to finally out-fish the man who taught him how to fish. And as we cleaned fish that day, the message was reinforced by fileting males and females and allowing him to see their seasonal milt (sperm) and eggs.

Clearly the most poignant anecdote I know of the spring's surrealistic means to affect a coming of age actually turned out to be a prolonging of age. And perhaps, just perhaps, I pray, the spring was both sanctuary and catalyst, preparing a rebirth to come. I pray that what happened in the spring that day was the beginning of a story with an ending not yet written.

The occasion was a somber one. A cancerous mass had just been discovered on my father's pancreas. If the initial reports of pancreatic cancer were correct, as our prominent oncologist suspected, my father had about three months to live. Before the final biopsy results were to arrive and a desperate round of chemo to begin, we decided to take my dad to his favorite place in the world for his last fishing trip: Bennett Springs State Park. All of our family turned out—my brother came in from Chicago; my dad's brothers met us there; and my dad's father also made it there for this spontaneous trip. There was an unspoken rationale about the gathering. We all knew the reason and importance for this trip without having to voice it.

The trip was important for me for a host of reasons. My dad taught me how to fly fish. But in our hundreds of outings, my dad never lived to see me catch a "lunker," which is a trophy trout weighing over three pounds. My inability to produce was really a sad way to repay a good teacher. I'd seen my dad catch plenty of lunkers in his day, but he had not lived to see the "coming of age" and passing of the torch manifested in my lunker.

The day was quintessentially beautiful. Overcast clouds adorned the sky. They unveiled the perfect profusion of light, accentuating our flies. Wind was nonexistent. The stream was predictable, flowing with a steady, colloquial eloquence. And the quality *and* quantity of fish empowered us to ignore the chill of this March morning. Cast after cast landed fish after fish. Not just any fish, but *nice* fish. Buxom rainbows glistened from the net, writhing and flashing their exquisite scales in a display of organic gemology. The collocation of colors shone with extra brilliance on this day, like a gelatinous ruby mash spread between speckled jalapeño backs and opal-glazed bellies. Everyone in our group got in on the rampant action. It was as if God had stocked the spring and ordained the conditions just for us, just for this special occasion. My brother ended up catching what my dad would call the single largest stringer of fish he's ever seen for one morning's work.

But the real spectacle was unveiled after the onslaught of fish. My uncles and grandfather, hungry for breakfast and beyond satisfied with their haul, emptied from the stream. My father, my brother, and

I remained together in the water for a few more minutes. Our attentiveness waned with calls from our empty bellies. I told myself, in my traditional countdown, "three more casts." And with those final casts, coming when least expected, a breakthrough moment burst forth. In one sharp instant, I felt a voracious strike attack my black jig. As the line squealed and peeled, hijacked by a sub-surface missile, I knew that the big one had finally come.

I fought that fish for over five minutes. Scared to death I was going to lose it, like I had others before, I heard my dad's soothing instructions like they were a background movie score. "Breathe easy . . . Rod tip up . . . Don't horse him . . . Let him take it . . . " Finally, the fish surrendered, and in a fitting end, it was my dad there by my side who netted my first lunker on what might be his final venture to the spring. I could hardly hold back the tears. My father's legacy had finally been realized. He could depart in peace. The spring had provided again.

My dad entered the spring that day as a grim, doleful, dying man. He left as a changed man, one who finally got to see his much-anticipated legacy rise to reality. Only the spring—or, more accurately, its Keeper—can dispense this new sense of life. But the ripple effect did not end that day in the spring. The next week, we got a call back from dad's oncologist; the cancer was not pancreatic cancer at all but, rather, a form of lymphoma. While formidable, it was treatable. Now, perhaps, it was just a fortuitous coincidence. Maybe it was psychosomatic—the events of the spring that day jilted his psyche to such an extent that it overcame physiological malady. But maybe, just maybe, it was ordained as the first stage of a renewal of life, with the theology of the spring writing the opening chapter.

There is something to be said, beyond existential soothing, for the psychological byproducts that come from encounters with the spring and other areas of nature. Dr. Stephen Kellert of Yale University maintains that humans possess a dependence on interactions with nature. Specifically, Dr. Kellert asserts that connections with nature are "fundamentally related to our capacity to think, to feel, to communicate, to create, to problem solve, to form a secure and meaningful identity, to mature and develop, to heal, to be healthy and productive."[180]

A 2012 research study commissioned by Dr. Dan Witter for the Missouri Department of Natural resources cited copious health benefits for people interacting with the outdoors: "Sick persons who experience greater contact with nature recover faster and require fewer painkillers"; "rates of obesity, diabetes, and myopia decrease when children spend more time outdoors"; communication skills improve because "our language and personality development [rely] heavily on images and representations of nature, wildlife, and the outdoors"; and "camping, hiking, fishing, and other outdoor activities and adventures lead to better physical and mental health, increased self-esteem, and positive character development."[181]

It is tragic that the vast majority of people in our day are missing out on the abundant life the spring and outdoors have to offer. According to Kellert, ninety percent of Americans now spend their time indoors.[182] Children devote considerably more time inside on electronic devices than they do playing outside. Over a thirty-year period from 1972 to 2011, recreational visitors to Ozark National Scenic Riverways, from which towns like Eminence subsist, decreased by 55.6 percent, from 3,081,256 in 1972 to 1,365,960 in 2011.[183] Missouri's largest trout fishing destination, Bennett Springs State Park, saw its total attendance drop by twenty-seven percent from 2001 to 2015.[184]

Granted, the above data comes from a small, localized sample, with various factors that make a generalized extrapolation difficult. Consider also that the United States National Park Service has reported record numbers of visitors for 2015, which offers hope. Perhaps more people will get off the couch and enter the spring's ecoverse to come away changed. By now, we've seen plenty of the ethereal prowess of the spring. Like a divine messenger, it draws and infuses theological, physiological, and psychological life to those coming into its waters. For our final discourse, we will examine how our ultimate hope, the only hope that matters, emanates from the spring, coming into spiritually dead people, radically imparting a fountain that flows eternal life.

DRAWN TO ABUNDANT LIFE IN THE SON

J. Gresham Machen was strikingly right (and ahead of his time) when he wrote, "At the very centre of Christianity are the words, 'Ye must be born again.' These words are despised today. They involve supernaturalism, and the modern man is opposed to supernaturalism . . . ."[185]

Machen wrote these words around one hundred years ago, but they ring true even louder today. The words "you must be born again"—the very words of Jesus in John 3:7—rankle us not only because they point to a supernatural act, but also because at the heart of the issue lies an implied assertion about our very nature. This assertion cuts against the grain of the modern humanist mind that believes humanity is inherently good, and *if* we even need to be saved, we possess the self-sufficiency to save ourselves.

Recall the succinct anthropology found in the theological allusion to springs in chapter five, where we referenced Proverbs 25:26, a truth teaching that the heart of man is like a polluted spring. Polluted springs and aquifers, as we've learned, are often impossible to cure. A polluted spring does not flow forth pure water. In fact, it can't do anything but spew forth contamination, which flows downstream, permeating all the stream channels and, in short, the entire watershed. And the spring certainly cannot heal itself, if it even can be healed. It requires the intervention of an outside agent to purify the heart of the spring in order that all the downstream effects can once more be pure, good, and life-giving.

The human heart functions much the same way as the spring. Our native, polluted hearts corrupt the moral faculties that flow forth from it. Historically, as well as philosophically, the heart is seen as the seat of moral operations that drive the human soul. The heart controls our moral faculties through interworking components. John Owen delineates these moral components as the mind (what it can cognitively discern and evaluate to permit action), the affections (what we desire or are averse to), the conscience (what warns, persuades, or dissuades us), and the will (what affects the acting upon by choosing or refusing).[186] Thus, if the components comprising our heart are corrupt and polluted, how can righteousness possibly flow from them?

Theologically, the Bible supports the polluted spring analogy. Jesus taught, " . . . Whatever goes into a person from outside cannot defile him, since it enters not his heart . . . What comes out of a person is what defiles him. For from within, out of the heart of man, come evil thoughts, sexual immorality, theft, murder, adultery, coveting, wickedness, deceit, sensuality, envy, slander, pride, foolishness" (Mk. 7:18-22). We also read that " . . . the hearts of the children of man are full of evil, and madness is in their hearts . . . " (Eccl. 9:3). In an age where pop culture tells us to "follow our hearts," the Bible is countercultural, saying, "The heart is deceitful above all things and desperately sick" (Jer. 17:9a). The human heart is so desperately sick and diseased that Jesus gave another analogy, noting, "A healthy tree cannot bear bad fruit, nor can a diseased tree bear good fruit" (Matt. 7:18). Unfortunately, this affliction of a polluted heart is a universal pandemic to all of humanity. "None is righteous, no not one . . . no one does good, not even one" (Rom. 3:10b-12). Far from neutral, we are rotten to the core.

I am sure many readers are protesting at this point, arguing either that the human heart is not really that bad or that our sin and unholy behavior are just acquired tangential reactions to social stimuli. Such a reaction is, fittingly enough, a symptom of our heart's corruption. All we really need to do to dispel that notion is to take a trip to the spring with a young child. Make it into a fishing trip. Spend only a couple of hours, and just watch this cute child come to naturally exhibit unseemly and evil characteristics you never taught—such as coveting, deceit, theft, or pride. No one has to teach children to covet the stringer of fish another child caught. They'll just do it. No one has to teach children to practice deceit, like lying about strikes they had on their lure or embellishing the size or number of fish they caught.

They'll just do it. No one has to teach children how to steal or to just take the brightly colored Snoopy pole from another child. They'll just do it. And no one has to teach children to be proud and boastful when they catch fish or to be envious of other kids catching fish when they are not. They'll just do it. In short, no one has to teach us how to sin. We just do it as the natural overflow from polluted hearts. We sin because we are sinners by nature.

But it isn't just that our hearts are polluted with a disposition toward our own desires, as if we are making honest mistakes. Our "mistakes" are acts of cosmic treachery against the God of the universe. Such rebellion is born out of a nature that the Bible says is hostile to God (Rom. 8:7). Owen makes a piercing distinction, noting that we are more than just enemies of God because "enemies may be reconciled, but enmity cannot; yea, the only way to reconcile enemies is to destroy the enmity."[187] The Bible describes us as "by nature children of wrath, like the rest of mankind" who live in the "passions of our flesh" (Eph. 2:3). We are creatures who prefer darkness over light so that our evil works won't be exposed (Jn. 3:19).

It would also be a mistake to surmise that our sad state of affairs is one that simply requires more head knowledge to make better spiritual decisions. Not only do we not desire God, we lack the spiritual ability to even discern spiritual truth. The Bible says that we are "dead in trespasses and sins" (Eph. 2:1), a condition that restricts any further activity. We are spiritually dead people who can only act as dead people act, passively rotting away, while incapable of any spiritual action. It would be wrong to conceive this state as a sort of spiritual coma that is able to inertly ponder spiritual truth because we are told that as spiritually dead beings with no spiritual life, we are not able to even understand spiritual truth or spiritual things (1 Cor. 2:14). Our natural condition is hopeless beyond repair. What we need is to be purified with a new heart. What we need is for a supernatural miracle to occur, birthing us into a new spiritual life, which radically changes the disposition of our nature.

A supernatural miracle is precisely what the God of the universes grants to the redeemed through the new birth, called regeneration. Regeneration is the most grandiose exercise of grace the cosmos has ever seen and, strangely enough, in my opinion, one of the most neglected doctrines of theology. While the word "regeneration" is used only twice in the New Testament (Matt. 19:28 KJV,[188] Titus 3:5), it is foreshadowed in much of the Old Testament, such as in God's promise in Ezekiel 36:26-27, "And I will give you a new heart, and a new spirit I will put within you ... And I will put my Spirit within you, and cause you to walk in my statutes ..."

In short, regeneration is the radical purification of our corrupted hearts and the creation of a new spiritual life imparted into us by God the Holy Spirit. Regeneration not only inclines us toward God by changing the disposition of our hearts, but also grants us spiritual discernment, thereby making us new spiritual beings altogether. Louis Berkhof summarized regeneration well, calling it "a creative, hyper-physical operation of the Holy Spirit, by which man is brought from one condition into another, from a condition of spiritual death into a condition of spiritual life ... which under the influence of the Holy Spirit, gives birth to a life that moves in a Godward direction."[189] John Murray described it: "A revolution, a reconstruction takes place at the center of man's moral and spiritual being: sin and pollution are dethroned in the citadel of man's being, and righteousness takes its place."[190]

Regeneration is where it all begins. It is the watershed moment, defining the life of a believer. Therefore, given the paramount importance of regeneration, here are four key points on the doctrine. To aid in your understanding of this doctrine, I recommend you reread one of the capstone biblical texts teaching regeneration, John 3:1-10, which began this chapter.

First, regeneration is essential to salvation. Jesus goes out of His way to emphasize this fact, telling Nicodemus, a religious leader, not once but twice that unless one is born again, he cannot see, and later cannot enter, the Kingdom of God. Regeneration is essential to salvation because it gives us spiritual life and the ability to discern spiritual truths. Only when we are able to discern spiritual truth can we respond in faith and repentance upon hearing the Gospel message (Rom. 10:17). Salvation is by faith alone, yet our faith is made possible only by regeneration. Without regeneration, none could be saved because none *would* be saved.

Second, regeneration is instantaneous. One minute, we are spiritually dead people, whereby the words of Scripture make no sense to us, and our sin does not bother us. But in a decisive, supernatural instant, our sin grieves us, and the words of the Bible suddenly leap off the page and make sense to us in a way we could not previously understand. Regeneration is an instant, one-time act, not something that develops over time like our sanctification. Jesus makes good use of the analogy of the wind in John 3:8, telling Nicodemus that it "blows where it wishes, and you hear its sound, but you do not know where it comes from or where it goes." We can't see the wind, control when it comes, or control where it goes. A fly fishing example is our strike indicator out on the water. The wind—in an instant, without warning—comes and goes, invisible to us. But we know it was there on the water, acting on the indicator, due to the change in its motion, caused by the wind.

Our regeneration works the same way. We don't see it coming and can't control when it comes on. But we know the Holy Spirit has entered and stirred us, as we are instantly transformed into what the apostle Paul called a new creation (2 Cor. 5:17). The ripple effects of the Spirit, the efficient Cause, acting upon us evidences itself in a new movement toward God.

Third, regeneration is an act of monergism, whereby we, the object, are passive participants. Monergism is a compound word with Greek etymology that literally means "the work of one" (*mono* = one, root suffix *ergon* = to work). The previous text of John 3:8, where Jesus uses the analogy of the wind, is also helpful in illustrating this point. Just as we cannot control when the wind comes and where it goes but are passive objects that it acts upon, neither can we control the cause of our new birth. To put it another way, just as we have no volition or participation in our physical birth, so we are likewise passive in our spiritual birth. We can't cause ourselves to be born, which would be a logical impossibility because we would have to exist before we are born in order to cause our existence. The better answer is the theological answer, which the apostle John offers in John 1:13, that our spiritual birth is "not of blood nor of the will of the flesh nor of the will of man, but of God" (cf. Jn. 6:63).

While our regeneration is based solely on the sovereignty of God to grant spiritual life to whom He wills (Rom. 9:15-16; Eph. 2:5; Phil. 2:13), it is not to say that human volition does not come into play afterward. Regeneration is the first act, initiated by God, by which He supernaturally draws us to Himself (Jn. 6:44, 65), like humankind has been drawn to physical springs for survival. But later acts, such as sanctification and ongoing repentance, expressly require the cooperation of the believer. Regeneration removes the polluted spring that once flowed within us and replaces it with a new spring of truth, from which flows the living waters that Jesus spoke of to the Samaritan woman at the well (Jn. 4:14). Unfortunately, a polluted watershed remains, which seeps into our moral faculties from time to time. Because our fallen nature still remains within us, believers are called to actively put to death those polluted branches within them through the cleansing water of the indwelling Holy Spirit (Col. 3:5).

Fourth, regeneration both purifies and indwells. Jesus makes a cryptic statement to Nicodemus that has been the source of much confusion over thousands of years. He states in John 3:5b, "Unless one is born of water and the Spirit, he cannot enter the kingdom of God." While the immediate context tells us He is referring to the act of regeneration in general, many theories have been offered up to explain what Jesus means by "born of water and the Spirit."

Clearly, by "born of the Spirit" Jesus is referring to the new, spiritual life we are granted as newly-created spiritual beings indwelt by the Holy Spirit. But the more difficult part of the interpretation is what Jesus meant by "born of water." Some speculate He is referring to physical birth from water in the womb and spiritual birth from the Holy Spirit. Others believe He is talking about water baptism and regeneration. However, such a construal fails to reconcile with the overriding truth being taught—the passivity of the regenerate. Furthermore, such an argument is anachronistic. While Jewish baptism had been in practice for a long time, Christian baptism, a sign of one's already having been brought to faith through regeneration, had not yet been instituted.

The explanation that makes the most sense is that which would have been obvious in the context of the original Jewish audience and easily understood by Jesus and Nicodemus in an idiomatic, if not ritualistic, sense. Jesus is using water in the symbolic sense of purificatory cleansing, such as the rites of purification the Jews ceremonially followed to be cleansed of any defilement. If a Jewish woman were to become unclean (through the touch of a dead animal, certain bodily discharges, etc.), and, thus, unfit for Sabbath worship, she would often have to go through a series of purifying cleansings involving water rites. The verb used in John 3:5 is in the aorist tense, indicating an act completed once and for all. Thus, Jesus was saying that upon our regeneration, the Holy Spirit comes and purifies our hearts once and for all, making them not only fit for His indwelling, but also rendering us as capable to worship Him through our daily lives. Being purified for all time, we are now fit for adoption as His children and for service as God's people. This does not suggest we will live without sin on this side of Heaven, but it does mean that the natural pollution of hearts has been purged and made anew.

At this point, one may see the effects of regeneration but not understand how it acts as the operative cause that radically alters our disposition. Furthermore, it might be asked if it is even possible for the effects of regeneration to be brought about without doing damage to human free will. I must preface my answers by noting that regeneration is just one of the mysteries of God, Whose ways are not our ways, and, thus, pretending to know any more than He has revealed to us is the height of hubris. That said, what God has revealed to us systemically about regeneration goes a long way toward answering both questions posed above.

Regeneration loosens us from the bondage of sin by changing our desires. As demonstrated above, human nature is not morally-neutral; we are inclined toward sin and rebellion. We desire these inclinations freely. Our will was always free, both before and after our regeneration. But what determines the will? A.W. Pink astutely answered, "The strongest motive power which is brought to bear upon it . . . varies in different cases. With one it may be the logic of reason, with another the voice of conscience, with another the impulse of the emotions . . . with another the power of the Holy Spirit."[191] Essentially, Pink is saying, much like Jonathan Edwards before him, that our greatest desire at the moment of choice determines the will (though Edwards' view was certainly nuanced).

Prior to regeneration, our motive was to please ourselves in a will to power. Our fallen motives drove our greatest desires toward unrighteousness. All of the moral faculties that John Owen cited—the mind, the affections, the conscience, and the will—are at work, complicit in propelling the corrupt heart. Inexplicably, in a moment, the Holy Spirit arrives on the scene and radically transforms these faculties of the heart, changing our disposition away from sin and toward God.

While changing motives, the Holy Spirit illuminates the mind. Awakened from darkness, the mind now apprehends God's truth with luminous joy. We can understand God's special revelation and revel in the insatiable beauty of holiness like fresh spring water that we can't drink from enough. Owen called this aspect of godly enlightenment of the mind "a candle of the Lord unto the soul, enabling it to search all the inward parts of the belly. It gives a holy, spiritual light into the mind, enabling it to search the deep and dark recesses of the heart . . ."[192]

Because the Holy Spirit supernaturally changes our affections and desires, our sin inscrutably begins to bother us. Our desire to gratify our sinful motives is replaced by a new, alien desire to please Christ. The Holy Spirit now works within us, helping us to not gratify the old desires of the flesh (fallen nature) but to cultivate godly desires (Gal. 5:16-17). The new desires of the Spirit give us peace that we couldn't understand prior to our regeneration. It's as the psalmist wrote, "As a deer pants for flowing streams, so pants my soul for you, Oh God" (Ps. 42:1).

Equipped now with a mind that discerns the holy and a desire that craves righteousness, the conscience is better equipped to act as the heart's barometer to identify wrongful acts. Once buoyed by weighing matters against the standards of men, the conscience now uses the proper litmus test in moral matters—the standard of God. Informed of the vileness of sin, the regenerated heart now has a conscience with a stronger clutch to prevent harm, like a father holding his child from crossing an intersection. The Holy Spirit aids our conscience to convict us of sin and, thus, steer us toward holiness.

Finally, with the collaborative input of the mind, the desire, and the conscience, the will can act accordingly. Upon regeneration, our wills are altered forever because we now possess the Spirit of Christ. Christ Himself, without flaw, lived in accordance to the will of God the Father (Jn. 4:34, 6:38). What greater confidence can the regenerate have than to know "it is God who wills and works in [us] for His good pleasure" (Phil. 2:13)? After the Holy Spirit purifies the polluted heart and renews our hearts, mind, and conscience with inclinations toward godliness, our will follows suit, freely. The will is now able to choose holiness, driven by a motive that seeks Christlikeness as its greatest desire at the moment of choice.

Thus, we find no violation of our "free will." The Holy Spirit has simply liberated us as new creatures from the willful addiction to sin. And after drawing us to Himself with an irresistible glory that enables the soul to discover the incomparable beauty of the Holy, He implants within His new creatures a new heart that wills to flow with the living water of abundant life.

The spring. It's both a relic of the past and a cathartic ideal. Talked about more than visited, it sits on the environmental periphery like a faddish, bucket-list destination. To the modern eye that has delayed pilgrimage to its waters for too long, its turquoise smile awaits with a hint of nostalgia, like a reunion with an old acquaintance. It awaits to stir us theologically, physically, psychologically, and spiritually. We've now penetrated the depths of its bosom to see the life it gives. We've seen its streams selflessly provide physical life for entire people groups. We've seen its aura ceaselessly nourish the psychical development of the soul for those seeking rest. And we've seen its ancient blues as an enigmatic type pointing to the ultimate infusion of abundant life through regeneration. New life awaits you in the spring's waters—waters that, when read as the theology of the spring, reveal the glory of its Creator.

Reflection Questions

1. In this chapter, I cite a number of examples of people who came away from the spring with a change in their very psyche. Have you ever had any encounters with the natural world that changed your mindset? What was it like?

2. We were told in this chapter our hearts are deceitful above all things. However, as I noted, we live in a world that encourages us to follow our hearts. Has your heart ever deceived you? What potential problems could occur if we base all of our decisions on the subjective inclinations of our hearts instead of grounding our decisions on absolutes?

3. Do you believe humanity is increasingly averse to the supernatural? If so, why do you think this the case, and would spending more time in the outdoors change this belief?

4. Shai Linne, in his song "Regeneration," artfully raps, "It's kind of like the wind which is free east to west/ Can't perceive the steps, you can only see its effects . . ."[193] How does this line apply to describing regeneration as we have seen in this chapter?

5. Jesus compares regeneration to the wind—we don't see it come or go, but we know it has been somewhere by the visible effects it

leaves on an object it acts upon. How does this speak to the new desires we see play out in a person born-again by the Holy Spirit?

6. Why should our regeneration through monergistic means prevent us from boasting of our salvation?

7. John Owen warned about those who mistake the effects of regeneration with its cause, writing, "These have their use in the business at hand; but whereas they are all to be looked on as streams, they look on them as the fountain."[194] What are some possible ill-consequences of seeing our outflow of good works as the cause or spring of righteousness?

Part Three

THE CREATOR'S COMMISSION
FOUND IN THE SPRING

CHAPTER SEVEN

CATCHING FISH, PART ONE: CALLED AND EQUIPPED TO CATCH FISH

"While walking by the Sea of Galilee, he saw two brothers, Simon (who is called Peter) and Andrew his brother, casting a net into the sea, for they were fishermen. And he said to them, 'Follow me, and I will make you fishers of men.' Immediately they left their nets and followed him."

—Matthew 4:18-20

THE DAY BEGAN WITH THE fervor of pre-dawn optimism. Not unlike a child on Christmas morning, I awoke in a reverie that sprang out of the still-dark ambiance. My mind raced in full bloom with my faculties as a realist not yet fully engaged, and in its suppression, the fanciful was unleashed. Anything seemed possible.

Such was the mood when I met my friend Joe in the parking lot of a local grocery store, our rendezvous point that would launch us out into the day's fishing trip. Typically, single, college guys out at this hour are winding down from a night of chasing girls. We, on the other hand, were winding up for a day of chasing fish. And like true college kids, while we may have been wrong, we were never in doubt that we would catch many fish and catch big fish. The early-hour confidence was ductile, being stretched and extended as we made conversation over that long drive to the stream.

Opportunities like these to catch up with Joe were rare. He was a boyhood friend, and it seemed like we had already conquered the world together. We both came from broken homes and were not well-off. But we won a couple of state baseball championships as kids, and later, we reeled off two consecutive undefeated seasons while winning state football titles our junior and senior years of high school at one of the most elite programs and under one of the most elite coaches (Pete Adkins) in the country. So, given our background and synergistic triumphs, you might understand why—in our minds—the conquest of trout was never in question. Our time together on this morning was all the more meaningful since Joe, a much better football player than I, went out of state on a football scholarship and rarely made it back home. But on those occasions when he made it home, we tried to make it count. This trip was no exception, as our conversation on that early-morning drive to the stream resumed naturally, as if he had never left. How rare it is to be gifted friendships like these from a Creator, Who Himself calls us "friend" (John 15:15).

However, what transpired that morning may well have required me to examine my credentials and surrender my friend card. Now, I could shirk culpability for the matter on account of being a poor college kid. Unlike today, when I love to take people fly fishing and have accumulated enough equipment for my guests to use, I barely had enough resources to have my own rod, let alone foot one for someone else. Therefore, Joe had brought his own gear—gear that taught an object lesson: the spring has little tolerance for conspicuous imposters.

Let me back up a second for greater context. My friend Joe grew up in a rural setting outside of town. While he enjoyed venturing into the outdoors, his exposure to the world of fishing had been essentially confined to farm ponds and, perhaps, a couple of lakes. Whether farm pond or lake, both tend to utilize a "chuck and duck" strategy of fishing that impales live bait on a hook, hurls it out into the muddy water, and hunkers down, hoping for the biggest fish in the proverbial sea to come along. Fishing flies for trout on the lower Niangua River—which means "many springs," as christened in the native Osage Indian language—is a different culture altogether. But Joe was a kindred soul, more than willing to spend time with his friend, so he jumped at my offer to take him to a place with a style of fishing completely foreign to him. Since Joe didn't own a fly rod, much less any flies, I told him to bring his spinning rod and said he could use some of my streamer patterns.

To ensure that you don't get lost in the jargon of fly fishing but actually learn it yourself to better enjoy this book, throughout this chapter I will define new fly fishing terms as they are introduced. So, to elaborate on the previous paragraph, a pattern is simply a fly that is tied to imitate a specific organism but might have minor nuances favored by the tier such as color, size, and added effects. For example, a new midge pattern might incorporate using a gold head instead of a black head. A streamer is a type of larger fly that is fished beneath the surface of the water, typically tied with marabou feathers or deer hair, made to resemble smaller minnows and fish in the stream.

But it was at the point of departing for the stream when I first became negligent. The instant I saw Joe load his big ol' "farm rod" into the back of my car should have triggered a mandatory line inspection. You might be asking, "What's so important about his line?" Recall from a prior chapter that trout have ultra-keen, near-sighted vision. This vision enables instantaneous distinction between legitimate food and charlatan imitation. Likewise, the thicker the fishing line, the better trout are able to see the line that is connected to an authentic-looking fly. That one anomaly, this foreign line running through the water—even if transparent in color—is sufficient grounds for skittish trout to reject the fly. Moreover, fishing line comes in varying thickness with a tradeoff—the thicker and heavier line is more resistant to breaking, but is more visible. On the other hand, the thinner line is less visible to fish but easier to break. Line durability is measured by pounds of pressure required to break it. Thus, ten-pound test line requires ten pounds of pulling pressure to break, and it should be able to easily handle fish ten pounds in weight and more. However, two-pound test line requires only two pounds of pressure to break, but it is more difficult to see. You can land fish larger than two pounds on two-pound test line, but you must be extremely delicate in how you play them off the rod and apply perfect tension.

Sure enough, the issue of Joe's line came into play nearly as soon as we started fishing. We arrived at a more remote, yet proven reliable, access and waded in, still bullish about our prospects. Within the first couple of casts, I landed a fish. And then another. And then another on the next cast. Joe, on the other hand, was having no such luck, even though we were using the same lure—a black marabou jig. (Similar to a streamer, a jig is technically not a fly. Jigs are measured by weight of the metal-cast head atop the hook. Flies are measured by hook size and are headless.) In spite of the results, Joe remained cool, though his confidence was waning.

About twenty minutes and six or seven fish later (for me), Joe, still without a strike, asked if I had anything else he could use to match my success. I offered him a different pattern—this one with heavy streaks of yellow tied into it. Joe gladly took it, tied it on, and went to work. Fifteen minutes later, the fickle trout still refused Joe's offering. Now frustrated, Joe kicked at one of the sculpin that had inched up toward his feet.

"I wonder if I can even catch one of these simple little things," Joe said. So, in a maneuver of part frivolity and part surrender, Joe dangled his jig down by his feet and caught this undiscriminating, little sculpin.

"Haha! Gotcha, simp," Joe bellowed. "Guess I'm going to stick to trying to catch these simps the rest of the morning, while you catch real fish with your magic touch."

"Let me see it," I told Joe, still staring at my line as I manipulated my jig. Turning toward him, I could see the line glistening in the air with the "simp." (Joe still refers to sculpin as "simps" to this day). And that is the thing. I shouldn't have seen that line, at least not so easily.

"Dude, let me see your line," I told Joe, as I quickened my shuffle through the current toward him. I could now see the reason he was not catching fish. He must have had at least ten-pound test line on his reel, while I was using two-pound test. His line was so big that it looked like the brother was doing a CrossFit battle rope exercise.

"Oh man, there's your problem; your line is too big," I told him.

"How can that matter? They're just little fish," Joe replied.

"Yeah," I said, "little fish that see the littlest detail. Why don't you just try using my rod for a bit and see what happens."

Joe skeptically and reluctantly traded rods with me (though I had no intention of even attempting to fish with the line on his rod and reel). "I think you just know how to hold your mouth just the right way," Joe sardonically joked, launching his first cast.

A couple of casts yielded no results. "See! You've just got some kind of magic going on here," he jeered, his voice now bordering on surrender.

I watched Joe make one more cast, and after observing his quick retrieval, I instructed him to let the fly sink to a ten count before reeling, in order to get the streamer down to the depth of the fish. Joe, desperate to do anything at this point to salvage the morning, applied this advice. Two casts later, the trout ceased their careful scrutiny; Joe at last had a fish at the end of his line.

Catching fish. There are few phrases known to humanity that can rival "catching fish" in terms of timelessness and utility. For generations and millennia, this phrase has invoked broad meaning. For some, it's economic. For others, it's recreational. And in some cultures, it's a matter of vital survival. It can be an obsession or a hobby. It can be a science, applied as an empirical, almost mechanical, means to an end. It can be an art, with no objective means and no end beyond blurring the distinction between art and life. Used as a question, it disarms passing strangers as a verbal peace treaty. Used as an invitation, it deepens relationships and fosters cohesion between parents and children, or friends on an annual excursion; or it spawns a reawakening to those treated to a trip to the spring by those who care about them.

But when used as a metaphor, the way Jesus used it two thousand years ago, "catching fish" takes on a transcendent meaning with infinite value. Coming from the lips of Jesus—the Truth incarnate—the phrase is both command and invitation and represents the invaluable means of how a fallible vessel of a fisherman is used to help reconcile a wayward creature to the Creator. Preparing for the central theme of the next chapter, "catching fish" may also refer to the supernatural transformation affected by the Creator of the spring in a rebirth conjoined in union with the Creator. Perhaps most astonishing and artistic of all is that the Creator would use fallible fishermen, such as us, casting out into humanity, to draw afflicted creatures to Himself. The next two chapters will deal with catching fish literally in the stream and metaphorically through evangelism.

I love fly fishing for its simple pageantry. Like studying theology, it's both artistic and objective—a craft governed, ultimately, by something beyond us. I've yet to find anything more invigorating than the rush of catching fish. It bequeaths a certain ecstasy, delivering an intimate perspective as both participant and spectator to the grand stage, where true life pours forth. The purpose of this chapter is to exhort you to get out and seek the joy found in catching fish. This begins with the necessary equipment I would recommend to help you get started.

Before we wade in, it's integral to understand what we mean by "catching fish." The method used must always include respect for the object, whether it be a trout or person. There's a reason it's not called "trapping fish"; we who have been quickened by the Life-giver of the stream realize that forceful manipulation never leads to the changing of heartfelt desires in affinity with the Creator of the spring. In spite of the best intentions of some fishers of men, trapping fish into a life insurance policy requiring no premium, with promises of relocation, never pays out. And there's a reason it is not called "collecting fish"; it flows contrary to the magnanimous spirit of the spring to partake in action that ultimately exalts self at the expense of the spring.

People, like fish, are not prizes to be won for purposes of ego, nor objects to be collected for a charity project. People don't generally submit to becoming a project and, like trout, can smell that spirit a mile away. And there is a reason it isn't called "conquering fish"; we could easily throw a stick of dynamite into the stream if our call was a "win at all costs" approach that delivers the most bodies. But such a strategy betrays the most fundamental reason why we go to the stream to catch fish. We go out of a genuine and enduring love for the stream, which permeates us in a genuine and enduring love for the stream's Creator. And in a cyclical fashion, we find ourselves immersed in one out of love for the other.

Thus, to be true fishers of men is to act out of the same precept—one that demonstrates a genuine, enduring love for people (the image-bearers of their Creator) and, therefore, a greater love and reliance on God Himself. That is the purest essence of "catching fish" when pursued in full obedience and submission to the Creator. To catch fish with this eternal, rather than temporal, perspective, is to realize that like the sparrow does not fall apart from God's will, no fish can be caught unless God grants it (Jn. 6:63). To this end, it is incumbent upon eternally-minded fishermen to offer the most genuine presentation possible that mirrors the ultimate "real" life in Jesus that fish cannot resist. Out of love for the Life-giver, we imitate Him that others would desire Life. Jared Wilson said it best in his book *The Prodigal Church*, "What you win them with is what you win them to."[195] We aren't fishing to win people to a cheap counterfeit that becomes expendable when the next fad comes along. We win them to an immutable Truth, issued by an immutable Love that changes hearts, reconciling people to this Love in fusion that slakes their souls for all eternity.

We love fishing because we can do no other. Our love to spread morsels of hope is stronger than our fear of ridicule. Within us lies a conviction that triumphs over our timidity, an unction that cares more about seeing people freed from the bondage of the appetites of this world than it cares about its own reputation. Even in our weakness, the source of Truth works through us, moving us to action like the prophet Jeremiah, who wrote, "If I say, 'I will not mention him, or speak anymore in his name,' there is in my heart as it were a burning fire shut up in my bones, and I am weary with holding it in, and I cannot" (Jer. 20:9).

We love fishing because we understand our efforts are futile, apart from a change in the fish's inclinations to abandon its natural diet in favor of our presentation, tied to act as an authentic insect fashioned by the Creator Himself. It is art imitating life—ultimate life, if you will. When the barometric pressure drives fish to the stream bottom or when the full blaze of the sun drives trout to cover, we still love fishing. We love fishing because when the results don't fully depend on us, we can better enjoy the engagement, as our participation as creatures is itself an act of grace. We love fishing because we understand that "apart from [Him we] can do nothing" (Jn. 15:5).

EQUIPPED TO CATCH FISH

You might have heard the maxim, "It takes money to earn money." This principle certainly applies to fly fishing, which, like any recreational pastime worth its salt, requires an initial investment in equipment. However, after your initial outlay, a whole new world within the stream is available for you to discover. While there is no dearth of amenities and supplemental gear, it is more important to know how to use base outfits well with fundamental techniques than to be average, using all the upgrades. So, although the "Cadillac" of fly rods is available to you, I'm more concerned to put you in the stream with the "Ford" model and to do so with functional mastery. Cadillacs are great *if* you know how to use them.

I'm fond of the allegory of the old man and young man who would both rise each morning to cut wood. The younger man's strength and energy far surpassed that of his older counterpart, as he cut twice the wood of the older man on the first day. On the second day, in spite of his vigor, the younger cut only a fourth more wood. On the third day, they cut the same amount of wood. Astonishingly, even starting after the young man on the fourth and fifth days, the older man produced more wood. Perplexed and embarrassed, the younger man asked him how he was able to out-produce him—in spite of his youth, strength, and amount of time spent cutting. "It's quite simple, actually," the old man responded. "I rise each morning and sharpen my axe before doing anything else. As I sharpen my equipment, my equipment sharpens me for the task ahead."

Whether using a fly rod to catch trout or providing the Word of Truth to catch men, it is important to keep our equipment sharp. We don't need flash; we need function. The following list delineates the specific fly fishing equipment you need, from sizes to manufacturers, to get you into the stream, functionally, to begin catching fish.

The Fly Rod

The magic wand and chief tool of the fly fisherman, fly rods generally run anywhere from six to ten feet long and vary in weight, flexibility, and material. The primary purpose of the fly rod is to deliver the fly to the fish in the most natural, transparent manner possible. The length, weight, and type of fly rod that is right for you depends mostly on what type of fishing you plan to do. Rod selection is important—mostly because your rod becomes not just an angling extension of your arms, but eventually, it becomes an extension of you.

A fly rod is your connection to a new dimension of drawing fish to yourself. For many, it becomes a sixth sense, granting access into a world that you could not otherwise perceive. There's nothing like the tactile sensation of feeling a trout through a fly rod. It becomes a newly-grown limb, whose nerve endings are grafted into the fish it clutches. Each fiber of the rod converges in your grip; and through its connection to the fish, you feel every joust and jerk, every twist and surge, every life-fighting pulse, and every final capitulation. An author's words do no justice to the sensory value of a fly rod. It is your most important and most intimate tool.

Most fly rods come broken down in pieces—those typically being two-piece, three-piece, and four-piece rods. Each piece—from the handle and grip at the bottom to the end tip—gradually gets smaller. The pieces fit together through conduit pieces called ferrules. Each piece must be lined up with the small rings that your line runs through, which are called guides. The pieces are stored and transported in a tube. What dictates whether you wish to buy a two-piece rod? It may be as simple as how often you travel and need a small container or how long you want to take to dress your rod before hitting the water. The other variable is the length of your rod, as longer rods require more pieces for portability. Fly rods are longer than conventional spinning rods, given the nature of fly fishing being more akin to hunting fish. The longer length of the fly rod gives you precise access to the prey while remaining unnoticed, like a portable sniper's post.

Given the matter of rod length, how does someone know how long a rod to purchase? Again, the answer to this question lies in the environment you plan to fish. A shorter rod is often more advisable in tighter quarters, such as narrow spring creeks, where your cast may not exceed thirty feet and where trees and other overhangs are easier to avoid with a shorter rod. Longer rods, on the other hand, can get your fly to places that a shorter rod can't and have the length to punch your fly into more precise casting locations. The primary job of the fly rod is to funnel kinetic energy into the fly line and, when fully loaded, deliver the fly with the energy captured by the rod. Thus, the longer the rod, the greater its capacity to be fully energized to deliver the fly where you want it to land. Longer rods also produce greater line control of the fly in the water. For example, a longer rod can high-stick a nymph dead, drifting through a fast run or mend line to prevent drag on the fly's presentation.

Length is not the only factor, however, in the way a rod casts. The line weight a rod can handle also plays a vital role in delivery. Fly rods are manufactured with a specific casting weight that is suited to cast a specific weight of line. The lower the rod weight number, the smaller line and flies it will cast. For example, a one-weight rod is more petite and can cast only light-weight line and extremely small flies (such as those on a size number eighteen hook and smaller) and will, accordingly, catch smaller fish. You would typically use a one-to-two-weight rod to fish for bluegill and small pan fish. Conversely, an eight-weight rod can cast heavier line, which can shoot out with greater velocity and deliver larger flies to a target farther away. A rod of this size can be used to catch larger fish, such as bass, steelhead, and bone fish. A fifteen-weight rod, then, will require even larger and stronger line and will catch larger fish, such as tarpon and small tuna.

The classic and most natural order of fly rods was originally made from bamboo, which gives rods a more flexible feel with the strength of an organic soft wood. British military officers are said to have brought back bamboo to make fly rods as early as 1700.[196] Bamboo split-cane rods have gradually given way to fiberglass and graphite rods, which are the predominant composition for fly rods today. Rods are manufactured with specific flexibilities, called "action," which are rated as either slow, moderate, or fast action. The faster the action, the stiffer the rod shaft. The slower the action, the more the rod bends. Beginners typically prefer slower action rods because they are just learning to feel the rod move during their back cast to help them load up their line.

What should you buy? There are some great fly rods out there at entry and mid-level price ranges. As with most things, you get what you pay for, but a beginner doesn't need all the extras before knowing how to use them. One should also consider the warranty and serviceability of your prospective rod. Given that, I recommend and endorse the nine-foot/five-weight Redington Classic Trout Rod as the entry level fly rod of choice. You can get into this rod for about $150. I cut my teeth on this rod and have come to love it for a host of reasons, among them its versatility to catch small pan fish and land large trout, as well as the maneuverability of a nine-foot rod moving five-weight line in tight quarters with superior control. Even better is that the rod comes with a lifetime warranty, which I have greatly benefited from. Redington is an American company, located in Bainbridge Island, Washington, and I have always found their customer service and timeliness to be top-notch.

(On a side note, no one enjoys having a rod broken. But if you are a father or mother of children, if you go fishing enough with your kids, it is inevitable to have a rod stepped on, slammed in a door, or broken in some other creative way. A lifetime warranty takes a bit of the sting out of a broken rod. But the far greater travesty is to never have a rod broken at all by your children because you are not bringing them with you. To that end, we need more broken rods.)

Those who survive the trials of a beginner fly fisherman will, at some point, be ready to make the foray into a more advanced, mid-level rod. I also have a couple of recommendations. While you will pay significantly more for a mid-level rod, as you become more fluent at casting, you will realize that there are things you can do with a more expensive rod that you can't do with an entry-level rod. However, until you gain the experience with an entry-level rod, you will never know what those enhanced capabilities are. Once you become proficient, you may find the outlay into a mid-level rod to be a sound investment. To that end, I would recommend rods such as the Sage Accel ($650) or the Winston Nexus ($485) as great options. Both manufacturers are giants of the industry, and these rods provide smooth and forgiving casts that seemingly bestow on the adept user a super power of tactical precision. Both Winston and Sage also back their products with a lifetime "original owner" warranty. As a final note, I'm also a huge fan of the six-weight rods offered by Orvis and Temple Fork Outfitters.

Finally, any imperative to move you out into the spring would be remiss to not offer a recommended fly rod for children. Fly fishing is the ultimate family legacy. Fathers and mothers that deny their children time in the water with them are denying a piece of themselves to posterity. I look back at moments when four generations of my family have waded into a run together, and in that portrait, fly fishing becomes an adhesive, tethering generations together. A fly rod can become like a patriarchal staff, passed down to a child coming of age. Therefore, I encourage you to get your children exposed to fly fishing early. I recommend you do so with a short, slow action rod that is easy to handle, such as the six or six-and-a-half foot, four-fifth weight rod by Eagle Claw. You don't want to break the bank on a piece of equipment that your child may take no interest in. This two-piece, entry level, fiberglass rod is made in Colorado. I gladly started both of my boys on it.

The Fly Reel

After God the Holy Spirit changes the appetite of the heart, God the Father uses His truth to draw men to Himself. Likewise, the fly fisherman uses a reel to draw fish that have been hooked to himself. Fly reels do not come as diverse in their purposive customization as fly rods; but as the keeper of the line, reels are too important to not possess unique enhancements that cater to a fisherman's tastes. Regardless of nuances, it should be understood that the fundamental purpose of the reel is to efficiently store, release, and retrieve line.

So, what are the distinguishing characteristics you should look for when shopping for a reel? For starters, consider that your reel is susceptible to being submerged in the water at countless times during your outing—such as negotiating a path through the stream or releasing fish. Even the reel's most basic function of retrieving line from the water naturally pulls moisture into the reel cavity. Therefore, you will want to purchase a stainless-steel reel—one that is water and rust resistant. And while most reel manufacturers have come to eliminate most unnecessary crevices within the reel, you will not want a product with a design that lends itself to retaining water in the nooks and crannies, which can jam up the reel. A jammed reel can be a heart-breaker, especially at moments when you most urgently need clean line release because you've hooked into a nice-sized fish.

While it probably goes without saying, you'll want to purchase a reel with sufficient line capacity within the reel spool. Reels are typically just circular pieces of machinery, just a couple of inches in radius, so there shouldn't be too much of a worry here. But you don't want to purchase a smaller reel and put nine-weight line on it. The heavier line-to-reel proportion will cause the line to burst out the spool and jam up. When in doubt, consult the salesperson at the fly shop when buying a reel to match you with the right line.

The third characteristic you'll want in a reel is to make sure the reel is compatible with your retrieval hand. What do I mean by that? Well, it sounds like common sense, but some reels are made to be cranked by a left or right hand only. "Old school," or traditional, fly fishing methodology taught to reel and crank with the same hand you cast the rod with. If you can picture this in your head, you'll see that it causes you to switch hands after the cast, which, in my opinion, is inefficient. It runs the risk that you miss strikes "on the drop." That is, after the fly lands on the water, a fish strikes just as you switch the rod to your non-casting hand to reel. It's like when a hockey team gets scored on when they get caught in transition changing players.

Therefore, I recommend reeling with the hand opposite your casting hand. I am right-handed; therefore, I cast with my right hand (because I need my casting hand to be the one I am most accurate with) and reel with my left. Thus, I don't have to switch hands and miss potential strikes. As a prospective consumer, you should buy a reel that is cranked with the opposite hand or buy a reversible reel that allows you to change the crank lever to either right or left-handed positions. Most non-reversible reels are manufactured to a default of right-handed reel operation. There is nothing worse than to buy a reel, fasten it to your fly rod handle, and realize it looks odd because it is upside down as a left-handed reel, for it is really a reel for a right-handed retrieve when you turn it right-side up.

The final, and most important, factor to consider when purchasing a reel is the matter of drag. Drag is simply the resistance the reel applies to the line as it is released. Drag is not just important in how it enables you to shoot your line out during a cast, but it becomes chiefly important when a fish is on the line. Back in the late sixties, The Buckinghams sang that it was "kind of a drag when your baby says goodbye."[97] It is even more of a drag to say goodbye to a fish because your drag was not set or maintained properly. Drag helps you remain in a state of "constant contact" with the fish after you hook it and often must be manually adjusted during your fight as the fish's intensity ebbs and flows. Therefore, I always want a reel where the drag settings are easily accessed and palpable by touch. When I have a fish on the line, the last thing I want is to take my eyes away from the fight to try to find the drag adjustment dial. Most reels come with a default drag setting, which is also something you'll want included, but more important for my money is easy drag adjustment.

What should you buy? Like rods, reels come in both luxury models and "blue collar" models. But unlike rods, the upper-tier reels don't come with the value-added functionality; the ceiling for what a great reel can do over a moderate reel is relatively low. Some expert guides advise that you save your money and purchase a basic reel, instead of the high-priced model, and use the cost savings to take casting lessons. While the value of a good reel in seamlessly adding or recalling line is certainly noticeable, I agree with the former advice and recommend getting a basic, but serviceable, reel. The Okuma SLV 4/5 is a great entry-level reel that can serve you well with a mid-range rod, too. Okuma prides itself on providing quality gear at a price that won't make you skip a few meals in order to balance your household budget. You can get the SLV 4/5 for right at about $65, which is very reasonable, given you'll get many years out of this stainless-steel reel. This reel has served as a close confidant to me during many excursions, with its conveniently-located drag dial always there, like a boxer's cornerman when you get into the heat of a battle.

Flies and the Fly Lines That Carry Them

Considerable attention has been given to the two primary tools of the fly fisherman—the fly rod and the reel—and for good reason, as these are not only the two most expensive pieces of equipment you'll need, but also the two most dynamic rigs that impact your success or failure. But while we will present the more ancillary components of fly fishing equipment in the following pages, it is not to say that these other members of the team are not integral to your success.

Case in point: your fly line. Without line, you couldn't deliver your fly to the fish, let alone have a means of apprehending the fish after you get it hooked. "But it's just simple line; why spend time talking about it?" you might ask. Fly line is not so simple, and, in fact, I would advise a beginner to have their fly line assembled by a specialist at a local fly shop before trying to tackle the feat on your own. Why is it so complicated? Because the line that goes on your fly reel has four very different segments bonded together that make up the composite whole.

The first component of the fly line, and that which is seldom seen or called upon, is called the backing. Backing, as the name implies, is essentially the back-up "muscle" that is on call should you hook into a fish that goes on a long run and would otherwise outstrip your supply of fishable fly line. Your backing is your extra supply of line but is not ever intended to be actively used in presentation of the fly. Backing is usually made of braided nylon, a strong material that compacts concentrically when wound up first onto the reel. The fisherman attaches the backing to the fly line by tying a tube knot, one of the many hosts of knots that the fly fisherman must be adept at tying. I often joke that Boy Scouts must make the best fly fishermen, given the myriad of nimble knots that the fisherman must learn to tie. I can't emphasize enough that one of the most underestimated skills in fly fishing is the ability to tie minuscule knots.

The next section of the fly line to be wound into the spool of the reel is the biggest—the fly line itself. When people fly fish, the casual observer sees the fly line tossed back and then rolled forward into the water. Fly line is most often yellow, green, or orange in color. The primary function of fly line is to get the fly to the fish, and to that end, fly line comes in two types—floating and sinking. As you can imagine, the type of fly line you use depends on the type of fishing you will be doing. If you are fishing deep lakes, or combing the bottom of deeper stream pools with streamers, or imitating stream bed prey, such as sculpin, you will want to use sinking line that quickly gets your fly down to the depths of the fish. Sinking fly line is produced with specks of lead and tungsten within the outer coating to increase density and, thus, reduce buoyancy. There are varying degrees of sinking line available that are designed to sink at a given number of feet per second.

Floating fly line, as you might suspect, is primarily used when fishing dry flies that are presented on top of the water, as well as flies imitating insects emerging from their hatch inches below the water surface. I like to use floating line when I'm "nymphing," the technique described in chapter six, which gets its name for the insect stage abiding in the middle depths of the stream with their commensurate appearance and stage-specific motion of feebly drifting through the water. (Typically, the rods best suited for nymphing are four, five, or six-weight rods). Floating fly line permits the fisherman to inconspicuously deliver the fly to the fish without it detecting the line intruding through the water column. The fly line floats because it is crafted with numerous air pockets surrounding the line's core.

The selection of fly line, as in evangelism, depends on where our intended recipient can be found. At times, we must get deep and quickly present our message of Life in a gripping, piercing manner, calling for immediate conviction. For others, we gradually drift our presentations to them, so they can see it coming and digest it mentally before swallowing it wholly. The truth of the presentation is not altered, but the manner in which it is delivered must be capable of getting to the fish as they are. The fisherman must present his fly, a model imitating the truest insect life, as the fish most naturally encounter it in the stream.

One final consideration before you purchase fly line is to determine what form of line is best for your rod and casting ability. Fly line is shaped with varying physical deviations to best suit different situations. For example, you can purchase line with its weight distributed in the casting end (weight forward line), which helps shoot your line through the rod guides to make longer casts and reduce the air resistance encountered by larger flies. Line tapered at the front helps flip flies over in a gentle, tantalizing presentation. Rear tapered line serves to provide a gradual taper transition to abet a smooth cast for longer range targets. If you have any questions, again, ask your local fly shop expert who can get you outfitted with proper line. For my money, I have always had great success with Rio fly line products.

Transitioning beyond the fly line, we come to a new section of line called the leader. The leader is sometimes called "tapered leader," due to the fact that most leaders come as a gradual reduction in size from where the butt of the leader adjoins the fly line. The leader is a clear, stiff piece of line that functions to facilitate the placid transferal of energy coming from the fly line toward the end of the cast to affect a soft, nondescript landing of the fly. The butt of the leader can be affixed to the fly line through an assortment of different knots—the most effective, perhaps, being the needle knot. Leader material is generally the same type of line as monofilament, a clear, flexible line that is nearly buoyant-neutral. A leader typically comes nine feet long, with the thick section that adjoins the fly line possessing a thickness/strength of around twenty-pound test, tapering down to about a four or five-pound test at the end.

The spring water filling the sub-surface worlds found in the Ozark streams, or the famous "Fly Highway" streams spanning the northern Rockies into Oregon, is unmatched in its pristine clarity. The bellies of the stream are so pure, they appear filled with molten glass. The clarity of these underwater vistas not only provides an open window for predators, but also enables fish with already laser-like vision to more easily spot charlatans. Thus, you can see for yourself the impasse posed to the fisherman by trying to attach his fly to the end of leader that has the thickness of five-pound test line; they face the same end as my friend Joe, as the trout will invariable reject a fly—no matter how authentic it looks—when connected to a highly discernable line. Thankfully, our final piece of line—tippet—comes to our rescue.

Tippet is a thin, transparent section of line that is tied to the end of a leader—I use a simple loop knot to join the two—with the fly tied on the tippet's other end. As the last line before the fly is presented, your tippet must be both strong and imperceptible. Tippets can be as long or as short as the situation dictates, often two to four feet long. Given tippet must be small enough to avoid detection by the trout, it conversely is more fragile and, thus, through breakage and tying on new flies will need to be replaced multiple times throughout a fishing expedition. Tippet can be purchased at varying sizes designated by an "X" rating, where the lower the number indicates the larger tippet. For example, 7X or 8X tippet is extremely small and used for the smallest of flies, while a 1X tippet is used for larger flies such as number four to number eight size hooks. To translate tippet "X" size into strength, 7X tippet typically carries about 2.5-pound test, while 6X will generally hold about 3.5-pound test.

Tippet material can get moderately expensive, depending on the type you purchase. The primary materials that comprise tippet line are fluorocarbon and monofilament, and both compounds possess different attributes. Fluorocarbon, for example, sinks better and is less flexible, which makes it a better option for sub-surface fishing techniques, like nymphing. Monofilament, on the other hand, floats well atop the water and stretches better, making it more ideal to fish top water with dry flies. Fluorocarbon tippet is also more expensive than monofilament. One cheaper alternative I have found to work almost as well is simply to purchase one or two-pound fluorocarbon fishing line that I keep in my vest and tie on as tippet material.

At the end of our tippet rests the object of truth, that morsel of mock-organic life presented to convince the fish of the truth it represents. Much more could be said about flies, which would exceed the scope of this book. Given the limited purview of this chapter, we will focus on the dynamics at play in how the fly catches fish. That said, I could not provide an exposition of the fly's use in the catch without, by extension, how the fly has caught me.

As a submitted disciple of the Creator of the stream, I'm able to see differently. I'm now enabled to see the abundant life offered by Jesus, not just in the physical portals of worlds He has crafted for our enjoyment, such as the spring, but also in His image outflowing through my own life by imitating Him out of love, obedience, and gratitude for the transformation He has affected. A life resigned to Christ is a life no longer bound by the mores and man-established values of this world. We don't have to worry about fitting into social circles or wearing masks like an actor to play the part of someone we are not, but who our social circles expect. We no longer have to be consumed with how the world measures achievements, nor do we have to be consumed with conforming to the standards of man. And what a relief, what a liberating thing that is! My only concern is born out of my new desire to please the One Who has set me, once a captive, free. That concern is our call to be imitators of Christ (Eph. 5:1), to conform ourselves to the image of Him Who gives life (Rom. 8:29). One way we do that is to pour into other people to help bring about their transformation into Christlikeness. I like to facilitate this life renovation on a one-on-one basis by taking people to the spring to discover this abundant life for themselves. But even that pairing together of disciple and spring, like that which unites God and man, requires an intermediary.

For me, tying flies is a means of discipleship with the natural world. I can never create life; that ability falls on Him alone, Whom I seek to emulate. But one means of emulating the Life-giver is the art of using organic material—such as feathers, fur, and hair—to create something that resembles the handiwork of the Creator as closely as possible. This fly is my imitation of Christ's true insect creation. But even more, to tie the fly that brings about a connection between the created world and a new creation in Christ is as edifying and challenging an art as one can find. My life is an imitation of Christ's new creation in me. To imitate Christ, I point people to the life found in Him. And yet, paradoxically, I find Him more myself as the undeniable Life-giver through imitating the simplest of life forms He creates. I find His Divine hand clearly present when I seek to artistically recreate the minutia of the simplest of insect life that He creates. So, while I could spend the money to simply buy flies, tying flies easily profits me more.

Many fishermen approach the spring with a vast arsenal of flies at their disposal. I've found that while it is good to always be prepared, if you know your environment, the natural diet of the fish, how heavily they are pressured, and what seasonal food is available, you don't need to pack the entire kitchen sink. Rather, pack those battle-tested flies that you know will work within their respective genres. I like to bring top water bugs, such as a good mayfly and a good caddisfly imitation; nymphs; a good stone-fly, in case the stream has these bottom-dwelling flies; the always-versatile midge pupae, given most every stream has midges that are always hatching; a good scud imitation that mimics freshwater shrimp; and some small jigs, woolly buggers, and streamers. Two other important additives you should have at your disposal are split shot, which are small weights that you fasten to your tippet about eight-to-nine-inches above the fly to get it to sink, and a floating strike indicator (or the common moniker "bobber,"), which is affixed to the leader and floats on the surface with the fly submerged below (not used, obviously, for top water flies). The fisherman knows a fish is taking the fly below when the strike indicator moves, stops, or is pulled under the water. Naturally, the size of your strike indicator should also be commensurate with the size of your fly, as a large indicator requires more force to alter its course and, thus, may not indicate light, sensitive strikes to a small fly below.

When tying your fly onto your tippet, I always like to use what is called an "improved clinch knot," a knot I have been tying since I was old enough to walk. However, flies can be tied on in sundry ways, with certain patterns being more amenable to the motion permitted by specific knots. The size of flies is classified by hook size in a manner similar to tippet size, with the higher hook number specifying a smaller size (the exception being for big hooks). I generally tie flies on hooks ranging from size fourteen to twenty, but I will tie streamers on larger number eight and number six hooks. Hook sizes increase in increments of two in even numbers (thus, there is no size fifteen hook, for example). The size of a fly is more important than even color. It has been said that going up one hook size—say, from a number sixteen to a number eighteen hook—represents, roughly, a twenty-five percent increase in size of insect being imitated. Fish can easily distinguish an imposter when it is twenty-five percent larger than the steady diet of bugs it has been eating. Thus, it is imperative to use the size of fly that best approximates the size of insects in the spring ecosystem.

How can you tell what kind and size of bugs are present where you are fishing? One easy way fishermen determine what type of insect is present is simply to survey the surface of the water. Another tool used by some fishermen is a sieve. They simply dip it in the water and examine the insects it has sifted. Finally, to get data straight from the horse's mouth (or in this case, the trout's stomach), some fishermen will use a stomach pump to literally draw out the contents of a fish's stomach to see what it has recently eaten. Fish stomach pumps are designed in such a way that allows the interrogated fish to be released back into the water, unharmed. When in doubt about trout feeding preferences, you can always talk to a local fly shop about current insect hatches and the dietary staples of a specific stream. Sometimes, I do wonder how the outreach in many American churches would appear if they were to make better efforts to determine what ideals were being consumed by their neighbors?

Ancillary Equipment

At this point, a purview of the *primary* equipment necessary to catch fish has been presented. That is not to say, however, that there is no other supplemental equipment available to assist you in catching fish. Therefore, the following additional equipment items should be considered valuable tools worth accumulating.

Waders

Some prefer the sanctuary of a boat, or the stability of remaining on the bank; but for me, there is nothing like stepping out into the stream and melding into the environment I seek to reach. I want to be where the action is, to feel the stream's foundation beneath my feet, and to watch the life burgeoning within arm's length. Waders are the vessel that yields the best of both worlds—the warmth and dryness of the bank with access to the inner sanctum of the stream. Simply slip the waders on over your clothes, and you are ready to immerse yourself. If fishing in colder environments, you might consider purchasing neoprene waders that retain heat much better than nylon. However, neoprene can get extremely hot in the summer. You also have the option of purchasing waders with boots built into the foot or those cut off at the foot with built-in booties, which require you to purchase wading boots. (You can, in turn, use your wading boots to fish warm-water streams without the need for waders). Wading boots, even with waders, afford you a much greater range of motion and, in turn, confidence—an invaluable asset as you navigate the stream. Many fishermen appreciate the arch support wading boots offer, which aids foot comfort and diminishes pressure on the lower back.

Waders are one accessory where you definitely get what you pay for, as nothing is more frustrating than to buy a new pair and find that they've sprung a leak the third time you've used them. For my money and for a big-picture investment, I recommend the Orvis Encounter as a stocking foot wader, which is as durable as it is comfortable, produced by an iconic name in fly fishing. Or, if you'd like to save some cash, the Hodgman H3 comes as a comparable alternative, albeit with some diminution in quality. A final option is Simms, the "Rolls-Royce" of waders, which will cost you plenty up front but are of such high quality you should never need another pair of waders. Simms hand stitches its waders in Montana for premium comfort and durability. If you prefer bootfoot waders, the Cabela's Neostretch chest waders, which I use, get my vote.

Vest

While certainly not an essential item, if you are a fiend for organization, like I am, you'll want to wear a vest that conveniently houses and organizes your gear. With a vest, you don't have to hunt around for your flies, strike indicators, line clippers, hemostats, etc. Nor do you have to worry about lugging around a tackle box. A good vest is a non-cumbersome way to neatly organize all your gear in assorted pockets and compartments (but not too many pockets), so that you move about your work like an expeditious surgeon of the water, reaching for your tools without having to take your eyes off the target. While I prefer the traditional vest appearance, newer chest pack vests have taken on more of a front and rear-sided backpack look, which, in my opinion, renders a more comfortable fit. I also prefer a vest with mesh paneling to provide ventilation on those days when the sun is beating down.

Preferences aside, one quality I insist upon is that your vest be an earth-tone color. The meticulous vision of trout is too discriminating to allow you to get away with a vest color that is unnatural to their home turf. For my money, I recommend the Yellowstone Pro Series vest, sold by Bob Ward's. It offers unmatched "bang for your buck," with a seemingly infinite supply of pockets and pouches. I love this vest, which is a milestone of comfort meeting functionality. If you prefer a very inexpensive model, the White River Journeyman mesh vest, the "house brand" for Bass Pro, might work. It is a traditional model, and while not flashy, it's durable enough to get you started and meet your needs for some time.

If you prefer higher-end quality, Fishpond makes some great vests. If you prefer to try a chest pack, I would check out the L.L. Bean Rapid River Vest Pak or the Fishpond Sagebrush mesh vest, a product that incorporates amenities you appreciate more the longer you're in the water—such as padded shoulder straps, breathable material, and tippet dispensers.

Glasses

As the scene from chapter one proved, a quality set of polarized glasses can transform you from a stream interloper into a stream resident with an underwater view of the world. Remember, your glasses need to be polarized in order to unlock a whole new world of optical discovery. Best of all, you don't have to spend a lot of money for an operational set. The Strike King S11 fits the bill nicely to equip you with the clarity you need at a price that won't blind you from sticker shock. If you don't mind spending a few extra dollars, Costa prides itself on making the clearest sunglasses on the planet and backs it up with a superior and stylish product backed for life. Costa targets more of an open-water market but can still equip you for the stream.

Nets

Our second-to-last stop on the equipment tour, aimed at getting you out of the book and into the spring, represents (hopefully) the last stop for the fish. Nothing can kindle a dour mood more quickly than losing a "once-a-generation fish" because you didn't have a proper net. Likewise, there is perhaps no greater revenge for a fish than to tangle your line or snag your fly in the braids of a nylon net, thus delaying your reentry into the action as you untangle the mess. Both of these disasters have happened to me and are easily preventable with the right kind of net. I recommend using rubber netting, which is not only less abrasive to the fish's skin and eyes, but also has a much lower proclivity to tangle your fly. If your hook gets caught in the rubber lattice, it's much easier to extract, which gets you back into the water quicker.

I generally agree with the overriding philosophy of purchasing clear or white rubber netting, as opposed to dark rubber netting, simply due, again, to the superior vision of the trout. However, by the time the net comes out, the trout has probably been alerted to your presence anyway. It is worth your money to purchase a net with a hoop diameter appropriate to the size of fish you wish to catch, as well as one with a long-shafted or extendable handle. I've made the mistake of using a net with a hoop that was too small, wistfully watching a fish swim off that seconds earlier flopped right out of my net. So, spend the extra money for a larger hoop size and longer handle, such as the Nomad El Jefe.

Fly Box

The keeper of your arsenal of flies is your fly box. It sounds simple enough, so why does a small, plastic container warrant discussion? Because your potential success is at stake if your weapons are not protected. When buying a fly box, remember these three important attributes: size, water-proofing, and clasping. Size is important because you want the box to fit snugly into the specific dimensions of your vest, but not so snug or loose that pulling it out becomes a balance-sacrificing ordeal in fast water. Spend a few extra bucks for a waterproof box. It is deflating, after wading out deep, to find the water level permeated your fly boxes and either rusted your hooks or saturated your flies. Finally, buy a box that clasps shut all the way with a firm latch to open/shut the box. It is easier than you think to whip out a fly box, only to have its chamber swing open and depose loose flies into the water.

A word of caution: take a deep breath before making a shopping list of the items above. Enumerating the equipment to outfit your fly fishing endeavors can cause severe heartburn for some when considering the cost. But remember, you start one piece at a time and accumulate gear. Moreover, you are investing in the livelihood of people, not just incurring expenses to catch fish. Even better, you are accumulating a legacy of intangible value. Your equipment becomes the tools that allow you to reach, bind, and build organic relationships with fish and men.

I believe Neil Young's 1972 album *Harvest* is one of the greatest albums ever made. The album, a hybrid of musical and social art, delves into issues shaking the core of humanity—such as addiction, racial reconciliation, and the need for genuine relationships that are anchored by unconditional acceptance. It captures the spirit of raw, organic relationships better than any album I've ever heard. My favorite song on the album addresses the maturing and changing dynamic between the older generation and the younger. It's called, "Old Man," and it always makes me think of my grandfather, given the theme of a young man discovering that he and a certain old man really aren't that different. I first heard the song in 1993, ironically when the Missouri River experienced a monumental flood that buried the highway, trapping me on the opposite side of the river from my home. I bought *Harvest* on a cassette tape and took up refuge at my grandparents' house for over a week, until the highway was restored. Through a Divine Providence working things for good, the river might have closed down a highway, but it opened up a relationship.

The story in the song progresses eerily similar to how the relationship I have with my own grandfather has matured and progressed. When I was a young teen, listening to my grandfather's stories on our two-hour drives to go fly fishing seemed like an exercise in captive torment. One line early in the song echoes that sentiment, "It doesn't mean that much to me, to mean that much to you."[198] Whether riding in the car, wading downstream from him, or sitting through his coffee cup at breakfast, I didn't find much meaning in my grand-father's instructional maxims. The only thing that mattered was my self-gratification and catching the biggest fish.

But over time, echoing the maturation in "Old Man," those trips to the spring with my grandfather fostered something else—empathy. I heard him talk about "love lost, such a cost," in being widowed at an early age. I listened to his aphorisms while standing near him in the stream, such as, "Boys, the fun and games end when the animal hits the net,"—a reference to the work of cleaning fish. He spoke about hard times and the humble sacrifices made to support a family "like a coin that won't get tossed."

As I matured, these things became real in my life, and I yearned for my grandfather's wisdom—not just nuggets, but those prolonged periods of time with him when he had time to expound. As I experienced the hurt and alienation that comes with growing up, along with the triumphs and successes, Grandfather was always there, willing to pour his understanding into me. His interest in my sporadic comings and goings was steadfast, always awaiting me like a friendly front porch. My attitude toward him became like the line in "Old Man" that bemoans, "I've been first and last/ Look at how the time goes past/ But I'm all alone at last/ Rolling home to you."[199] I grew and became more autonomous at Grandpa's side in the stream. I grew and learned to drink (and like) coffee while listening to him at breakfast. And I grew to better see the central motif of "Old Man": "Old man, take a look at my life/ I'm a lot like you/ I need someone to love me/ The whole day through."[200] For good reason, Harvest is my favorite album to listen to when embarking on a fly fishing trip.

My grandfather began slipping away as I began writing this chapter. And as I closed out this chapter, he ended up closing out eighty-six years of life. He'll leave a legacy that will not pass. Those times with my grandfather in the spring, bound by the equipment we accumulated and shared, cemented this legacy, teaching me much more than just how to catch fish, but also that I was a lot like him—much more than I realized as a disinterested teen. But as much as I cherished my grandfather, the one thing he could not do is "love me the whole day through."

We humans, as hard as we try, cannot love perfectly, with perfect "other-centeredness" at the core of our relationships. We fail to uphold our end of relationship parameters. When people fail us, we carry hurts and grudges, even the most minuscule, that cycle through the treadmills of our minds. Hard as we try, we all fail to love others perfectly through the duration of our relationships. Only the perfect Being, God Himself, with perfect, infinite love can love us the whole day through, in a way that we all desire. He doesn't need us yet, in lovingkindness, brings us into a covenant relationship with Him, loving us unconditionally while fulfilling the covenant terms on our behalf. It is He Who makes the first move to love us (1 Jn. 4:19). We simply love Him back in appreciation, and one way this is done is fishing for men with tools we are given.

Like any hobby, there are countless other tools and toys available to help you spend your money in the realm of fly fishing. We have simply covered the basics. My hope was to arm you with some practical information to equip yourself as you begin your journey into the spring. This chapter is just one more step to encourage you to get away from the dehumanizing bane and banalities of urban grind and into the revitalizing waters of the spring, where, through it, you come into a greater recognition of our Creator. Perhaps other readers—those once engrossed with a primal attraction to the spring—will be reacquainted with the love and enchantment that water once held. May this chapter be the springboard that launches them out into its depths once again.

Before you move on, consider this simple truth: while there is a plethora of equipment needed to catch fish and copious presentations to hook them, the fisher of men requires only one thing in his arsenal. He or she must have the Word of Truth and must know it inside-out and deliver it unabashed, without wavering or compromise, so that the Word of Truth will be the words of eternal life, as they were intended to be. We must know the truth so intimately as to write it on our hearts, so that it can be unsheathed on demand, to give life when we encounter those who are dying. Peter had an unrivaled acquaintance with the Incarnation of Truth, Jesus, and experienced the power of His words as life. After others turned away from Jesus' hard sayings, Peter remained, confessing, "Lord, to whom shall we go? You have the words of eternal life" (Jn. 6:68).

Peter's affirmation of the Lord's words as life reveal two things about the Word of Truth we handle. First, truth itself is given by the eternal and unchanging One, so His truth cannot change. It is as ludicrous as it is arrogant for a creature to proclaim a "personal truth" apart from, and in contradiction to, the truths governing the universe given by God, Who grants the creature tenancy. Second, the Word of Truth is both redemptive (the truth of how we are reconciled to our Lord and Creator, the Giver of life and truth) and preceptive (indicating how we pursue holiness that results in abundant life).

Often, truth is hard to swallow, as its foreign holiness always clashes against our natural desires. That should be expected and is the essence of the juxtaposition of the holy and the fallen. But our creaturely resistance to truth, no matter how visceral, doesn't make it any less true. The created cannot rise above its Creator, and, thus, all truth is God's truth—that can't be changed. The wise fisher of men understands how to properly handle the Word of Truth and need not rely upon gimmicks or huckster histrionics. Nor does sappy emotionalism or playing on sensitivities make a presentation truer. Relying on external stimulus draws the focus from truth to a man-centric salvation—a prescription bound to fail when the music's over. It becomes window dressing in lieu of heart transformation. Nothing can be added to ultimate truth to make it truer. Anything we add to truth actually dilutes truth, making it less true. Truth is not a quick-fix.

Truth doesn't need us, nor does it require the accumulation of equipment to be effective. It rests on itself. And that is where the metaphor between fly fishermen and fishers of men becomes divergent. There is one Truth, one Gospel, one Good News for people. Our job is to cast that Truth and leave the results to the Truth-giver (1 Cor. 3:6).

The wise fisher of men understands that while Truth is unchanging, the ways we present Truth must vary depending on the fish we seek to catch. The theology of the spring has much to teach us about the application of this Truth, as we will find in the next chapter.

Reflection Questions

1. In the final page of this chapter, I stated, "Truth doesn't need us." How is this so?

2. I made the point that just as fish see line attached to that what is baiting them, people, too, see through disingenuous pitches and schemes. Recall a time when you were given a disingenuous sales pitch, and recall the emotions you felt when it was over.

3. Some people, whether playing golf, riding motorcycles, or fly fishing, live out the adage, "Gotta look the part to play the part." How can this philosophy, when taken to extremes, work against your efforts of genuinely relating to people?

4. Three staging areas for catching fish were listed: fishing from a boat, fishing from a bank, and wading in and fishing from the stream. Which way best reflects your preferences in building relationships with people and why?

5. If we value being people of substance over being people of style, how does that impact the amount of equipment we accumulate and rely upon to catch fish in an evangelistic sense?

6. Why is humanity incapable of loving perfectly?

CHAPTER EIGHT

CATCHING FISH, PART TWO: STRATEGIES FOR EFFECTIVE FISHING

For though I am free from all, I have made myself a servant to all, that I might win more of them. To the Jews I became as a Jew, in order to win Jews. To those under the law I became as one under the law (though not being myself under the law) that I might win those under the law. To those outside the law I became as one outside the law (not being outside the law of God but under the law of Christ) that I might win those outside the law. To the weak I became weak, that I might win the weak. I have become all things to all people, that by all means I might save some. I do it all for the sake of the gospel, that I may share with them in its blessings.

–1 Corinthians 9:19-23

YOU HATE THAT GUY, BUT you love to be him. As paradoxical as it sounds, it perfectly fits the profile of a fly fisherman. You know the type—the person who breaks the curve in a tough economics class; the sub who comes in for a rec sports team and blows all the regulars away; or, in our case, the fly fisherman who approaches a stretch of water and immediately begins catching fish within eyesight of those laboring for hours without a single catch. You despise those guys. But, oh, how you love those days when you are "that guy." Don't get me wrong—a fly fisherman loves to lay claim to a stretch of water that can be fished unhindered from others. But when other fishermen are present, the pride in all of us swells a bit when we start plucking fish out of the water upon arriving on the scene. When juxtaposed to their futility, we see their heads turn as we land each fish. The humble ones tip their caps. Those interested in self-improvement glance over in an attempt to figure out what fly you are using. The proud won't look at all.

I openly admit I am not a good fly fisherman. I want to be. I love the prism of life seen through the sport and relish every chance I get to be in the water. I just wish I was better at it. The days of "skunking" those around me, like my morning with Joe in the prior chapter, are few and far between. But I'm ever too hopelessly in love and bullheaded with fly fishing to ever give it up. Ironically, my stubbornness often serves as one of my greatest weaknesses, as I am too slow to switch to another fly when not catching fish.

I yearn to be the deliverer, who arrives on the scene to open the flood gates of harvest, the one who unlocks the mystery of the right fly and right technique needed to compel the sub-surface audience to succumb. But more often than not, I am the spectator, watching someone else enter the water and start slaying fish. Humbling moments like these are easier to digest when I'm not on my home turf, and immaculate beauty surrounds me. Sarvis Creek, nestled in the lush pastures of the Yampa Valley near Steamboat Springs, Colorado, is one such venue that softens the agony of defeat. Jagged emerald uplifts, clothed in evergreens, line the horizon as the slashing, icy mountain stream flows unbridled through the bosom of the valley. The scene is a surreal one that begs to have been cut by a divine Rocky Mountain gemologist, unveiling verdant lucidity.

Given the backdrop, one can find solace when failing to land a fish. Granted, traveling a great distance to engage this fabled water puts more at stake for a fly fisherman who dreams of fishing such a stream. Even more is on the line if one leaves the beauty of a 4,000-acre ranch retreat to take on the challenge of Sarvis Creek. Add rising at dawn to prevent missing the insect hatch that might take place, and you've put a lot on the line. I might be just a tourist, but I still intended to fish like a resident. After all, that is why people travel to fish these archetypal waters.

Imagine arriving early at Sarvis Creek. The sight of fish rising and swirling brings your pent-up enthusiasm to a near eruption. Imagine the nervous excitement that pulsates through your hands—hands that begin to shake as you dress your rod, like the long-awaited championship game you've dreamt of reaching. Imagine the effort of preparing for this foreign environment, equipping yourself with sub-surface nymphing flies, like the "yellow sally" stone fly pattern or the "black beauty" midge that seems to command universal success. Likewise, imagine the effort of bringing a number of top water dry fly patterns you painstakingly researched, such as indigenous Trico mayfly dun patterns and Spotted Sedge caddis. Imagine being equipped with a vast arsenal, ready for anything on a trip you've planned for months. Imagine, then, the chagrin of a moderately experienced fly fisherman of Ozark spring creeks and rivers who spends several hours shut out in Rocky Mountain water.

Deflated, but not quite broken (see the virtue of stubbornness above), imagine you see an older fellow stroll down the hillside upstream from you. You continue to work the water, and fifteen minutes later, you peer around a bend, only to find him reeling in a nice, fourteen-inch rainbow. Next cast, he pulls in another. Your pride tries to convince you not to watch, but you've been humbled enough beyond caring; you made the trip out here for the love of the sport, not to feed your selfish pride. After seeing him catch a third fish, knowing you have nothing to lose, you meekly interrupt your counterpart, praise his success, and ask what he is using.

"Barrs Emerger tied on a number eighteen hook," he says, with an affable smile. He puts his line in his mouth and raises his hand, motioning for you to wait. "Here, try one," he says as he reaches into his vest and pulls an extra fly out of his box. "I'm just casting out at a forty-five-degree angle and swinging the fly up with an elevated rod tip. They are hitting about six inches to a foot below the surface."

You gladly thank this man, who obviously knows the environment in which he toils, and scurry along back downstream.

The congenial spirit of this gentleman is not unusual. By and large, the fly fishing brethren are an amiable community. I have found that more often than not, when I am humble enough to seek the counsel of those who are catching fish, they will let me share in their success, not just by giving advice, but also often by giving me the very fly that they are using. In this case, my new friend not only helped me understand my depth was off—as I was fishing nymphs too deep, instead of emergers just below the water surface—but he also offered me a taste of what the local population was feeding on. Then, equipped with this advice, imagine my unrestrained joy, finally catching a fish on this long-anticipated pilgrimage. I could now retreat back through the shaggy green vale with my head held high. The breathtaking scenery that morning had made my woes tolerable; but beholding that trout was a gorgeous moment, and the lessons learned to land him were priceless.

TEN STRATEGIES FOR CATCHING FISH

The preceding scene brings us back full circle to the age-old question: how do we catch fish? When we focus on that story from a Colorado stream more closely, a certain parable proceeds about impediments to success. But the story also reveals lessons from our failures that make us more effective in our fishing. We are admonished to become more genuinely in tune with the fish we are trying to reach. The story is a discourse that the theology of the spring teaches—not just about catching fish, but just as much about catching men.

If we have been truly born again, the call to be fishers of men is not optional. By grace alone, we have been regenerated with spiritual life when we naturally desired darkness (Jn. 3:19). We, then, are to offer Light to those in that darkness (Matt. 5:14), with the confidence of catching fish not based on our own abilities. Rather, we rely on the Light that is in us, which illuminates spiritual truth and gives understanding in those on whom we shine the Light (2 Cor. 4:6). It is no coincidence that two of Jesus' closest disciples, Peter and Andrew, were called to be fishers of men while they were mending their nets. They did not stop to first contemplate the call, considering that as experienced fishermen, their methods would be more fruitful. Rather, these expert fishermen immediately left their own nets in recognizing the Incarnation of Truth and obeying His call to a greater type of fishing.

The remainder of this chapter will delineate ten keys to enhance your effectiveness in catching fish. Each stratagem carries a dual metaphor as an aid in catching fish and in catching men. If we are failing to catch fish, both in the stream and evangelistically, these ten tips will help us examine ourselves and our methods. Applying these strategies allows us to be faithful to our call, leaving the results to the One Who called us.

1. Know your environment and its appetites.

I have stood in incredulity at times, watching fishermen charge into streams and homes with the mindset of taking prisoners captive, rather than setting captives free. I've known good men who certainly meant well, but I have seen their hard-charging approach create barriers between them and the fish they seek to catch—rather than tear the barriers down. The truth of their message did not penetrate these barriers because the fish were already wary. The "foe" flag immediately came up because no gentleness or concern was remotely demonstrated.

It goes like this. A guy knocks on the door. The person on the other side demonstrates rare courage in this day and age by opening it for a stranger. Then, the fisher of men, who fails to make eye contact, launches into a canned spiel, a fixed formula that does not allow adaption or alternate courses of presentation based on feedback from the recipient. I've seen this fisher of men look down his nose, point his finger, and tell his listener he is a rotten person, who is living wrongly and going to hell (which is, typically, not untrue). Then, without making an attempt to see what the person believes, this fisher "casts his line," which is an attempt to put the person in the doorway into a headlock, until he repeats some semantic formula, which, upon utterance, bestows some magical get-out-of-hell-free reward. As soon as this captive person is compelled to repeat this formulaic expression, the fisherman checks a box and moves on to the next house.

Often, in a cynical maneuver of self-preservation, the recipient of the message just goes along with the evangelist's demands in order to get rid of him. There is no receiving of Truth and, certainly, no change of heart or regeneration. And sadly, no true Gospel is presented. The person just wants the evangelist off his porch and will say anything to get rid of him.

Other times, the person on the other side of the door gets contentious. Who could blame him when admonition is imposed before interest? If someone shows up at your door, with no real interest in you beyond seeing you as a project, you get defensive. It's not much different from trout defending their territory from other fish moving into their habitat. While it may not be intentional, the presentation comes off as superficial and/or adversarial, with no regard for the recipient beyond being their project or enemy. It doesn't matter how true the message is; it is seldom received when delivered in an abrasive spirit. Few fish would be attracted to a hook dressed with an ugly piranha at the end of it, gnashing away at passersby.

A good fisherman takes time to examine the environment of the fish—their habitat, food supply, and over-arching worldview—to determine how to best present the truth. Before storming the waters, stop and survey your surroundings before wading in. Drown out the cacophony of men, so you can hear the symphony of the spring. A heart that fishes out of genuine love for the stream listens to that which he seeks. What do you hear? We find ourselves spiraling through a consumerist culture that has lost the art of listening and, yet, has neither clue nor interest in recovering it. David Dark described the bounty found in listening in his book, *Everyday Apocalypse,* noting:

We are, in fact, made for this kind of listening . . . When we're committed to a necessarily nondefensive, apocalyptic receptivity we will see new life bursting through in everything from a pig founding a community of outcasts by rescuing a dog who is trying to kill him in Babe: Pig in the City, to a lone couple ushering in a new day by overcoming fearful normalcy with new dance steps in *Strictly Ballroom*. Life won't be confined to our expectations, so we better get used to it.[201]

A shrewd fisherman examines where the sun is rising. Fish have no eyelids and are extremely light-sensitive. Thus, they feed and behave differently when the sun bursts through the stream. Likewise, listening will tell you just how saturated in darkness and receptive to light your human fish might be. Where are the fish? If they're feeding on top of the water, you correspondingly fish dry flies. If they are swirling beneath the surface, you fish emergers. If there is no surface activity, you start with streamers or nymphs.

Astute fishing is not only concerned with where the fish are feeding, but also on what they are feeding. Some fly fishermen will first scoop a sieve through the water and examine the insect life found in its waters before ever casting a line. We should do the same with people. Take your time and first determine what they are feeding on. The evidence of the resurrection might be a more enticing morsel to a Buddhist, who worships a "still dead" Gautama Buddha, than to an atheist, who might be more attentive to the cosmological argument for the existence of God. Both know God exists, in spite of how they suppress this knowledge. Draw that truth out. Perhaps you read closer and find a community plagued with a physiological oppression at hand, such as one laden with addictions. Offer them truth—the freedom from bondage found in Christ.

Do you see any boulders or overhanging foliage? Fish, like fallen humans, love darkness, where they are concealed, and their sin and vulnerabilities are shrouded. Are the fish being heavily pressured by outside forces? Jason Randall offers sound advice here, noting, "Pressured fish are anxious fish; they are suspicious of everything and much harder to catch."[202] So, in response, pressured fish will often flee to deeper pools, where they sense greater safety. In the same way, pressured people tend to withdraw and avoid strangers and new commitments. The fly fisherman and the fisher of men then offer their presentations in these sheltered "safe" confines where the fish are congregated. Do you see any fast-moving ripples? Ripples are the more heavily oxygenated part of the stream and, therefore, are flush with insects and are easy pickings for fish to feed. Do you see any people who are willing to examine the truth you cast before them?

The preceding were just a few tips in how to first know your environment *before* you begin fishing in order to better catch fish. Knowing your environment is integral to being a good fisherman. Wild trout and wild humans are naturally skittish. We must be delicate when approaching their environment. Taking time to know the waters in which we are fishing is to love our waters, our communities, our fish, and our neighbors. We're drawn to the stream to love its occupants and those we're graced to catch.

2. Go where the action abounds.

Who likes being left on the bench during the key moment of a big game? Who likes staying in the kitchen to cook when the entire party is playing games in the living room? Who really likes seeing others grow in joy and Christlikeness through small group studies, yet idly abstains from participating in these activities? And more specifically, who really prefers to remain fishing in a location with no fish, if they knew of a deep pool two hundred yards downstream loaded with fish?

Everyone prefers to be where the action is. In fly fishing, as in fishing for men, this truth plays out on both a macro and a micro level. On a macro level, we can become so beholden with particular spots on certain streams where there is no action, often for very insipid reasons, that we fail to get into the action. Perhaps some spots are more aesthetically pleasing. Others simply have better word-of-mouth popularity. Some spots are just the most easily accessible; and since we don't want to over-exert ourselves down a back road or by hiking a trail, we fish by the road.

Now, when I urge you to go where the action is, please understand we are talking about location (macro) and depth (micro). I am not talking about the lame act of crowding in on someone who is repeatedly catching fish. Nothing is more bush-league than the guy who rushes in to raid someone else's hot zone. There's plenty of stream around, so don't be that guy.

Chris Gates, fly fishing guide and owner of Ozark Sweetwater guiding service, has an oft-repeated maxim that bears repeating, "Famous water keeps people off the best water."[203] Gate's admonition is clear: fishermen are all too often self-impaired by preference or popularity instead of going to where the action is. Perhaps a famous location or spot highly visible from the main roadway once hosted much action. But as Yogi Berra once quipped, "Nobody ever goes there anymore— it's too crowded."[204] Such one-time hot spots fall victim to their own fame or location and, therefore, get over-fished to the point that little action remains.

A little research and effort into where action can be found never hurts. Fish will feed rhythmically and, often, contagiously, which causes an almost mob-like frenzy amongst densely populated fish during a hatch. This rhythmic feeding means fish become predictable and, thus, easier for fishermen to catch. For example, the full luminosity of the sun on the water helps to expedite late-stage incubation and hatching of insects in the spring. Therefore, if you know an access on a river has greater sky-to-surface exposure to the east at 7:45 a.m., and another access on the same river doesn't get any sunlight until 11 a.m., you should begin fishing at the access that is most likely to yield the first insect hatch, where the action will most likely be.

Ichthyologists have found trout so voracious during feeding frenzies that they gorge themselves to the point where bugs are backed up in their throats, yet they will *still* continue feeding.[205] Likewise, with people, it is prudent to present our truth during times of mass feeding receptivity. People are most comfortable conforming. This group-think proclivity is not always beneficial, but in this case, if several people in an area are receptive to entertaining the truth you present, many more passing by will typically be interested in finding out what all the fuss is about. That doesn't guarantee catching these fish, but it does mean more seed is sown through your presentation.

We are also prone to missing the action on a micro level. By that, I mean that fly fishing, like many other sports, is a game of inches. Trout will suspend themselves in the water column precisely at a level where food is floating along so as to conserve the most energy. Fish also feel safer in deep pools. The key, then, is to get your fly down to the precise level where the trout are stacked up and cast upstream, so that the fly inconspicuously drifts right into their mouths. The fisherman calibrates the depth of the fly with a strike indicator, which floats on the surface and, thus, regulates how deep the fly at the end of the line drifts. When you can see the fish, adjusting your indicator to their depth is fairly easy. But when you can't see the fish, depth adjustment to get your fly down to the action becomes a much more formidable challenge. You must, by trial and error, vary your depth until you come to the trout's level.

Another example of going where the action is on a micro level is when you spot fish tucked along the far bank underneath some low, overhanging brush or submerged logs. Reaching these fish requires a precise, but high-risk, cast, yet is often worth the reward because no one else makes any effort to reach them. But if we don't make our presentations where the action is, we shouldn't be surprised we're not catching fish. The fish won't come to us in an act of surrender.

Lamentably, and in a similar vein, the American Church has abdicated its mission to catch fish for the same reason: it has come to expect the fish to come to it. Rather than sending fishermen into its neighborhoods, it has sat idly by. Today's Church is not a fly fisherman, strolling through the streams of fish to proclaim Truth. It has become a lazy spectator, riding on a boat, hoping that the fish are Asian carp that will flop into its stern.

When fishing for men, we also need to be mindful to go where the action is on the macro level. How do we know where that is? We ask ourselves, "Where is God clearly moving?" This does not mean that we are to be frontrunner fans, eschewing the painstaking work of breaking ground amongst unreached people groups that often bears little fruit initially. Nor does it mean that we ignore clear calls by God to minister to the fish of particular streams, where a ravaged habitat produces small fish with discriminating appetites. It *does* mean that if we offer up ourselves, saying, "Here I am! Send me" (Isa. 6:8), the most efficient use of our time, talent, and treasure is to deploy our assets where the action is. Therefore, if I have $1,500 to spend on a short-term mission trip with a genuine desire to proclaim the Good News, I should go where God is moving and imparting life.

It's easy to get myopic over where you're fishing when it's "your turf" or "your mission." But shrewd fishermen understand that to be territorial is really an admission of naiveté. This immature attitude fails to realize grace; the waters we are allowed to fish are granted to us as fiduciary users. We are trustees of sorts, to cultivate and steward the parts of the created order that are yielding up life. When we shuck the yoke of territorialism, thinking less of ourselves, we become more agile to respond to places where the Creator of life is drawing people to Himself. The river, land, fish, and people are His, for His good pleasure; and by grace alone, He allows us to participate as His emissaries.

Going where the action is stirring, evangelistically, can also be demonstrated on a micro level. If you are an agent of Truth, proclaiming Truth wherever God has placed you, you will find receptivity to truth can vary as much by floors in an office building as it does levels in the water column. Before I surrendered to fulltime ministry, I worked in the banking industry, where I strove to be a missionary and fisher of men and women. The other employees and departments knew I was a staunch believer without my being militant about it. Without fail, it seemed like every time a colleague in another department came to me with questions about spiritual things, other people in that same department would soon open up with questions of their own. Soon, the entire department was swarming with questions and discussion about spiritual truth. Yet, the adjacent department would not have anyone with any spiritual temperature. Good fishermen put their hooks where the action is percolating.

One last tip is that you should always seek to be unassuming when the action begins. If the fish are becoming more and more aggressive in a certain pool, or you find the right depth, be as tranquil with your delivery as possible to avoid spooking fish. The same goes for when you are sharing the Gospel and fishing for men; let your audience get comfortable with you and gain your trust before you go to set the hook. I call this being a stream ambassador, and it grants you far greater access and keeps you in the game much longer if you remain placid and unassuming in your demeanor.

To be honest, I perfected this technique playing football, of all things. When most people think of football, they think of applying brute force and brawn to overcome their opponent. I tried to use a mixture of brains and brawn as the team ambassador, a strategy that my teammates initially mocked but came to see as ingenious when they saw the results. It basically worked like this: before each game we would get a scouting report of the other team. Specifically, I'd get the name, number, height, weight, and playing style of the player I'd be matched up against from the opposing team. At the risk of looking like a stalker, I would go out of my way in pregame warm-ups to greet my opponent by name in a show of friendly sportsmanship. My schmoozing would carry over when the game began, as I'd compliment him, pat him on the head, and call him by name. I found that by acting diplomatically and being unassuming, most guys would go easy on me. Then, just as they dropped their guard with me, when a play was called that came my way, I would steamroll this unsuspecting opponent. I'd help him up and act all nice, so as not to burn the bridge I had established, only to flatten him again the next chance I got.

Now, my point is not to be manipulative with people because we can't force what only regeneration can produce. However, we can set ourselves up to be more productive fishermen if we would act more unassuming when the action begins. And remember, unassuming does not mean laxity; you must be ready to strike quick when the opportunity arises.

3. Keep moving.

Fishing guide Chris Gates advises fly fishermen to use their feet. Bait fishermen typically like to set up a lawn chair and hope for the best, disconnected from the habitat they hope to pervade. However, adroit fly fishermen know of no such passivity, as they actively canvass their territory, discontent to sit back and miss an opportunity for presentation. Yes, there are some fly fishermen who will find a "honey hole" and remain there. But like wise fly fishermen working up and down the stream, the wise evangelist fishing for men and women uses his or her feet to deliver a new presentation to those who have not heard it. Undeterred by rejection, he or she should "shake off the dust" from their sandals, moving on to the next home (Matt. 10:14), just as the fisherman shakes off the dirt from his or her waders, moving on to the next riffle or pool.

I liken good fly fishing strategy to the classic game *Battleship*, which I love to play with my kids. Basically, they both employ the same strategy of finding a body of water and casting through different quadrants, hoping to get a hit. It is inefficient to spend too much time in one quadrant; as with *Battleship*, there are too many other areas to scour. With fly fishing, if a trout has not taken your presentation the previous forty-nine times, what makes anyone think the fish would strike on the fiftieth? Begin by casting upstream about ten feet away from your body, and work your way across, and then downstream. Continue to extend your cast outward about three or four feet as it floats downstream and presents your fly through different quadrants. Finish by covering the far bank, always sensitive to potential strikes that would cause you to remain in the area. After you have presented in each quadrant, move along to the next promising section of stream and repeat this method.

One of our biggest impediments to continue moving is that we get lazy, and, if you are like me, we get stubborn. We are not only depriving ourselves of the beauty that lies around the bend when we get lazy, but we deprive others of Truth. We've already talked about the laziness many churches demonstrate by not getting out into the heart of their neighborhoods and fishing for people. Yes, we will be rejected going door-to-door, but a genuine love for people remains unhindered by such rejection because we don't fish for our own self-worth. If we don't move on, we will miss those same encounters with fish, those elusive wild trout that can be relished only by those who step deep into the less-traveled throes of the stream.

I often cease moving because I get stubborn. I clench my teeth, vowing to show the fish who has more resolve. It really becomes a laughable portrait of insanity—ensconced in "my spot," refusing to budge, and, therefore, preferring my own pride to catching fish. It again comes back to submission and casting off the self-sufficiency we so stubbornly cling to. The fish belong to God, so when I've been faithful to present to them with no results, rather than force the results by my own doing, I need to move on to other fish that might be more inclined to bite.

Undoubtedly, the best example we have as fishermen to keep moving is that of Jesus, the greatest Teacher Who ever lived. He was known as a "peripatetic" Teacher, which means He walked around as He taught. He wasn't confined to any one location, so His students followed Him wherever He went.

In Jesus' day, students who desired a distinguished rabbi, or teacher, searched out their desired teacher and hoped to be accepted as a pupil. There were varying levels of prestige for rabbis, so imagine the devotion students would display if they beat the competition and were granted the honor to learn under an elite rabbi. The students would follow the rabbi around wherever he went, hoping to glean even the most trivial nuggets of knowledge that fell from his lips.

Jesus, being the ultimate Mover, shook things up by turning the teacher/student dynamic on its head. Jesus walked around and humbled Himself in an inconceivable manner in His culture by approaching people to be His students. Not only did Jesus make the move by going to those He chose as His disciples, but He and His disciples' entire ministry was devoted to itinerant teaching and proclamation of the Gospel Truth, being fishers of men. Jesus epitomized, as the great Teacher and great Fisher of men, to keep moving as we present Truth.

4. Make a genuine presentation.

People will accept mistakes, but they won't accept a fraud. I've found this to be generally true—the exception being social media, where it is just assumed that people are never as interesting, important, or pious as they portray. Deep down, humans are wired to value substance over style. We don't want superficial, insincere exchanges that make us feel like a target for someone else's success. Just as we like the tranquil ambiance of the spring, we want the security of putting our guard down and unmasking. We want a listener who is not taken aback by our missteps. At our core, we all long for those genuine, unmasked, one-on-one connections, where we can be vulnerable and challenged, yet always feel loved through a bond that is unconditional and not disposable.

Trout are the same way: they will take an imperfect presentation, but rarely will they swallow a cheap imitation. They get pressured so heavily by imitations that they become all the more cynical and selective. People and trout can spot a disingenuous approach from a mile away. They want the real and genuine, not a phony. So here are some tips to ensure your approach is a genuine one that passes the careful scrutiny of trout and men.

First, we should be careful to avoid using "churchy" vocabulary that can sound foreign and unnatural. I often call this using "Christian-ese," as it can come off as a sort of colloquial dialect. Terms like "washed in the blood," "be intentional," "lift you up," or even "accepting Christ"**** can confuse the person we are attempting to reach. Worse, when we imply they should know what these terms mean, many lose interest, feeling too embarrassed to seek explanation to what we gloss over as basic lingo. They get quickly disenfranchised, concluding they must already know the answers to follow Christ. Christian parlance can become a stumbling block by failing to genuinely deliver truth in a way that is natural for an unchurched audience to understand.

Naturally, given their adept ability to detect sound, we want to avoid talking too much of any jargon while fishing for trout. We want to be inconspicuous without causing alarm in the water. Likewise, we are genuinely fishing for trout and men when we avoid unnatural dress, which makes us stick out like we are salesmen. I always wear earth-tone colors when fly fishing to blend in with the environment and thus increase my odds of gaining an audience with the fish. This tactic should also be employed when fishing for men because, as people desiring dialogue, we should not wear anything that would impair our approachability by distracting people.

**** As a personal aside, I don't use the term "accept Christ." I don't say this to sound snide, because I know and love good people who use this phrase with the best of intentions. But if we believe the Bible, that Jesus "chose us in him before the foundation of the world" (Eph. 1:4) and that "we love because he first loved us" (1 Jn. 4:19), then actually He accepted us and not vice versa. It can come off as condescending to issue the imperative "accept Jesus," as if we hold bargaining leverage over the King of the universe, Who is feebly paralyzed, waiting for our acceptance. We see a consistent reaction of every person in the Bible after an unmitigated encounter with the Holy, and their response is anything but that of patronizing acceptance. So, when fishing, perhaps we should be careful to avoid potential confusion by explaining we receive Christ as the *effect* of Him accepting us (2 Thess. 2:13; 2 Tim. 1:9). Yes, we "accept" His offer and respond in faith, but only *after* we receive Him, via the Holy Spirit's indwelling. I understand what well-intentioned saints mean when using the term; but if we are bearing witness to Truth, let's do so accurately.

One time, I went out with a certain well-known ministry group to distribute Bibles at a local high school. I arrived at the site dressed nicely in khaki pants and a polo shirt, much like the students' teachers would be wearing. I don't say this to be insolent, but all of the other men showed up in stuffy suits and ties, some suits looking like they had to be forty years old. Many of the kids looked at these guys as if they had three heads, and little interaction took place. After engaging some students and teachers in conversation—evidently, I was somewhat approachable—one of the group's leaders walked up and not-so-quietly told me I was "out of uniform" and not to show up at the next event dressed the way I was.

Look, I am not saying we should not look sharp. I know too many pastors who take the other extreme because it's seemingly cool to look edgy, and as a result, step into the pulpits looking like they just crawled out of a dumpster. The message can be just as easily lost if we appear slovenly in handling the Word of Truth, as one trying to "look cool." Far be it that we should become the focus, rather than the message. We are handling a solemn message of life and death, a reflection of the very character of the Ruler of the universe revealed to us. If we truly understand that, we should tremble at the thought. And out of love for people, those fish we seek, it should be delivered circumspectly. We should exude a reverence commensurate with the paramount Truth we cast, buoyed by a genuine and winsome delivery.

When we tie flies, the truth presented to the fish of the spring, we want it to be as genuine as if we were Jesus Himself, sculpting an insect out of organic material before breathing life into it. We don't take shortcuts in our wraps that make the wings look artificial. We don't skip the step of palmering a thorax. We meticulously follow each step to replicate a fly as closely as possible to its real-life insect muse. It is no surprise to me that some of the best material for tying flies is organic material. Take, for example, deer and elk hair, which, being internally hollow, are buoyant. Many dry flies mimicking caddis and mayflies are tied with elk and deer hair to make the wings. Do you see why? This buoyant, organic material is not only natural in appearance, but also practical in preventing the fly from sinking, thus giving it a more genuine presentation. It is not far-fetched to imagine the deer, whose hair was used to tie a fly that catches a wild brown trout, once drank life from the stream holding that very trout.

It is popular with some fly-tiers to tie in "hot spots"—that is, flashes of vibrant color added to catch a fish's attention, making a fly stand apart from others. A hot spot can be effective, but only if you don't get so cute with it that the hot spot distracts from the fly itself. Whether it's cheap flies or excess drag, fish spot imposters. The same goes in how genuinely we profess truth to men, walking that fine line of being approachable, but not getting too cute and compromising the essence of the message. The point is, whether it be a fly tied to imitate an insect or a presentation of Truth to imitate Jesus, both should be as genuine as possible.

In John chapter four, Jesus Himself, gives us a perfect example of how to be genuine, winsome, and uncompromising in fishing for men. He meets a woman at a well, a woman of ill-repute who is an outcast of society. Jesus goes out of His way to strike up a conversation with her, to show interest in her. After affirming this woman's humanity by demonstrating a genuine concern for her, He has accumulated the relational "capital" to speak into her life. He not only confronts her about blatant sexual sin, but He offers her a solution: springs of living water "welling up to eternal life" (Jn. 4:14). The woman didn't rise in a huff and lambast Jesus for judging her. She left in joy, telling others about Him. This amazing portrait shows how we should love our neighbors, even our enemies like this woman, who, as a Samaritan, would have been loathsome to the Jews. Jesus didn't compromise His presentation of Truth, but He also didn't share it without love. He spoke the Truth in love of her greatest need: spiritual, not physical, thirst. Jesus was genuine in His concern for both her human and spiritual needs and conveyed what we lack so much today in sharing Truth—that it's not what you say, but how you say it.

Two other actions of Jesus in this account bear mentioning. First, notice how He deployed questions to show interest in leading the conversation. Questions are one of the most powerful means we have to both demonstrate legitimate concern for those we meet, but they also serve to provide us with information that we can use to best address any needs in that person's life. I am grateful for Greg Koukl's book *Tactics*, which is a must-read book on how to share truth via the art of asking questions. Koukl advises that questions are the best way to advance a conversation in an inoffensive way, and therefore, "never make a statement, at least at first, when a question will do the job."[206] Hugh Hewitt encourages people to ask at least six questions in every conversation.[207] This is great advice to show genuine interest. Genuine people ask questions.

The second thing Jesus did could best be articulated by what He didn't do. He didn't come out guns blazing, immediately imposing His agenda. He didn't lasso and round the Samaritan woman up in order to meet His daily catch quota. He listened to her; and as the Master of conversation, organically guided the discussion to spiritual matters. I've found that if you care enough about the person and have some semblance of conversation skills, God will present an opportunity for spiritual discussion, often from the most unlikely of topics. Just this past spring, I've had varying topics—such as the rock band, The Smashing Pumpkins; tacos from the fast food chain, Jack in the Box; and children's baseball—all lead into spiritual discussions. Because these things mattered to the people with whom I was speaking, and as I was content to listen, God opened up a place in each conversation for a spiritual angle to naturally develop.

I cringe when hearing accounts of well-intentioned fishers of men taking a disingenuous approach that treats people like projects. I was contacted once by a lady who had recently been at a local hospital because her father was having surgery to remove a cancerous mass. After the surgery, the doctor remorsefully came into the waiting area to let her know the somber news that the situation was much worse than they had thought, that they could not get all the cancer, and that it was likely terminal. Devastated, the woman got on her phone to call family members with the bleak news. While on the phone, a man came out of nowhere and began intently tapping her on the shoulder. Flustered and interrupted, she put her phone down for a second to see what the man needed so urgently.

"Hey, do you go to church anywhere? If not, I want to invite you to my church . . . "

Good intentions, most certainly. But tactful and genuine it was not. We should be careful not to be rushed when we witness, making sure our Gospel presentation is sensitive and complete. Proverbs 19:2 warns, " . . . Whoever makes haste with his feet misses his way."

The lady knew that I worked at the church the man had invited her to. She wasn't mad but called to tell me about it so that perhaps something could be said to spare someone else from being turned off by the man's bad timing. While his heart might have been in the right place, a better response would have been to wait until she got off the phone, then express genuine concern after seeing her tears, and gently ask if he could pray for her family. Who knows where the conversation could have gone from there?

The old adage that "people don't care what you know until they know that you care" could not be truer. I've seen this truth manifest itself in local missions, as well as internationally in places like Senegal and Mexico. There were times on these missions that a sterile feel pervaded the air. We'd spent a couple of days, and I didn't feel like much of a connection had been made with the natives. Through our translators, they would just give a perfunctory nod out of courtesy to our presentations. Finally, I decided I truly wanted to genuinely know these people. I abandoned the translator and would simply start pointing to objects to ask how to say the name in their native language. I'd point at a chicken and learn to say, "seesay." I learned that a female was "musso." Dogs, cattle, friend, etc. You name it, I tried to learn it. And in doing so, in taking interest in these people, the spark was struck for a genuine relationship to kindle. Their eyes lit up. We asked about family. We began laughing at mispronunciations. A connection was struck to such a degree that these very prim, proper men were hugging me when I left, all because I put my guard down and took genuine concern in them. Only after knowing I cared about them, did they care to hear the truth I came to share.

The above anecdote leads me to the final point about genuine presentation—a presentation does not have to be perfect to be effective. God can use an imperfect presentation. In fact, He must use an imperfect presentation if any fish are to be caught. My delivery in the bush country of Senegal was far from perfect—from its source being my own sinful heart to the language barriers it passed through. However, I trusted God to use that imperfect presentation to His glory. I've left conversations feeling like a complete moron to subsequently hear, to my shock, that God used some portion of the exchange to stir in the hearer's life.

The reality is that in order for people to be converted by faith, they must first hear or see the Word of Truth, which necessarily comes by immediate means delivered by an imperfect being (Rom. 10:17). The power in the efficacy of this presentation, therefore, points to the Sovereign Power behind the imperfect presenter. People, like fish, will never accept what they don't desire. It is as Jonathan Edwards taught— free moral agents *must* always choose according to their greatest desire at the time of choice. They can do no other. Think about that, and it will make your head spin. It will also likely make you think of times when you choose to exercise instead of eating cookies, but the reality is that your desire to work out won out over your desire for the cookies, even though you *really* wanted to eat them. So, our presentations must be authentic, given how easily fish and people see through a fraud. But without a change in desire—a change in appetite—a brook trout in the Nesowadnehunk stream in Maine will never bite on a hot dog, just like an unregenerate person, who loves darkness, will not desire the light of Christ. God uses our external genuineness to foster the genuine *internal* change of heart He produces.

Likewise, when fishing for trout, we too often give up on a cast because our presentation didn't hit the intended location. Plenty of times, I have caught fish four feet out in front of me, most unexpectedly, while retrieving my fly. Or, in combating our constant nemesis in fly fishing—drag, which causes the fly to drift unnaturally—we mend our lines and inadvertently turn the fly over, making an unnatural fly appear even less genuine. After giving up on a cast and looking away at such instances, I've been shocked to glance back and find my strike indicator submerged and taking off. The lesson is clear: don't be discouraged by mistakes in your presentation. You never know how God will use the Truth you are presenting.

5. A go-to is important.

Every fisherman needs a go-to fly, like every fisher of men needs a go-to line. A go-to is that ace in the hole, the slugger off the bench that is the great equalizer when the chips are down. A go-to fly is the one you unveil when nothing else is working. There is no question in your mind if the go-to will catch fish. The questions are when and how many?

My dad used to always tell me, "Presentation is king, but confidence compensates." By that, he meant I could overcome errors in my presentation through the enhanced manipulation in delivering my fly, innately imbued by my confidence. When you *know* you will catch fish, you feel freer and less restrictive in how you fish a particular fly. Loosened in your approach, much of the foreign, human element that adulterates the fly's interaction with the fish is removed.

My go-to lure is called a "John Deere Green" mini-jig. It is a simple, olive, chenille body cast on a one-sixty-fourth-ounce jig head, which is painted green with a big yellow eye. My father can't stand it and is quick to note that he has never caught a fish on it. He also points out that the only reason I catch fish on it is because I am [unexplainably] confident in it.

Case in point: my father and I were fishing at Maramec Spring, near St. James, Missouri, when we were about to bump into our drop-dead departure time. I don't always keep fish, but I hoped to catch and keep my limit of four on this occasion in order to provide for a fish fry we were planning that weekend. Fishing had been slow for the last hour, so with five minutes remaining to catch two fish, I whipped out my John Deere. As I tied it on, my dad just stood there, expressionless, shaking his head. Sure enough, on my second cast, BAM! I landed a beautiful, thirteen-inch rainbow. Then, on the very next cast, in the very same quadrant, BAM! I caught another.

"Well, there's my limit with two minutes to spare," I said, while stringing my last fish.

"Unbelievable," my dad wryly muttered, as he turned and walked to the bank.

Fly fishing is circumstantial business, where success varies on conditions, so don't ever underestimate the value in having two or three go-tos. I would add that midges are always a sound go-to, as they have universal appeal, being found in most streams and drifting at all hours of the day, at all times of the year. Therefore, my second go-to is the brown harvester midge, given its universal versatility. For those times when conditions on top of the water get hot, it is always wise to also have a dry fly go-to as well, which, for me, is a size number twenty renegade.

Correspondingly, you should also always have a go-to when fishing for men. People are more complex and less predictable than trout. You never know what kind of worldview, background, and reception you are going to get. I've called on people who visited our church to be warmly greeted by some and vigorously challenged by others. Likewise, when I go door to door, some people invite me in for a three-hour spiritual discussion, and other people debate me, seeking to humiliate me. It is easy in those hostile situations to get flustered. That is where a go-to line comes in handy.

Your go-to line not only gets you back on track conversationally, but it should be something akin to your fly fishing go-to that gives you a boost of confidence to amiably stand in the fire as you deliver Truth. I don't generally recommend scripted presentations when sharing the Gospel—the Good News of the Person and work of Christ. But when you get flustered, having a go-to on standby is an effective tool to get you back into the flow. The effectiveness of your go-to is rooted in your confidence and familiarity in its presentation, which comes with practice.

My go-to line combines two texts of biblical truth. After talking about the holiness of God, I share Romans 6:23, which reads, "For the wages of sin is death, but the free gift of God is eternal life in Christ Jesus our Lord." In particular, I try to connect the dots between a holy and perfect God, Who cannot tolerate imperfection, and flawed humans, who need perfect righteousness. One imperfection is enough to separate us from God for eternity. Whether people have transgressed His law one time or one million times, the same fate awaits both. I also try to bring in a common denominator about wages—about how they are things we earn and are owed and how we are all owed death for rebelling against the perfect Being. And then I drive home the doctrine of the sinfulness of humanity by pointing to Romans 3:10-11, which states, "None is righteous, no, not one; no one understands; no one seeks for God." I ask the person questions and dialogue about the universality of sin, inquiring if anyone ever had to teach them to lie, covet, or slander. As I then empathize with our shared, hopeless, human condition, I talk about the remedy a holy God provided without compromising His holiness, the great exchange made by the substitutionary atonement of Christ to redeem His people. And, eventually, I find myself back on track, more often than not, with an attuned listener, thanks to my Romans 6:23 and 3:10-11 go-tos.

6. Examine your fly.

No, this subtitle is not intended as a double entendre, though it could be. Comfort can be more dangerous than apathy. This is particularly true when comfort leads to false assurance. The apostle Paul appealed to the church at Corinth in the first century not to rest on their laurels or to get comfortable in their spiritual development. Writing from the imperative mood, Paul implored his readers to "examine yourselves, to see whether you are in the faith. Test yourselves . . . " (2 Cor. 13:5). Centuries later, John Calvin commented on this passage, noting, "It is with good reason that they are called to look into themselves, that they may discover there what they despise as a thing unknown."[208] Calvin knew all too well the propensity of the human heart to deceive itself. The cloak of comfort can gradually lull us to sleep, unaware of how lifeless we've become.

Holding a fly rod in a stream doesn't make us a fisherman any more than holding a Bible in a church makes us a Christian. Jesus, with cutting brevity said, "You will recognize them by their fruits" (Matt. 7:16). We should always honestly and introspectively look at ourselves to see that we are bearing the fruit, the natural outward expressions of a fly fisherman or fisher of men. By extension, we should examine our fruit to see that it is healthy or sterile.

Undoubtedly, the area of fly fishing most often in need of examination is to examine our fly. This is important, due to material in the stream that can contaminate the appearance of the fly, such as moss. You are dead in the water when you have moss on your fly. Fish won't touch a fly with moss. Why? Go back to genuine presentation—you are imitating a natural insect in the water. Insects don't naturally adorn themselves with a sleeve of moss. Thus, fish know there is an imposter at hand when they see moss on your fly.

The problem is, if you get too lazy to bring your line in to check for moss, you can waste ten or twenty casts by presenting a fly that doesn't have a chance to be received. I realize, as an ardent fisherman who wants to make the most of his time in the water, you don't want to continually break up the action. But consider that trout can be crueler than people in their rejection. They will break your heart in how they go about shooting toward your fly like a missile, only to pull up at the last moment. If you see this, it should be a primary red flag to recall the fly and check for moss.

Moss is not the only thing that should cause you to check your hooks. To my embarrassment, I've had times fishing small egg patterns when I've gone over five minutes without a strike. I pulled the fly in to discover all I had was an empty hook—the fish had cleaned me out entirely by stripping the fly material from the hook shank. Equally regrettable, I've pulled in my fly after getting a number of strikes but being unable to set the hook. Upon review, I found the bend of my hook completely broken off. It's a cruel game those trout play.

Finally, and in line with our earlier theme to keep moving, if after checking your fly during spells of inactivity, you find nothing wrong with your fly, you need to be willing to change to a different fly. We often get so beholden to a certain fly that our allegiance to tradition is stronger than our mission to catch fish. Swisher and Richards advise in their classic manual *Fly Fishing Strategy*, "One cardinal rule—don't waste a lot of time on the wrong pattern, especially in simple rises where there aren't too many insects on the water . . . So if after two or three minutes you are not getting any action, switch flies."[209]

When fishing for men, we should be equally humble to examine our presentation and make a change if it is not catching fish. Fishing for men is a life or death proposition, and while we don't dictate the results, eternity hangs in the balance after the seed of Truth is proclaimed. Therefore, in a heart that loves people, there is no place for valuing a particular style of presentation over the recipient's eternal destination.

This does not mean we ever dilute the integrity of the message. It is as Alvin Reid said, "We must be uncompromisingly conservative in our theology and unashamedly progressive in our methodology."[210] Astute discernment should be applied when talking with people, specifically to perceive how they are responding to the presentation of the Good News of Jesus Christ. If a certain approach is consistently garnering the same stale, unfruitful reaction, you should check your hook and make changes where needed.

For example, in speaking with baby boomers, you might find many who have been "de-churched," meaning they previously attended church long ago but fell away. Perhaps they've been hurt by a church in the past. With this in mind, you might consider altering your approach toward a greater emphasis on repentance or the primacy of the local church. Or you could point out that attending a church or being a "good" person does not reconcile anyone to a holy God.

Conversely, one method of evangelism I prefer, called "The Way of the Master," developed by Ray Comfort, can appear irrelevant to millennials and younger generations because it presupposes the existence of God. Thus, when questioned about transgressions against the Creator of the universe, some people in this generation are unmoved because they deny the core premise that a Lawgiver even exists, much less absolute laws He promulgates. When I spot this, instead of jettisoning the approach altogether, I will tweak it by removing the moss and starting with a reasoned argument about why an eternal Being must exist.

Jesus Himself was not bound to one specific style of evangelism. With some, like the Samaritan woman at the well, He was gentle and inquisitive (Jn. 4:7-30); but He firmly tested others, like the Syrophoenician woman, in order to manifest their faith (Mk. 7:24-30). With some, like the rich young ruler, He used object lessons about the law to convict (Matt. 19:16-30); and with others, like the fastidious religious rulers of His day, He was direct and confrontational (Matt. 22:36-40). And with others, like Herod and Pilate, He kept completely silent (Lk. 23:9; Jn. 19:9-10). These are just some of many approaches used by the greatest Fisher of men. We would be wise to follow His example and examine our lure, clean up any impurities in it, sharpen our hooks, and be willing to change to a different approach if necessary.

7. Where's the hook?

You can tell a lot about fish by where the fly is lodged in their mouths. More specifically, the hook location gives some visual indication as to how your fly is being received below the surface beyond your vantage point. Therefore, it is wise to determine where the hook is at in the first couple of fish that you catch, which can help you proactively manage your strategy for greater success.

Consider the trend of trout taking a fly "deep." This term means that when you land a fish, the fly is lodged deep down in the caverns of its mouth. This often requires using hemostats to "surgically" extract the fly from the fish in a safe manner that inflicts no long-term harm. When the hook is being taken deep, it often suggests that fish are hungry and aggressive. They are striking hard and sucking the fly in with less discrimination. If this is the case, you can take a little more time in setting the hook, rather than the oft-frantic reaction of setting the hook as quickly as possible when a strike is detected. When hooks are taken deep, it can be a harbinger of a good day. So, stay in the water, and strike while the iron is hot.

Hook location can also reveal as much about flaws in your mechanics as it does the appetite of the fish. Setting the hook should always be done under control, with a steady upward lifting of the fly rod. If you land trout with flies consistently hooked in the side of their jaw, it might be an indication that you are unknowingly setting the hook by pulling the rod to the right or to the left. Another common mistake is made in conjunction with doing something right. While correctly pointing the rod tip at the strike indicator, following the flow of the stream, some have a tendency to set the hook by jerking the rod in the direction of the stream flow. However, setting the hook in the direction of the stream flow simply obeys the laws of physics and works against the fisherman, as it pulls the fly away from the fish's mouth.

You know you are on your game when you are hooking fish on dry flies at the front of their mouths, right in the nose. Not only does this indicate you are setting the hook by bringing the fly straight up, which ensures it isn't being pulled away from the fish to the left or to the right, but it points to the fish consuming your fly as naturally as they consume real flies with a quick, head-on sucking down of the bug. Such response indicates your presentation is dead on in its imitation.

One other tip that aids in setting your hook is the ability to recognize natural movement and, therefore, spot unnatural movement. This is important on those days when the fish are not hitting the flies aggressively, as they will ever so discreetly tap at the fly as a kind of reconnaissance mission before they strike in full. When the fish are making such gingerly contact with your fly, there is very little reaction to your strike indicator; perhaps only the slightest reverberation can be seen as it floats through the current. As a result, it is very difficult to know if there is a strike at all, let alone when to set the hook. Therefore, experienced fly fishermen learn to be in such deep concert with a strike indicator that they perceive the faintest stoppage, pause, or minute shift in its flow. After studying water currents to know the natural drift of the indicator, they are quick to react when they spot unnatural movement, thus ensuring the hook can be set.

When we are fishers of men, we should also examine where we are hooking people. The reasons are twofold. First, if people are hungry for the Gospel, taking the hook deep and swallowing it in force, we need to keep casting it out. We also need to make sure we are hooking them to the true Gospel and not winning them to programs and quick fixes or playing on emotions. If we are hooking people with the guise of liberty in Christ, only to release them into the bondage of programs and works, then we are not catching fish. We are trapping lackeys, which will inevitably lead to a Gospel-less culture that smothers people, ultimately leading to their frustration and burnout. Sadly, grace is choked by works.

Equally lamentable is the loss of fish we had hooked. One of the most frustrating things is when a trout spits the hook just as you are about to land it. Perhaps it is due to a dull hook that needs to be sharpened. A sharpened hook easily penetrates and cinches deep into the fish's oral cavity, where it can't escape. On the other hand, a dull hook loosely cinched in the fish's mouth might often be a symptom of a dull, lazy presentation. Such a hook fails to retain people as well. If we are relying on the sufficiency of Truth, which is sharper than a two-edged sword or any fishing hook, then we can rest in greater confidence that those men or women hooked by it will land in the doors of our churches (Heb. 4:12, Isa. 55:11). Why? Because it wasn't us that "caught them" in the first place, but rather, the acuity of the Truth that was presented which convicted them. Conversely, if we find, during our fishing for men, that we are hooking but never landing people, we should examine our hooks to see if our presentations have strayed from the sharp Word of Truth that pierces the conscience toward a dull hook that tickles the ears.

Sometimes in evangelism, we set the hook too early, trying to force a decision that is too much too soon for a skittish person, effectively pulling the Truth away from the person before it has time to anchor and flourish. The fisher of men needs to be careful to let the seed first sprout and let God be God before prematurely rushing anything. Just as important, the fisher of men needs to be perceptive to spot unnatural movement in people, such as questions or responses that are not normal to natural humanity and might be a sign of a regenerated heart that God is calling to Himself—such as deep-felt remorse over one's sin, a desire to know God more intimately, or the first steps of repentance, seen in a submission that finally renounces self-reliance and turns from bondage to sin. So, whether we are fishers of trout or fishers of men, we are wise to look at where we are hooking fish before we begin reveling in the grace revealed with the catch.

8. Look beneath you.

Sometimes, while fly fishing, wading into the water stirs up the habitat. This can stimulate fish, who intuitively troll the area as nymphs, eggs, scuds, and other food sources once tucked in the bottom, are now loosed and flow into the open water. It isn't uncommon after fishing in state or federal parks about fifteen minutes to look down and discover "tame" trout stealthy suspended right at your feet. Overcoming their fear, these fish swoop in unnoticed, anticipating your departure, so they can feed on what you might stir up.

The same concept can often be seen in our churches after concerted revival efforts. In effect, the Lord stirs people with the message, causing them to reconsider some things that have been neglected. Or, as people pass through different epochs of life, seeing struggle and decay more closely, they might be more open to the bigger questions of the cause and ultimate destination of humanity. Situations like these are ideal times for members of the church who fellowship in small groups to be on the lookout, "sight fishing" for those who have been shaken free from strongholds or false securities. The objective, then, is to invite them into your small group community before they begin to drift away beyond reach.

Like fishing in the stream, we sometimes get so focused on what is "out there" that we neglect to look down and see whom God has brought to us. For whatever reason, these outliers have shucked the angst that held them back, mustering the courage to turn away from their inhibitions to approach you with spiritual hunger. These fish are ripe for truth, especially after a life-changing or major revival-oriented event, and we should be ever so sensitive to their presence, not neglecting to cast a presentation before them.

When I'm fly fishing, I always try to survey downstream of my feet before leaving a location to see if any fish have congregated around me. If I have an audience, I will always make a presentation to them. Please note, I'm not advocating the controversial "San Juan Shuffle," where fishermen shuffle their feet along the streambed, chumming fish with the food they stir up. I'm simply suggesting we assess our environs for fish that have naturally let their guards down to settle in our midst. Tie on a little scud, pupae, or any kind of natural food that gets jettisoned from the gravel you displace, and you'd be surprised at how easy this close-range catch can be. It may sound strange, but I sometimes feel a much greater reward in catching those fish I hunt and catch by sight than those I blindly present my fly to out in the deep. There has been a visual connection made that makes a potential meeting more meaningful.

I carry the same general philosophy in my ministry. My wife and I don't feel called to fish out in the deep for those who might come along. Rather, I feel compelled to look around for those standing out on the periphery and reach out to them. Instead of the foreign mission or the safe confines of fellowship amongst friends, I want to offer community to those who don't have community—a community where one can grow and find identity in the ultimate Truth of Jesus. Sadly, I've seen the all-too-predictable end result play out concerning those standing on the perimeter: if those seeking truth and community do not forge a meaningful relationship in the church within four to five weeks, they will not return.

So, look beneath you. Sometimes the fish God has brought to you, ripe for the catch, are right beneath your feet. Sometimes, they are your closest family and friends, who are often the hardest to reach, with the most awkward conversations. But God may provide an opportunity for you through tragic events, such as the death of a loved one, which causes many people to begin considering their own mortality and asking questions. Look around you, and you may find God providentially working out situations that use you to draw fish to Himself.

9. Maintain perfect tension.

You've hooked into a fish you've been working for some time. Now what? The fisherman's quest doesn't end upon hooking the fish. There is a very fine balancing act that must occur to consummate the catch and land the fish in your net. The perfect equilibrium you strive to maintain is perfect tension.

Tension is an essential product of physics that makes it possible to complete the catch. As we noted in the previous chapter, you should always purchase a reel that enables you to readily adjust the drag as needed. The more the fish fights, jumps, or runs, the more opportunity it has to break free, especially if your drag (which regulates tension) is not properly set. Thus, as your see-saw battle to land the catch of a lifetime rages on, any adjustment to drag morphs into an intense chess move. Each calibration grows more harrowing because too much or too little drag can leave you holding an empty net and telling dubious stories of yet another one that got away.

Here lies the importance of line tension: if you set your drag too high, applying too much tension restricts line movement and elasticity, so the line will break if the trout exerts enough force. If, on the other hand, your tension is too low, the fish can work your fly loose and spit it out. Or with slack line resulting from lack of tension, the fish makes a run, creating a whip effect with tensile stress that snaps your tippet. Thus, during the ebb and flow of wrangling a fish, you are perpetually assessing whether or not you have sufficient tension in order to land the fish. For example, if you are fishing with two-pound test and hook a five-pound trout, you've got to be extremely careful with your tension to compensate for the fish-line strength disparity.

Tension is also important in fishing for men. By tension in personal evangelism, I mean the personal relationships and counsel that come once the hook of the Gospel of Truth is set. The natural person will not automatically surrender and submit. Our old, fallen nature, which resides in us until the day we die, will be at war with this new righteousness that has gripped and renewed us (Gal. 5:17; Rom. 7:21-23). As we are transformed inside out, like fruit budding from a tree, it takes time for old habits to die. But for those hooked who are truly converted, our guarantee that we will be brought to completion is the depositing of the Spirit of Truth within us (2 Cor. 1:22), like an earnest, money-down payment in a real estate transaction. While not overnight, our tastes and affections gradually change because the Holy Spirit gives us new spiritual life and, with that, the outworking of a new will congruent with those things in which He takes pleasure (Phil. 2:13). My longtime pastor and mentor, Dr. Monte Shinkle, used to say, "If you are truly saved, you don't have to stress over whether or not to leave bad habits; those bad habits will leave you."

The problem, however, comes when we catch men and apply too much or too little tension as they are landing on the solid ground of life in Christ. I've seen well-intentioned people err in both directions. One takes a very dogmatic approach that applies too much tension upon conversion. As the discipler, these people rigorously watch over new converts, letting them know what parts of their lives are out of bounds and what parts are in. They immediately introduce and require specific disciplines that must be adhered to in order to be in the faith. Ignorant of liberty in Christ, the convert feels the suffocating weight of never living up to Christ when they turn in a weekly report to a discipler. Christianity becomes a never-ending, joy-robbing, perfunctory checklist of sorts that inevitably leads to burnout. The line of discipleship eventually breaks under the immense tension being applied to the new convert, who is left disillusioned.

As sad as that all-too-real account of applying too much tension to a new convert sounds, an equal risk exists if too little tension is applied. This often occurs when disciplers want so badly to make the new convert "like" church that they eschew what it means to be a church member. They care more about not offending or grieving the person than they do about grieving the Holy Spirit. In the process, liberty in Christ is perverted at the expense of the personal holiness Christ calls us to pursue. The discipler cares more about showing a loving non-judgmental Jesus than showing the person a holy, just, judging Jesus (Who *must* be loving to be just). The lack of tension ultimately results in the person swimming off, never really feeling a hook set within them, never feeling any life-changing conviction, never having really lost anything, but, most tragically, never truly gaining Christ.

The best means of landing the fish is accomplished through applying perfect tension that allows for individual growth in grace, while also speaking the Truth in love to see the fish grow in holiness. Applying too much tension can result in a line that breaks under the weight of legalism that sees God as Lord of our lives without understanding we can never perfectly obey Him in this life. Applying too little tension can promote licentious behavior that demands no holiness because it is happy to make God our Savior but not our Lord. Both approaches fail to complete the catch.

10. Make a peaceful landing.

The fish has arrived! After all your hard work, scouting your environment, making a genuine presentation, getting to where the action is stirring, setting your hook, and maintaining perfect tension, the time has come to land the fish. Okay, this sounds pretty straightforward; what directions could possibly be necessary at this point?

Experienced fly fishermen understand the importance of positioning themselves downstream from their fish to better ensure a gentle landing. Why? Because they know the fish will resist final submission and will make sporadic runs away from them. If the fisherman is situated downstream, the fish is the one doing all of the work, fighting against the current, and fatiguing itself in the process. Once it relents, the fisherman can prevent the fish from tumbling out of control and being swept away by the current if he is wisely positioned downstream, allowing the fish to flow into his net. Likewise, the people we mentor will stumble and resist as they are being drawn to Christ. Loving discipleship dictates that we position ourselves downstream from the torrents of their lives in order to catch them when they fall and, ultimately, to be positioned to ensure a peaceful landing for their first steps in a new life.

Like people, fish are prone to making one final, last stand at the point of being apprehended. Getting cold feet is out of the question for them; but like people, when the moment of final surrender comes, trout can make a frantic, final push. I've seen many act like Chandler on the television show *Friends*, who, after months of meticulous wedding preparation and pep talks to confront his fear of commitment, makes a jailbreak escape from his friends just moments before his wedding.[211] I'll grant the show was hilarious, but I've never understood how someone who is truly submitted to becoming one flesh with another human being, whom he professes to love, can flee at the moment of matrimony. I can only surmise that such a person never was fully committed to the other if unable to fully submit at the point of union.

The cold feet "fight or flight" concept shouldn't be so alien to me. I've lost some nice fish by rushing to net them before they were fully submitted. Showing a lack of patience, I've lunged for a trout while it was still fighting, trying to force that final commitment before it was ready. The only problem is, if the trout has not submitted, it will not commit to being taken. Praiseworthy trout have had the last laugh by either spitting the fly out or breaking my line by a final thrash right before my net.

Or you can get lucky by netting a fish that has not fully submitted, only to find him spit the fly while in your net. You might feel a brief feeling of relief that you got him netted just in time, before you realize that he, again, got the last laugh by getting your loose fly tangled in your net. You might have captured him, but he succeeded in buying his buddies some time because it will take you ten minutes to untangle the mess he left you. This mess would not have occurred had you shown patience. Given all that can go wrong, as a personal confession, I still struggle to learn the necessity of a gentle landing.

A good fisherman doesn't rush "the decision" of netting a fish before it submits. He deftly maintains tension and lets the fish work the fight out of itself without forcing the matter. The fisherman gradually draws the fish to himself during the respites of the fight, all the while being ready to respond to jumps and runs the fish will mount. Finally, when the fish has submitted and can resist no more, the call for commitment is made, and the fish is landed, gently.

Fishers of men act much the same as a wise fisher of trout in eliciting a gentle landing. They let God be God and simply enjoy the privilege of being used as His vessel to draw another fish to Himself. They don't use coercive methods but use spiritual discernment and spiritual understanding before there are signs of spiritual life. They are patient and gentle with the fish, leading it with proper tension to a point of surrender. Together, fisherman and fish, discipler and disciple, examine the Word of Truth and seek ways to apply it to their lives. To the fisher of men, there is never any past conduct too repulsive, no conversation too disturbing, nor any question too dumb, nor any sin too foreboding to discuss because the fisher of men recalls they, too, were once dead to righteousness, "following the course of this [fallen] world" (Eph. 2:2). Thus, knowing grace, the fisher of men knows better than to force a submission that risks a last-second insurrection. The Holy Spirit must do the work, convicting the person of their need for full submission to Christ and, upon doing so, providing a gentle landing.

Finally, one all-too-neglected component of a gentle landing is celebration. Fish do not naturally seek to be caught. And fishermen are not owed the joy of catching fish. The fish, the spring, the crisp ambiance, laden with enthralling vistas and silent ruminations that convey the theology of the spring—none of them belong to us. Therefore, we would be wise to recognize the grace present in these ephemeral blessings, celebrate them, and worship God accordingly.

Jesus said that "there is joy before the angels of God over one sinner who repents" (Lk. 15:10). I often point to this passage when I baptize people, letting the witnesses know that there is more going on here than what we see. There are more interested parties to a baptism than those confined to the church sanctuary. The gentle landing of baptism, where someone makes a public profession of faith depicting their identifying with Christ's death and resurrection, is a big deal. As such, we should be moved like a current to the person who is baptized, overflowing with greetings of joy, encouragement, and celebration. All fellow believers and, by association, fellow fishermen should make room for this new member of the family. What greater cause for joy is there than observing a supernatural work that brought life out of death? We should all celebrate these occasions.

It's unfortunate that fellow fishermen and fellow believers do not always celebrate the landing. Both are often too jealous of the newfound joy they observe in another, or they are too self-absorbed in their own lives to pay homage to the Creator who permitted the catch in the first place. I've seen fishermen crowd in between members of my family, fishing side by side. These boorish goons have refused to budge as I'm trying to net a fish to secure a gentle landing. Such behavior demonstrates a profound lack of stream etiquette, which unfortunately appears to be on the rise. It not only refuses to celebrate the gift of the catch and the gift of the spring with others, it is downright selfish, robbing others of the gift of the spring. I lament that my dad's second-to-last time ever fishing with his father was curtailed by a man who waded out in between the two where he could literally breathe on them both. The final memories of a son and his father, interacting through the one thing they loved doing for decades, were spent in broken fellowship from the selfishness of another. Don't be that guy. Give room, and celebrate the catch of others, whereby you participate in another gentle landing.

Considerable attention has been given in the last two chapters about catching fish, and for good reason. The spring has much to say about catching fish; from its waters flow symbiotic discourses intended for the benefit of the fish, as much as the fisherman. The spring has presented ten strategies to help catch fish, whether those fish be trout or men and women. While stark differences abound between fish and people, the theology of the spring teaches us that the methods we use to catch both may not be all that different. But should we really be surprised that common methodologies are utilized to draw both fish and man, pointing to a common source of life—a source where life both emanates and converges in its living water?

Reflection Questions

1. In what specific situations do you find it important to practice the axiom, "It's not what you say, but how you say it"? How can you personally implement this counsel in a sensitive manner to get the desired result of speaking the truth in love?

2. One strategy mentioned in this chapter was to "go where the action is." But I would also caution that in the ecclesial context

of the church, we generally don't look to take fish off someone else's stringer to put on our own. In what circumstances would this be acceptable? In what circumstances would it be wrong?

3. Some have said that fly fishing is like golf in that it looks much easier than it actually is. Why is that moment of setting the hook with a trout, or with a person, much harder than many realize?

4. What kind of go-tos have you used in your life, and what purpose have they served?

5. In your own words, what is the importance of examining your lure? How often do you examine yourself, and what do you typically find?

6. I mentioned that twenty-first century American culture has lost the art of listening. Do you agree? If so, do you believe this is due to a lack of humility, a lack of focus, or something else?

7. What relationships in your own life can you list that need a better balance of tension? In what way?

8. Good fishermen use their feet. Given record rates of obesity and general malaise within our populace, why do so many people, if they get outdoors, decline to use their feet (i.e., take a passive posture instead of actively engaging the outdoors)? What is the greatest thing they are missing by neglecting to do so?

CHAPTER NINE

EATING OUR OWN: ECCLESIOLOGY IN THE STREAM

*Bless those who persecute you; bless and do not curse them. Rejoice
with those who rejoice, weep with those who weep. Live in harmony
with one another. Do not be haughty, but associate with the lowly.
Never be wise in your own sight. Repay no one evil for evil, but give
thought to do what is honorable in the sight of all. If possible, so
far as it depends on you, live peaceably with all. Beloved, never
avenge yourselves, but leave it to the wrath of God, for it is written,
"Vengeance is mine, I will repay, says the Lord."*

—Romans 12:14-19

A BEAUTIFUL FISH CAN EASILY become a fixation. The fixation waxes
all the more pronounced when showcased by a young boy—particularly,
when the youngster has caught little all morning, but was continually teased by the swirling entourage of rainbow trout, with seemingly no appetite, other than to follow around their big fish leader.
Understandably, that big leader of the pack became the object of the
boy's fixation. And that boy was my son.

Naturally, bringing your son to the spring means that when he
grows obsessed with catching a fish, you automatically get deployed
as a mandatory accomplice. Casting my equipment aside, I gladly embraced my role as first mate in helping my son Jonah accomplish his
goal: to catch "Big One." "Big One" was the name he gave to this alpha
trout that paraded through the shallow portions of the spring with his

smaller lackeys in tow. The fish likely weighed just below two pounds and stood out with his flamboyant colors. Big One knew it, too, teasing the boy with his cocky gait as he swam back and forth, seemingly mocking him from the water. Each time Jonah cast something in front of him, Big One would feign interest, only to snootily turn away at the last second. The boy's spirits grew dimmer with each pass.

I knew we faced an uphill battle. The more a fish is pressured, the more discriminating it becomes. I tied on mini jigs, leach patterns, and small zebra midges for my son. Yet nothing could entice Big One. His minions seemed to grow in audience, like a band of peasants out to watch their king successfully return home from battle. But then, after tying on a red and white egg pattern, the unexpected happened. Jonah swung a perfect cast about six inches out in front of Big One's smug face, and he took it.

Big One was hooked, and my son stood there, momentarily incredulous about what to do next. He obviously never expected to end Big One's reign; but with my coaching in his ear, he snapped out of his star-struck reverie and went to work. After the trout thrashed a bit, my son maneuvered Big One to the bank, where I put the final nail in the coffin by netting him. You've never seen a seven-year old with a larger grin; it took several weeks for that grin to wear off.

Now, while I do enjoy eating trout, more often, I prefer to catch and release. However, if you take a kid fishing, you'll quickly find that catch and release is an inconceivable concept. In a child's mind, catch and release defeats the entire purpose of going fishing. And when you've just landed the object of your fixation, a fish brimming with beauty and (just moments before) bursting with confidence like Big One, there is no question whether or not to keep him.

Yet the most unexpected sight of the day was not catching Big One. The most unexpected sight of the day was the unsettling phenomenon that occurred after we caught and cleaned Big One. The phenomenon is the concept I call "eating our own," which we saw play out in the raw, unrestrained self-interests of trout. A lesson commenced on the ecclesiology of the stream.

Trout that live in state parks acclimate to a different mode of survival than trout in the wild. For instance, trout become tamer to human presence. They tolerate people's intrusion into the stream to the point of adapting their diet, taking the quick and easy fix that humans can provide. Trout become scavengers. There is no better example than when you clean a fish and pitch the remains back into the stream. Trout voraciously devour the gutted fish they swam with just moments before as one of their own.

My son came to grips with this unnerving reality with Big One. Driven home by the monarchial behavior Big One displayed while alive, with smaller fish clamoring to swim alongside him, Jonah was shocked to see the other trout immediately start gobbling the remains of their fish-king after I filleted him. These loyal subjects transformed into mad anarchists, launching into a feeding frenzy on the one whom they seemed to obey and adore just moments earlier. As he gazed into the spring, the polish of my son's conquest of Big One momentarily dimmed. A startling truth from the theology of the spring confronted him: trout eat their own.

Unfortunately, trout are not the only species that eat their own. As the annals of time would attest, it might seem that the church has specialized in eating its own. Stories, appalling or sadly hilarious if not true, have caricatured the church in how it has unbiblically responded to the behavior of its members. Sometimes, the response has been negligence by offering no response to correct aberrant behaviors that inevitably lead the wayward to despair. Other times, the church over-aggressively and painfully repudiated members for moral failures with no sense of love or restoration. During some instances, the pastors and leadership are the perpetrators eating their own. Occasionally, cliquish lay members viciously rebuke and scorn weaker members of the congregation.

I must sadly confess that the church's reputation for eating its own is well-earned. Almost anyone who's been moderately involved in church can recall a story of people being mistreated, exploited, or manipulated. As a pastor, I don't have to look far for instances when people from within have tried to devour me. I've had a personnel committee chair (serving to "support" personnel) undermine my efforts to teach people how to share their faith. I've endured my wife being nastily yelled at while serving as a volunteer greeter at a *fellowship* chili cook-off. I've had church members take to social media to distort the truth and blast me for refusing to *not* follow policy (and the Bible). I've even had people be so "honest" to tell me in front of my wife and kids that I need to lose weight (I don't disagree), that they didn't like my voice, or that I had an ugly haircut. We could go on—and most pastors have stories worse than mine—but that's not the point. The point is that the church eating its own is regretfully pervasive, and yet it is not the design Christ gave His image-bearers to nurture His church.

I would also make the point that these and manifold anecdotes across the world do not invalidate the church or its mission. Stories of eating our own don't prove the church a fraud and render it useless. In fact, it proves quite the contrary. The church is a body of imperfect people, who come together to pursue Christ, albeit with the vestigial sinful nature remaining within them. The church is the only organization on the planet that requires you admit your fallibility and wretchedness in order to become a member. "The church is full of hypocrites!" you might charge, which has become a trivialized rebuff. But while the church isn't perfect, it also doesn't claim to be. If it did, the "church is full of hypocrites" charge would make a fair point.

For the remainder of this chapter, we'll build on what the spring has to teach us about eating our own. First, we'll examine how, unlike trout, we assume far heavier consequences with moral and eternal implications when we eat our own because we are God's image-bearers. Furthermore, our fellow Christians have even greater value as people redeemed by Christ at great cost to Himself. Second, we'll see how the

Word of Truth flows forth with a timeless prescription for conflict resolution in churches, so that those who drink of its waters may avoid eating their own. Finally, we'll discover how we unwittingly promote the eating of our young through unbalanced nurturing in the stream of life.

MADE IN THE IMAGE OF GOD

The closer we draw to the spring, the more we see with crystalline clarity just how delicately life hangs in its balance. Resting in its blues, the dichotomy of nature exists, where sheer beauty intertwines with the raw brokenness of a creation gone awry. This dichotomy is not hard to spot. Not only found in the spring's tranquil water columns, it is reflected on the water's glassy surface, staring back as the image of ourselves. But just as our reflection in the spring is simply a facsimile of ourselves—an incomplete image that says something about us without "being" us—so, too, is the image of God in man. This image, while imperfectly fulfilled in fallen mankind, has much to say about our anthropology and consummate fulfillment in the God-man, Jesus Christ.

What is meant by the long-debated term, "the image of God in man"? And how does the spring help us flush out its meaning? Let's return for a moment to the vignette of the spring that opened this chapter. In that story, we saw a big fish in the spring—"Big One"—who commanded the respect and following of many other fish. We also saw how quickly the allegiance to Big One gave way to the self-interest of his subjects after he was caught and his remains were tossed into the spring. Instead of giving their king a proper burial, his loyal followers launched into him with a frenzy of feeding.

And you know what? While they could not communicate audibly, I never sensed one inkling of remorse out of those trout. Not a single one displayed any reluctance to rip into the flesh of the dead leader. And not a single trout showed any grief when it was over. None of those trout were aghast at eating their own. Yet, conversely, I know of no human being—once they come to their senses after metaphorically eating one of their own by way of demonizing, slandering, overtly ridiculing, etc.—who does not either feel a sense of guilt or self-justification, which, either way, expresses a moral action.

You might be laughing at this example by now, but it illustrates the clear, but intangible, point of where we differ from trout or animals in our anthropology. And that divergence emanates from the existence of something we have, but trout lack—moral faculty. Since we as creatures did not create ourselves (see chapter four), that moral faculty that exclusively resides within us must have been placed there by our Creator. This moral faculty, the capability of making moral decisions that reflect the character of their Creator, is the primary vehicle that uniquely distinguishes humans as God's image-bearers, the *imago dei* in Latin.

Differing schools of thought have pontificated over the years as to what is meant by the term "the image of God." The phrase first appears in Genesis 1:26a, which reads, "Let us make man in our image, after our likeness." The following verse, Genesis 1:27, summarizes the climax of God creating mankind, this time using only the word "image." The theme is not visited again until Genesis 5:1, when only the word "likeness" is used, but 5:3 comes back to using both "image and likeness" together. Are these two words just synonyms used for emphasis, or do they mean two different things? The meaning is important because it has implications that lie at the very root of our human anthropology.

Divergent views over the term "image and likeness" have abounded over the centuries. Some theologians tend to separate the two words, with *image* meaning "the ability to reason" and *likeness* meaning "the ability to express natural gifts, such as spirituality, freedom, and virtue." Other camps believe that mankind has altogether lost the image and likeness of God in the fall through sin. They believe these two attributes are reacquired when people are saved, donning a new nature distinct from, but similar to, angels. The early church fathers, such as Irenaeus, believed "image" meant human characteristics, such as "personality, reason, jest," while "likeness" referred to matters of ethical conscience that humans can enact.[212]

Peter Gentry and Stephen Wellum, in their 2015 book, *God's Kingdom through God's Covenants*, posit a very scholarly argument that image and likeness mean two different, but related, things in a dual vertical and horizontal relationship. "Image" is said to speak to man's relationship to God as a son; and because of man's sonship, "likeness" speaks to his role as a servant king to creation.[213] Gentry and Wellum go to compelling lengths to prove this theory, citing many ancient Near Eastern artifacts, inscriptions, and linguistic evidences that reflect this motif through a physical statue or engraved mandate; the king is the image of God because he has a relationship to the Deity as the son of the God and, therefore, a relationship to the world to rule it as God's vicarious vice regent. Another point is that man alone is the sole creature God made to have a relationship with Him. Thus, given our gift of Divine relationship, the creation ordinance to "subdue" the earth and have dominion over it (Gen. 1:28) as His stewards is the natural extension of our relationship to God.

For example, consider the fact that the Hebrew word for garden (*gan*) means "to fence off or protect."[214] This protective sanctuary theme squares with the biblical account where man was first created outside of the garden, but afterwards, placed inside the garden's protective confines to flourish (Gen. 2:8). The Garden of Eden, the spring of creation, is presented as the center of blessing to the world. Moreover, in ancient days of Near Eastern civilizations, gardening was a royal vocation. For example, in ancient Mesopotamia, "gardener" was a title for monarchs. So, Adam's role as gardener could be construed as Adam being a type of priest-king with the garden as his sanctuary. To their credit, Gentry and Wellum are careful to point out that the definition of image and likeness is not just functional, but ontological and structural. They note, "The character of humans in ruling the world is what represents God," and later, "Man rules as a result of being made as the divine image; ruling is not the essence of the image itself."[215]

Gentry and Wellum make a cogent argument that more fully develops humanity's anthropological job title and is not incorrect in principle. However, I, like many old and new scholars, believe that the words "image and likeness" are merely synonyms expressing the same over-arching ideal that we should mimic the moral character of our Creator. The exclusivity and imperative management of moral faculty is indispensable to the Bible metanarrative.

Possessing moral faculties makes us uniquely moral beings, able to discern moral truths, which come from God and, therefore, reflect His perfections. By virtue of that special dignity of perpetuating holiness, we exist as image-bearers of our Creator. So, while there is weighty merit to the horizontal "dominion element" advanced by Gentry and Wellum, there can be no dominion exercised in accord with the King's commands if we do not have a moral connection to the King. This connection reflects His moral character by which He tasks us to rule over the domain He entrusts to us! Our dominion mandate, then, becomes gratuitous. Thus, the dominion ordinance, while related, seems much more a byproduct or office that comes with being in the image and likeness of God.

Consider further how this unrivaled moral quality of being made in God's image and likeness pales in contrast to any other creature. Animals, plants, robots, etc. don't live with an intrinsic sense of "ought." Trout don't feel a sense that they "ought not" _____ (fill in the blank with "eat eggs a female just laid," "spawn with another trout's mate," etc.) They lack moral faculties. None of them feel innate guilt as a natural response to what would be wrong for humans. They have zero inhibitions about inflicting harm on another; it's what makes them only animals. Conversely, humans are innately programmed to know this conduct is wrong, in part because an assault on God's image-bearer is an assault against the design and plan of God Himself.

This is not to say that an animal, such as my dog, won't hang her head if I catch her doing something wrong, such as getting into the trash. But her head-hanging comes only *after* I get on to her, and her reaction is not a moral response, per se. It is a rote, punitive response, known from many repeated acts of trash can sedition, for she has learned that transgression is not in her best interests. Her "remorse" doesn't proceed from a heart that loves God—or her owner, for that matter—but from her frustrated desires. She is simply manifesting her sad realization—gained from prior consequences stemming from the same act—that her desire of culling food from the trash will not be met. In other words, her response comes from self-serving, not self-guilt, and does not flow from moral faculty.

Humanity, made in the image of God, can ultimately be summed up as mankind's endowment to exercise moral faculties reflecting God's holy character in stewardship and government of the garden (Earth). At this point, you might argue, "Aren't morals just a product of pragmatism, the convergence of cultural customs and values that work to achieve the common good?" This question ultimately implies a relativistic original for our moral faculty instead of an absolute one. John Murray provided one of the best responses grounding moral faculty to an absolute, ultimate Being. Murray said, "The term 'moral' in this discussion refers to responsibility. Man lives and moves and has his being in the realm of 'ought,' of duty, of obligation to be consciously and freely fulfilled . . . The ultimate criterion of obligation for man is likeness to God . . . To sum it up, it is the metaphysical likeness to God that grounds obligation, and the fulfilment of obligation consists in conformity to the image of God."[216]

"But," one may respond, "there are some things that *most* people just know you ought or ought not do, aside from God." But masses and the mobs have often been wrong, like a school of trout in a feeding frenzy. Truth is not dependent on the plurality affirming it. As Kevin DeYoung put it, "If any sense of ought is to have any binding obligation, it must rest on something higher than majority opinion." Therefore, because we are made in the image of God, we can peer into the spring, watch the trout eat their own, and know we ought not do the same.

There is, though, a second reason why we treasure, not eat, other believers: Christ died to redeem them. The visible wounds received from openly tearing into others with our words are obvious. However, a self-centered liberty that values doing "one's thing" above building fellow believers also devours them.

I can think of no better example than the sad story I once heard about a young woman who uprooted her entire life to become part of a new, vibrant church. She belonged to a healthy, but small, congregation that plodded about its way with consistency and commitment to Truth, valuing substance over style. But in the prime of her life, she heard about a burgeoning new church across the country, one that was growing fast and had much to offer young adults like her. So, without even lining up a job, she packed and moved to the city of this dynamic church to become part of its ministry.

But about a year later, the young lady shocked her home church by showing up one Sunday morning, dejected and broken. The radiant church that attracted her had unraveled at the seams and no longer existed. When asked what went wrong, she offered a terse response through quivering lips, quoting Romans 14:15b (NKJV): "Do not destroy with your food the one for whom Christ died."[217] She had been devoured in a community where Christian liberty became exalted above Christian holiness and Christian unity.

Because mature Christians can handle some matters that are not sinful in and of themselves, it doesn't mean that those same matters should be encouraged in less mature believers. If a specific social activity would provoke a less-mature believer to sin, the more mature believers should refrain and seek the less-mature believer's holiness over their own personal happiness. This abstention should be taken even if the more mature believer *can* partake in the activity without compromising personal holiness or committing any indiscretion.

The theology of the spring provides a practical example: only big trout should eat mice. While this may sound strange, mice that fall in or venture too far out into the stream often become hearty meals for large, mature trout. There are even mice patterns fly fishermen can tie that look so realistic, my wife can't bear to see them in the house. But like young Christians, young trout can't handle questionable food, such as mice. I've read many accounts of small trout swallowing mice; but because their digestive systems are not large enough, these trout die from obstructions in their digestive tracts, caused by the mice. Like gray areas of liberty to immature Christians, mice might initially taste good for immature trout, but because they are not mature enough to handle it, the mice end up destroying them. People are more valuable than trout. Therefore, may we never destroy those for whom Christ died, and eat our own, by flaunting liberties that could be destructive to others.

The people in God's church have double value, both as human beings made in God's image and as fellow believers for whom Christ died, Whose suffering secured for them a glorious destiny. This makes it even more tragic when Christians eat their own. And Christians eat their own by practicing sin that corrupts other believers, spreading salacious gossip, and by flaunting liberties that damage weaker saints. But when corruption breaks out among Christians, there *is* an alternative to eating our own.

CHURCH DISCIPLINE: A BIBLICAL ALTERNATIVE TO EATING OUR OWN

Church discipline—the words alone cause many modern American evangelicals to shudder. For some, the term evokes images of archaic castigation, sifted from a Nathaniel Hawthorne novel—a black eye of the church no more applicable to the modern era than the primitive means of Puritan living. The mere mention of invoking church discipline to many contemporary believers provokes a visceral reaction against any such affront to an individual's freedom of choice. Over the last one hundred years, American culture has developed an imbedded reaction that presupposes each individual's "inalienable rights" of personal conduct. Eventually, this entitlement was imported into the church. The "inalienable rights" of church members were inflated to trump the standards and expectations imposed by the holy Creator of the universe on church membership. As a result, many contemporary Christians believe that not only should their personal behavior be compartmentalized from membership in the church, but also even more striking is the implicit premise that personal conduct, regardless of how incongruent it may be with Scripture, is off-limits as a mark of, or even qualification for, church membership. The playbook response, replete with feigned outrage, typically asks, "Who is the church to judge?"

Others, however, quietly lament the church's abdicated expectations of holy living; surely, the same God who commands us to "be holy, for I am holy" (Lev. 11:44) would not permit His church to sacrifice such an exhortation on the altar of modernity for the mere comfort of its members. If the God Who created the universe is sovereign and has provided a means for eternal fellowship with His creation, then His absolute standards as an infinite Being must transcend the temporal standards of an oft stiff-necked, finite humanity. The same God Who appeared in flesh as the incarnate Christ requires full Lordship over our lives (Matt. 10:38). Therefore, claims suggesting a bifurcation of living standards—that one can live according to both God's ideals and the ideals of the world—are easily dismissed. His jurisdiction extends to all facets of Christian living, not just when one walks through the threshold of the church foyer.

However, some at the extreme of this continuum would be all-too-desirous to act as the final arbiter of church discipline by aggressively excommunicating all who do not subscribe to their ecclesial views or who struggle with holiness. With such divergent approaches, some Christians—particularly, those who are generations removed—may be understandably ignorant of the legitimacy of church discipline.

What is church discipline, and is it necessary today? American Christians need only belong to a church for a short while in order to develop their own anecdotal experiences and answers. Many share the same observations that have become almost caricaturized: manipulative powerbrokers shredding churches from within, worldly ideals branding entire congregations as hypocrites, unfounded gossip running a pastor out of the church, a personal liberty becoming a catalyst for division, etc. If this sinful conduct is left unchecked, such cancer can spread throughout the entire body with the perception of tacit approval, thus contaminating with impurity the very fellowship of the church.

Picture this all-too-common scene: you see a fellow believer mired in self-destructive, sinful behavior. Perhaps this is out of ignorance, or perhaps deep-seated issues of rebellion are playing out. Regardless, we've seen that eating our own is not an option in this case. Neither is abandoning the fallen saint. But confrontation is hard, especially given the way our fallen flesh has disfigured the concept of confrontation as the irreversible death sentence on a friendship. We either resist confrontation at all costs or fiercely go about it in a manner that maims rather than mends. Thankfully, God was not unprepared for situations of discord and laid forth a remedy for His people. Church discipline is that means God has provided to restore people to fellowship through loving confrontation.

Sadly, humanity has distorted God's design for confrontation, an act He created to demonstrate love and bring reconciliation. For those made alive by the grace of God alone, if we sincerely love our neighbor as we are called to do, what greater love is there than to gently speak words of Truth to wayward behavior? To be willing to selflessly risk our own likability for someone else's ultimate viability? And what greater privilege is there than to be used as God's vessel of conviction to restore a person's relationship with Christ and fellow church members?

Church discipline, in its truest sense, seeks to mimic God Himself, bringing fallen believers back into full communion with Him and other disciples. It addresses a matter of sinful behavior so as to produce conviction, sorrow, repentance, and restoration. Contrary to innate connotations as punitive, church discipline is fundamentally rooted in God's glorification and man's restoration—a motif that follows the ultimate example of the work done at the cross. Discipline exacted without these core motives is flawed because it falls guilty either to idolatry (action that displaces God as the object of its honor) or vengeance (action lacking love, which substitutes the will of the individual for God's will).

Aside, but not apart, from reconciliation, church discipline also exists to maintain fidelity of doctrine and to protect the church's witness to the world. While born-again believers are unable to cease impetuous acts of sin entirely, the "new man" eschews *states* of sinful behavior through repentance, which comes from his will to walk with God (1 Jn. 2:6). Membership in the local church is meaningful and, as the apostle Paul notes in 1 Corinthians 5:9-13, reflective of true membership in the body of Christ.[218] Therefore, Paul proceeded to indict the Corinthian church of corporate sin by its toleration of the blatant sin of one of its members. The church's lack of response compromised the very testimony of the church in the eyes of the world it was trying to reach.[219] Francis Schaeffer noted of the early church: "They practiced two things simultaneously: orthodoxy of doctrine and orthodoxy of community in the midst of the visible church, a community which the world can see. By the grace of God, therefore, the church must be known simultaneously for its purity of doctrine and the reality of its community."[220]

Church discipline is both formative and corrective. Formative church discipline is perpetual and can be best aligned with modeling behavior. Teaching, reading the Bible, and availing oneself to positive instruction all represent means of formative discipline. On the other hand, corrective discipline is confronting a fellow brother or sister in love over the entrapment of sinful behavior shown in their life. The confrontation can be as innocuous as saying, "Because I love you, it concerns me that you may not be attending regularly."

Formative and corrective discipline ultimately converge upon the universal form of discipline. When dispensed with the desire of restoration, effective church discipline can and should be equated as a facet of discipleship, as a disciple is one who voluntarily submits to the discipline of another, including loving reproof.

Partaken as a form of discipleship, church discipline begins at an individual level. Such an effort is aimed at preventing a large, emotion-fueled group from eating its own. The paradigm starts at the individual level, precluding any initial group involvement or, at worst, a corporate witch hunt. The burden of responsibility cuts both ways, as earnest believers know they are far from a finished product and seek to further their sanctification. Furthermore, initiating the process on an intimate, one-on-one level avoids the public spectacle that can impair the church's witness.[221] The church gets involved only when the offender refuses to cooperate.

One final aside about church discipline that often gets overlooked is that it applies only to Christians and not the unsaved world. It takes place within the church body, the local church, where a prerequisite relationship between the parties in conflict has already been forged. While God designed the church to be a true family, in order to achieve familial solidarity, discipline must exist.[222] Much like our earthly children, when love or discipline is lacking, church members will be greatly handicapped.[223] Ultimately, church discipline is a substantive, yet rehabilitative, process, emanating out of love and holiness, resulting in the exaltation of God.

A natural response, following the over-arching "what" of church discipline, is to ask where the biblical warrant for church discipline is found. Is this tool that prevents us from eating our own grounded in absolute truth? Or is it just a convenient solution the church thought up along the way?

We can legitimately cite the first biblical example of discipline as a consequence of humanity's first sin in the Genesis three account of the Fall. Here, we see God not only discipline Adam and Eve for unrighteous conduct by driving them from the Garden and imposing a life of labor and certain death; but reading on, one also sees God's hand of mercy at work to restore the relationship of mankind and his progeny with Him. In spite of their rebellion, God makes a promise to the first man and woman that redemption and full reconciliation with Him would come through One of their descendants, Who would forever defeat the stranglehold of sin and death—prefiguring Jesus, the Messiah.

God's loving kindness is then shown throughout the pages of the Old Testament, as God establishes a people for Himself from Adam and Eve's descendants, whom He raises up and provides for in miraculous ways. Equally miraculous is the chastisement and mercy God shows after they repeatedly turn from Him. Although God disciplines His people to protect His holiness, like a doctor causing pain to reset a wayward limb, His loving purpose is to reset His people from a wayward trajectory back to Him—back to true Life. God's love is shown mutually inclusive with His discipline.

Another excerpt from the Old Testament Pentateuch, Leviticus 19:15-18 lays the ground work for restorative reproof of a brother. Verse seventeen preempts conflict by encouraging cordial dialogue: "You shall not hate your brother in your heart, but you shall *reason frankly* with your neighbor, lest you incur sin because of him" (emphasis mine). The passage delineates an honorable blueprint of conflict mitigation—one that precludes talking ill of a brother—but goes one step further, requiring one to reprove that brother or neighbor before the contention has the opportunity to take root into a full-fledged conflict. The Hebrew context of the word "neighbor" in verse seventeen is identified as group, clan, or brother, as in a familial or communal setting.

The Lord Jesus Himself, seeing the issue of future fractures within His church, prescribed in advance the method of church discipline in Matthew 18:15-18:

> If your brother sins against you, go and tell him his fault, between you and him alone. If he listens to you, you have gained your brother. But if he does not listen, take one or two others along with you, that every charge may be established

by the evidence of two or three witnesses. If he refuses to listen to them, tell it to the church. And if he refuses to listen even to the church, let him be to you as a Gentile and a tax collector. Truly, I say to you, whatever you bind on earth shall be bound in heaven, and whatever you loose on earth shall be loosed in heaven.

The salient feature of verse fifteen is the foremost objective of winning one's brother. The basic precepts can be summarized as a four-step process consisting of 1) private reproof ("reproof" in the Greek meaning to expose or show sin), 2) private conference, 3) public announcement, and 4) public exclusion.[224]

Confrontation by a group should be off the table until a one-on-one conversation with the offender has first taken place. The additional witnesses required in verse sixteen can serve a threefold purpose: 1) to hear the evidence to determine if an offense has even been committed, 2) to establish the facts and veracity of the offense should they need to testify before the church, and 3) to bring additional pressure to lead the offender toward repentance.[225] The public announcement of excommunication, treating one as a heathen or tax collector, ultimately calls on the church to treat unrepentant sinners as outside the circle of God's people, just as Gentiles and tax collectors were not even allowed beyond the outer court of the temple. The church should continue to reach out to these people as part of their witness, but not confer upon them the membership in the body of Christ.

Finally, verse eighteen has strong roots in Jewish culture and would have been clearly recognized by its original Jewish audience. First century Jewish authorities would adjudicate matters of scriptural precedent by either binding (restricting) or loosing (to liberate) the judgment. Calvin believed firmly that the object metaphor used by Christ was that the church was charged with binding (excommunicating) or loosing (receiving into membership) its congregation.[226]

First Corinthians 5:1-11 demonstrates the dangers of the church permitting sinful living to permeate its members. Conspicuous within the passage is that the erring member did not commit *a* sin, but rather, was deliberately living in a *state* of sin—one so carnal that it was capable of even appalling the pagans the church was trying to reach. The gravity of the situation is exemplified, given that Paul instructed the church not to eat their own, but to remove and hand the offender over to Satan. The purpose in doing so was twofold: first, to utterly convict him of his depravity in order to bring about repentance, and secondly, to prevent the sinful conduct from spoiling other members within the church.

In light of the formal proceedings mandated by the biblical text, Galatians 6:1 provides introspective precautions to avoid eating our own. It reads, "Brothers, if anyone is caught in any transgression, you who are spiritual should restore him in a spirit of gentleness. Keep watch on yourself, lest you too be tempted." The individual broaching discussion can show gentleness by expressing concerns in the form of a question, such as, "Do I understand this to be the case?"[227] Such an approach helps prevent the perception of a "holier than thou attitude." One cardinal rule to ensure gentleness is making sure the confrontation takes place in person. Much damage can be done by the exchange of texts and emails, whereby context is completely lacking and tone misunderstood.

This text upholds restoration as our end-goal of church discipline. Both parties more easily gravitate toward restoration if pursued with a spirit of gentleness, rather than a contentious demeanor that provokes hostility. However, gentleness does not nullify the need for the confronting party to exercise caution so as not to become likewise entangled in sin.

Hebrews 12:1-14 presents a final, significant New Testament angle on the matter of church discipline—it ultimately emanates from the *love* of God. The text conveys, amongst other things, that discipline should be viewed positively as God treating and molding believers as

His children. God expects us to discipline each other and to receive discipline favorably with an uncritical heart. Should believers cease to be disciplined, they then risk revealing themselves as illegitimate children all along.

When the American church turned away from discipline, her internal indiscretions were perpetuated without consequence. Ultimately, the church ashamedly found itself looking no different from the world. When contemporary believers are honest with themselves, they will concede what the church prefers not to discuss—that the lack of discipline today is the 800-pound gorilla in the room. With that confession, the matter of applying church discipline becomes all the more urgent.

"Okay," you may be saying, "I get that church discipline is biblical, but is it really feasible for churches in a day of consumerist Christianity?" Words like "excommunication" or "confrontation" smack our ears as radical, archaic alternatives. Our flesh, always seeking expediency, tells us it's easier to just duplicitously nibble on our fellow members. Moreover, don't we want bigger churches? "Bigger is always better," we are (deceptively) told, and, thus, wouldn't church discipline naturally result in our churches shrinking?

To answer that, let's return to a time when church discipline was regularly practiced. Records of meeting minutes from Baptist churches during the nineteenth and early twentieth centuries illuminate some counterintuitive results of church discipline. Of the total membership in those churches, 29.3 percent had been charged with an offense at some point, and 8.6 percent had been excommunicated. It is estimated that by the time of the Civil War, 40,000 people had been excommunicated by Baptist churches in Georgia alone.[228] Reason might suggest that such rigid discipline would impede the growth of these churches. But surprisingly, as Southern Baptist churches excommunicated at a rate of two percent annually, the church grew at an even faster rate.[229] Eventually, the explosive growth fatigued the church, so that by the early 1900s, it no longer had the stomach or the resolve to confront one another, opting instead to revel in its growth. The church's emphasis shifted to purifying society, and in its quest to reform society, it forgot how to reform itself, becoming infested with worldliness.

At this point, knowing how our human nature hates blows to our pride, you might be thinking, "Why would anyone tolerate such discipline and potential embarrassment when they can just go down the road and join another church?" Kevin Miller, assistant minister at Church of the Resurrection in Wheaton, Illinois, offers a surprising answer: " . . . We've found that almost never happens. Because what people want, in the heart of hearts, is to be loved so much that someone will say, 'You need to change, God will help you, and I'll walk with you.'"[230]

Adopting the practice of church discipline will likely not be initially received with a sanguine response. However, until the church musters the resolve to make some uncomfortable decisions in the direction of orthodoxy, it will struggle to appear and function as the full body of Christ, missing the blessings thereto. We will continue limping along as a self-amputating body, with the hands of the church chewing off the feet.

Regretfully, we live in a day when church membership means as little to some as the free admission they received walking through the narthex doors. Instead of seeing themselves as joint members of the body of Christ that would never entertain eating their own, some people attend church as mere consumers, a persona that justifies eating their own as an extension of their "inalienable rights." American churches enjoy standards of living with unprecedented levels of comfort—a comfort that has, perhaps, served as the accomplice to permitting poison in our holy feasts. Regardless of whether the cause is comfort or the self-concern of being perceived as "judging" another, when the cleansing blood through which Christ ransomed the church is watered down, the vibrancy of His Church—His body—correspondingly dissipates. While true discipline must be executed in love, when discipline is needed but ignored, this passivity becomes anything but love, rather appearing as something closer to love's counterfeit.[231]

HATCHERY-RAISED CHRISTIANS

We've seen the ravages and remedies of churches eating their own. We'll close with a final way many Christians eat their own—one often unseen and done with the best of intentions. I've ruefully watched many Christian parents throw their kids to the proverbial wolves (or to the predator trout, to keep with our spring analogy) with an imbalanced exposure to the world. Perhaps an object illustration from the spring will better explain how this occurs.

If you have ever fished at a state park or at a private trout retreat like Westover Farms—a top-notch destination near Steelville, Missouri—or any stream that is regularly stocked with hatchery-raised fish, you have probably observed a fairly obvious connection. Hatchery-raised fish are typically the first fish caught each morning. Always. And the reason for that is simple.

Hatchery-raised fish have lived their entire lives in a safe, self-contained environment that has enabled them to eat anything that hits the water with no risk of detrimental consequences. Therefore, they lose their natural fear of humans and their natural sense of discrimination for what goes into their mouths. These fish are protected and coddled until they grow large enough to stock into the stream—a much more hostile environment. Most state parks stock their streams each night with these hatchery "stockers" that are naïve to the ways of the stream. They typically have less than a one-day life expectancy because once released into the brave new world of the stream, hatchery-raised trout are oblivious to what awaits them.

And what awaits these unsuspecting fish are hundreds of artificial flies, luring them to their unbeknownst peril and eventual death. It doesn't take long. Hatchery "dummies" usually strike at the first lure they see, becoming easy pickings for a world out to get them. Therefore, fishing at state parks is usually easiest first thing in the morning. And then, when all the hatchery stockers have been caught, the fishing significantly slows because the remaining fish, those more "natural residents," are wise to the ways of the stream.

Ephesians 4:14, with its terse theology and marine fishing motif, provides a strong admonition to the spiritually immature, which also applies to Christian children. It advises us not to remain as children, "tossed to and fro by the waves and carried about by every wind of doctrine, by human cunning, by craftiness in deceitful schemes." But many Christian children are raised like hatchery trout. They live such insular lives, certainly out of a parental motive of protection, that—like hatchery trout just released into the stream that bite the first lure they see—these children never learn what deceitful schemes are present in the world to ensnare them. Even worse, others grow so accustomed to their "padded-room" atmosphere, tended to by "helicopter mommies," that they never transition from children to growth in Christlikeness. They are never weaned off milk for the solid food of a mature believer (Heb. 5:13).

The consequences of a hatchery-raised Christian can be disastrous. Like the stocker trout, I've seen many hatchery-raised Christian children, upon their first exposure outside of church life, bite at the first thing the world throws at them. Whether they are twelve years old and being let loose into middle school, or eighteen and whetting their first taste of freedom at college, countless hatchery-raised Christians literally go crazy. These kids suddenly discover a world they never knew existed and dive headlong into these unchartered waters, lacking the necessary maturity and discernment.

My heart agonizes every time I sit with broken parents, who no longer recognize the child they raised. What began with the best of intentions to protect, ultimately resulted in a child gobbled up by the world upon release. These kids lived in blissful ignorance of the seductive vices of the world—like the hatchery trout released into the stream without being apprised of enticing artificial flies or fishermen's lures that harbor latent, malicious intents. Whether it be pornography, promiscuity, narcotics, or a worldview that militates against the Christian worldview they were raised with, most hatchery-raised Christians get hooked because they not only were ignorant these temptations existed, but also never knew of potential snares accompanying these worldly pleasures. Not unlike the way our children get inoculated from various maladies in small, safe doses, these kids lacked safe, dose-sized exposures to the real world that awaited them.

So, what's the solution? Let me be clear: I am *not* suggesting we overcorrect in the opposite direction and pull our hands off our children and immerse them in the world from the earliest age. Today's world is growing increasingly hostile toward children, with more lurking sexual predators and the propagation of pornography available on demand through our electronic devices. Leaving our kids to fend for themselves from the earliest stages is strategy contrary to both the theology of the spring and the theology of the Bible—the Word of Truth.

The theology of the spring reveals surprising care for the young, who are unable to fend for themselves. Trout, even with their amoral faculties, have been gifted with an instinct to protect their redds (nests). Unlike the proverbial "deadbeat dad," who abandons the woman and child upon impregnation or birth, many male trout will stick around and guard the redd after they have fertilized it. Some males endure fights and battle scars while fending off would-be predators from eating the eggs. Doing their part to give their offspring a fighting chance in the world, these male trout resume life after the eggs hatch into fry and seek sanctuary under rocks in shallow water.

Granted, the male trout does not come alongside his children to disciple them through their full development. But their approach is impressively far from hands-off. Biblically, we parents are called to be very hands-on and to disciple our children through their formative years. One of the capstone biblical texts of parenting instructs us to, "Train up a child in the way he should go; even when he is old he will not depart from it" (Prov. 22:6). Such pedagogy speaks to active involvement in molding and discipling our children to spiritual maturity. Theologically, the element of stewardship that derives from the *Imago Dei* comes into play again. We see this because, ultimately, our children don't belong to us at all but to God, Who created them. We are simply stewards of the children God gave us; I'm a temporary father that is tasked to prepare and shepherd the hearts of my children for relations with their eternal, Heavenly Father. Being faithful to that call demands that I be far more than a parent who drops his children off upon arrival at the doorstep of the world.

So, if hatchery-raised Christians are not the solution, and immersing our kids in the world like eggs left alone in stream is not the solution, what is our parental paradigm? As I've hinted earlier, our approach should be a biblical one, modeling the approach of Jesus with His disciples. Jesus' approach was one of teaching, modeling, and guiding the spiritual children that He poured into each and every day. During their time together, Jesus was constantly exposing His children in doses to the world that both hated and needed Him. However, Jesus carefully guided their exposure to the world, while shepherding them in a protective capacity. Only upon their maturity did Jesus depart from them, praying to God the Father, "They are not of the world, just as I am not of the world. I do not ask that you take them out of the world, but that you keep them from the evil one" (Jn. 17:14b-15). This precept has been summarized as "being in the world but not of the world."

Jesus' express pedagogy and life example complements the entirety of Scripture, where no edict for either hatchery-raised Christians or evangelistic children is found. Regarding the latter, I've heard many parents offer the popular refutation that they place their kids in secular domains, so they can "be witnesses." Don't get me wrong: I don't doubt their sincerity and have no issue with a child's involvement in non-ecclesial activities. (I even encourage such an approach, so long as the parent is able to remain engaged as the shepherd.) But as pious as this parental rationale sounds, it misses the mark biblically. Our children are not instructed in Scripture to go into the world as witnesses. Only those who have progressed to spiritual maturity, as Jesus' disciples had after three years of *perpetual* discipleship, are called to go into the world as witnesses.

When we're in the world, we have to be wise, but children are not always wise or discerning. Fortunately, Scripture provides guidance in how we relate to the world. Colossians 4:5a advises, "Walk in wisdom toward outsiders" (cf. 1 Thess. 4:12). So now you might ask, "At what point do our children become spiritually mature?" I can't answer that because individual edification varies for each child. But what I can answer is that if your child has not been equipped to identify and counter worldly ideals—such as the irrationality of a creation without a Creator, the harm that drugs can inflict, or why promiscuity is not congruent with the best that God wants for His children through the gift of marriage—then they are not ready to be witnesses. Rather, they are ripe to be witnessed to by a world all too eager to give them skewed answers to topics we were negligent to broach.

Concerning further practical application, what does it look like to expose our children to the world in protective doses? In an active sense, it means to involve your kids in public activities. Soccer teams, track clubs, dance organizations, and local kid's choirs are all good options, where your children can participate under your watchful eye. These groups provide your child opportunities to interact with children of different backgrounds, which open doors of discussion with your own kids about what you overhear their fellow participants saying.

An even better option is to coach or serve as an assistant coach, where your child can watch you build relationships with the other kids, whom you can love without compromising your principles. Coaching enables you to be a light to the world—a light your own child sees and is able to replicate. One of my most rewarding moments as a baseball coach came during the last game of the season. I told parents at the beginning of the season I would pray with the team, but their kid's participation was completely voluntary. We had a kid at the start of the season that had never prayed in his life. We literally had to teach him what prayer was and how to pray. After I had just finished my send-off speech concluding the season, the boy spoke up, saying we couldn't dismiss because we hadn't prayed yet. This nine-year-old boy, who had never been to church, proceeded to lead the team in the final prayer of the season.

Another way you can give your child protective doses of the world is to involve your kids in your ministry activities. Plan a local family mission trip. Involve your kids in an annual day of serving food or treats to your mailman, garbage collector, bank teller, etc. I've taken my kids door-to-door with me, both inviting people to church, as well as "prayer walking," knocking on neighbors' doors to ask if they have any needs we could pray for. These direct engagements with the world are great opportunities to not only involve your kids as contributing members of the team, but also to afford you an opportunity to debrief at home about some of the responses and worldviews people have. Supplement these discussions with family devotions, or lead your household through a family catechism. Show your kids how truth outshines its counterfeit.

The primary responsibility of discipling our children, those Psalm 127:3 calls "a heritage from the Lord," does not fall on the church, the world, sports teams, or even Bible study groups. Instead, *parents* are tasked to be the primary disciplers of their children, a responsibility many Christians have outsourced far too long. The preceding lessons taught by the theology of the spring and buttressed by the Word of Truth steer us from producing cloisters of hatchery-raised Christians on one extreme or leaving unguarded nests at the other extreme. Instead, we will present our children mature in Christ and ready for the world. In doing so, we more fully reflect God's image and act as faithful stewards that prevent others from eating our own. After all, the most reprehensible act isn't that we eat our own, but rather that in doing so, we eat God's own.

Reflection Questions

1. This chapter began with a raw scene from the animal world, where a school of trout turned on and ate their own. What other examples from nature can you think of that demonstrate the lack of moral faculty in animals?

2. Recall some examples of organizations or teams that you have been a part of where you've seen people eat their own. What could have been done to potentially change the outcome?

3. John 4:24 expresses the simple truth that God is a Spirit. What does this short text have to say about how we are made in the image and likeness of God?

4. If man did not possess moral faculty, would sin be possible?

5. Think of five reasons why people avoid confronting someone with a grievance. Do you think the difficulty and our resistance to this confrontation would be decreased if it were done according to the procedures of Matthew 18 and if done after adopting some of the attitudes suggested in this chapter? How so?

6. If we expect our employers, our coaches, and even our parents to correct us so that we can contribute in a productive way, why would the church be any different?

CHAPTER TEN

SLIPPERY ROCKS: WHAT ARE YOU STANDING ON?

"Therefore thus says the Lord God, 'Behold, I am the one who has laid as a foundation in Zion a stone, a tested stone, a precious corner-stone, of a sure foundation: Whoever believes will not be in haste.'"

—Isaiah 28:16

THANKSGIVING IS, IN SOME WAYS, the quintessential holiday for the believer. Sure, Christmas and Easter receive most of the holiday hype. But cut through the commercial smog blanketing these two holidays, and at the core, you'll find that without grace—the unwarranted favor precipitating these events—they become meaningless expressions, celebrating ourselves. Thanksgiving, on the other hand, brings grace front and center, offering a special opportunity for humankind to look solely upon the God who provides for them during the grind of daily life. By carving out time to look upon Him and examine ourselves, we find a juxtaposition that reveals our utter dependence on God. We see ourselves as creatures who possess nothing beyond what He has entrusted to us. The essence of a proper view of grace is marked by a response of thanks. Thanksgiving sets the table with grace as the main entrée. And it is sufficient.

Naturally then, humanity does its best to pervert the opportunity to revel in grace. Rather than resting with a heart of thanksgiving that points to God's provision, we turn the holiday upside down as an opportunity to dash out for Black Friday deals, pointing to a stomach for acquiring more stuff. Grateful stewardship is overcome with rabid consumerism, often even before a meal is consumed or observance of thanks is offered. Therefore, you can imagine how a trip to a spring might serve as one of the most foundational ways for me to spend Thanksgiving. And on one particular Thanksgiving, I received such an opportunity. It was an opportunity the spring used to reinforce how foundational God's truth is to all matters of life.

Prior to traveling down near the Missouri/Arkansas line to spend Thanksgiving with my wife's family, I was advised by her cousin to bring my waders and fly rod for a special surprise. I didn't ask any questions. The hint of fishing was music to my ears. Don't get me wrong—I love my family, but a brief reprieve from a house full of yapping dogs, little kids, and frantic cooking was just what I needed to properly frame my Thanksgiving.

Bleary-eyed after a late night of card-playing, my wife's brother Todd, her cousin Rodney, and I awoke early on Thanksgiving morning to begin our excursion. I dressed in layers to combat the freezing temperatures, a decision that would later haunt me. The layers of clothes revealed my restricted mobility, as I waddled in and out of the kitchen to fill my coffee tumbler. It was still dark outside, and I was too tired to care.

It didn't take long to awaken. Rodney offered the invigorating news that he was taking us to an obscure access to fly fish on the North Fork of the White River. This announcement rendered my coffee no longer necessary. The White River is the home of some of the best fly fishing waters in the Midwest—a haven where legendary rainbow and brown trout have been caught, and many more have gotten away. Add to the White's indomitable reputation the fact that I had never fished this must-stop fly fishing pilgrimage, and you can see why my heart skipped a beat. I had plenty to be thankful for this Thanksgiving.

My mind bounced around—not unlike my body being flung about the truck cab as Rodney navigated the bumpy Ozark backroads—contemplating which sequence of flies I would use. But fishermen don't mind the ride, especially if the potential reward is worth it. After about forty minutes of rough terrain, the truck finally came to a stop in front of a pristine, new, stream playground, with no other vehicles or humans in sight. The frigid winter air of this wilderness silenced the hustle and bustle of civilization. I didn't notice the cold, hurriedly strapping on my waders to set out into unchartered territory.

Rodney knew the waters of the North Fork. I should have listened more carefully to some of the guidance he offered as we strode toward the stream. He pointed out some spots where he had caught fish, recommended some flies, and warned of some unsuspecting fast waters downstream. I would have been wise to build off the foundational advice he gave. Alas, too enraptured by the aura of these renowned waters, I haphazardly heeded Rodney's advice.

Initially, I stuck close to Rodney and Todd. But when my early presentations failed to provoke any strikes, I quickly became impatient. I was just sure this famed water should produce fervent hits. Unlike my brother-in-law, who stayed within close earshot of Rodney, I decided that I could improve my fortunes on my own. Gradually, I began making my way downstream to look for holding pools, brush overhangs, and other spots that might contain fish.

By now, the sun was coming up to my right, producing that iridescent morning fog lifting off the waters. The fog made for beautiful scenery but shrouded the topographical cues that would ordinarily guide me along a stream. I stubbornly tried a couple of flies, and when they produced no strikes, I maneuvered through the fog to try another spot. I continued this pattern of switching out flies while changing spots, trying to make it on my own, until I was so far away that I could no longer hear Todd or Rodney.

What I could hear, however, was the sound of fast water riffles. The morning fog still rose heavily from the surface and obstructed my view, so I wasn't sure how fast or how deep the water ran. But with no success thus far, I decided I knew better than anyone else and would make my own success in this stretch of swift water. Setting out into the unknown without the benefit of clear sight, I roll casted my way downstream. With my focus on my line, I didn't realize until it was too late how the stream had snuck up on me. Deceived by my own arrogance and blinded by the opaque fog, I had unknowingly, yet willfully, entered unstable territory. The stream floor had changed; large, slippery stones had suddenly replaced the smaller-grained rocks upstream that had provided an easily navigable textured bottom. And the sound of the riffles was not only due to choppy, shallow water, but also to a small feeder stream, which, concealed by the fog, had entered from behind me, resulting in a much faster current than anticipated.

There isn't a more paralyzing feeling in fly fishing than being trapped in the midst of an underestimated torrent. Mired in helplessness, you realize that the water level is too high to continue advancing forward. On the other hand, the current has become too fast to change directions and go back without losing your balance. Furthermore, remember all those layers of clothes I had put on? They restricted my mobility to such an extent that—when combined with frozen joints—I was as dexterous as an arthritic giraffe in the arctic. The rushing water threatened to topple me—top-heavy, with no solid base to stand on—if I didn't make a move. In desperation, I somehow forged my right foot about eighteen inches in front of me, perpendicular to the current, where it caught a rock.

I saw that rock as my salvation from disaster. Nature evidently saw it as a prop to consummate its final act of laughter. As soon as I hurled my body toward this rock that held my right foot, I felt my foot's contact with the rock disappear. Its surface was slick, and the transfer of my weight caused my sole foot on the rock to slide across it like a skating rink. The next thing I knew, my head was falling back, and my right foot—the one previously in contact with what I thought was stable ground—was eye-level with me. In final surrender, I extended my right arm, which held my fly rod, so that it would not get snapped under water by my falling body weight. That slippery rock had done me in.

Plunging fully submerged into the icy water is almost enough to shock the consciousness out of your body. The water wasn't overly deep— maybe three-and-a-half feet—but it was fast, roaring as it billowed over me. I struggled to set my feet beneath me, while being toppled by liquid frigidity. Finally, feet underneath me, I launched myself up out of the water while gasping for air, only to slip on another rock and go back under. The water carried me another ten feet downstream before I tried to stand again, only to slip once more on rocks slicker than snot.

By this time, I was downright scared. I gave up on my fly rod and focused on trying to save myself. Being tossed about, I still remember just rolling like a log until the stream spit me out, landing on my knees in shallow water about one-foot deep. I remained in this penitent position, panting and sucking in air, and, in my own way, worshiping the God Who had just spared me after I had sought my own way in His spring. It took a couple of minutes, but I managed to get on my feet and stand. Rising up felt like I was lifting a thousand pounds. Hoisting water-filled waders and layers of clothes soaked like sponges, I waddled out of the stream, as I had waddled out of the kitchen hours before. God showed His grace again, as my fly rod was snagged on a rock near the bank. Unlike my spirit, it was unbroken.

I laggardly drug myself back to the truck, as the frozen air went to work on my wet noodle of a body. It no longer shook from deep, exhaling breaths, but it now shook from deep, riveting chills. I reached the truck and yelled something to Todd and Rodney, still out in the water. I don't remember what exactly I said, but it evidently got through that I needed the warmth of the truck's heater immediately. Standing outside the truck, I stripped off the frozen, soaked clothes down to my underwear. I crawled into the cab and curled up into a ball, so cold that I thought my chattering teeth were going to break from their shivering collisions. Minutes later, Rodney and Todd arrived. They cranked the heat up full blast to thaw me. Given I had ended their fishing as well, we began the trip back home. I had plenty to be thankful for in the hearth of that truck.

The scene that played out in the river that Thanksgiving morning was terrifying. But if we take a step back, we realize something all the more terrifying. Viewed through the existential lens of the human lot, the events that took place in the stream that morning become a visual narrative, a narrative as familiar as it is applicable to every culture on the planet. What happened in the stream that morning represents millions of people who, by their very nature, attempt to maneuver through life on slippery rocks with no solid foundation.

We are delivered into the stream of life by One Who has not left us to ourselves, but reveals specific truths so that we might find life abundant in the stream. Our pride eschews His wise counsel, and we seek to find our own way. Turning our back on the Truth-giver, we hastily distance ourselves as far downstream as possible from any influence He might exert. But even with our counsel darkened, we quickly realize we're not equipped to navigate the chaotic waters awaiting us.

Willed by our self-aggrandizing desires, the stream carries us farther downstream than we ever intended to go. Our eyes are blinded, having not eyes to see nor ears to hear the truth that can restore us (1 Cor. 2:9). What we can see and hear through the fog of our pride are but distortions, appearing pleasurable for a moment, only to have their sweetness disperse upon consumption. In its place, the bait and switch of sin leaves us trapped in bitter, decadent waters. Only when it's too late do we realize that we've waded in too deep. In desperation, we opt for the quick-fix: setting our feet on slippery rocks with an unstable foundation, rather than on the Solid Rock that offers an enduring foundation.

Inevitably, our unstable foundation gives way. Now in over our heads, we fall fully submerged in the gnashing waters that seem hell-bent on carrying us to certain death. We thrash and fight, trying to get to our feet, as the waters of the world crash against us. Our efforts to regain control are futile, as we are further swept away. The current toys with us, granting enough of a respite to take a breath and then deluding us into believing we can pull ourselves up on our own before it sweeps us off our feet again. Struggling to gain a footing on the slippery foundation, we jettison our crutches and possessions as a final act of self-preservation. Spiraling into the unruly abyss, only as the slippery foundations fail us and our efforts to save ourselves are rendered impotent, do we realize our utter hopelessness. In that moment, we realize—contrary to our innate seeds of self-sovereignty—our ultimate destiny is out of our hands. We realize our need for grace.

But God . . . Two words that change the course of one destiny for all eternity. Just as we are about to drown in the maelstrom of the world and just as we concede that we have no hope in our salvation, God does for us what our self-efforts and unstable foundations could not: He comes after those of us who resisted and ran from Him. Changing our hearts, God pulls us out of the imminent death of the stream and throws us onto solid ground. He stands us back on our feet and shows us the way back to Him. Battered, broken, and bruised, we turn away from the stream and place our faith in Him alone as our Healer. We strip off the wet layers—the remnants soiled by the raw, fallen world—leaving ourselves naked and cold. But we trust that we are about to be clothed in His righteousness, a warmth that will sustain us forever.

The theology of the stream, as reflected in this book, has revealed some of those unstable foundations. Perhaps that unstable foundation you stand upon is that all beliefs are equally true? Or maybe you believed, before being confronted with the theology of the stream, that the universe just came into existence out of nothing. A logically-feeble foundation asserts that we are random accidents that arrived within a cosmos that exhibits purpose. The relativist foundation that there are no absolute truths destabilizes when faced with its own premise. Or maybe you stood on the humanist foundation that relies on our own desires and abilities in the naïve belief that man can save himself, thus rendering God obsolete. Each of these worldviews presents a precarious foundation, one that buckles under the pressures of logic, reason, ontology, history, and, ultimately, the weight of human inequity. We need to stand on a foundation that is not just stable. We need a foundation that transcends the created order. The theology of the stream points to such a foundation.

The Foundation to which the theology of the stream points is none other than its very Creator, Jesus Christ, and His Gospel. However, one *proviso* is in order. The theology of the spring, by its very nature of general revelation, cannot reveal the specific means to the Gospel of salvation. It simply convicts us of the reality of the spring's Creator, and by virtue of His existence, it mutually argues for our need of salvation. Ultimately, by way of its providential currents, the spring deposits us on the doorstep of special revelation—specifically, the Gospel of Jesus Christ. And while the theology of the spring cannot explicitly articulate this Gospel, plenty of Gospel pictures flow from it—pictures of all reality springing forth into existence; spring vistas of three subsistences existing in one essence; life forms showcasing inscrutable design; historical panoramas of living waters that draw and give life; vignettes teaching us how to catch fish; and many other pieces of Gospel scenery, framing the spring motif. But what is this Gospel, the special revelation that the theology of the spring is unable to reveal?

We hear this term "the Gospel" thrown about often, but what does it really mean? "The Gospel" is a term that has become unnecessarily blurred, due to excessive additions, subtractions, and qualifications. Simply put, the Gospel is the Person and work of Jesus Christ—how we are joined to Him and reap the wages of His work, by grace alone and through faith alone. Paradoxically, stating what the Gospel is, is simple. But stating how the Gospel is, is both beautiful and profound.

THE GOOD NEWS

The declaration of the Gospel comes as good news to humanity. In fact, it's the best news anyone could ever receive. The Greek word for "gospel" is *euangelion,* meaning "a good message," or "good tidings" through the Kingdom of God.[232] However, if the Gospel comes as good news to all who receive it, then by virtue of it being universally good, the condition of all who receive it must be universally bad. The bad news is because of the fall of the first human, Adam, all of humanity inherited a sinful nature—a natural inclination to rebel or sin against our Creator. It is this universal sin discussed throughout this book that separates us from a holy, pure, and just God. Because God is holy, He must punish and separate Himself from sin. A being that is perfectly holy cannot permit that which is unholy. If He did, He would be compromising the very essence of His holiness. A God that negotiates His holiness is not God. In the same way, a Supreme Court justice that does not punish the capital crime of the guilty is not just.

The just punishment for sin is death and eternal separation from God. The bad news is that our condition is completely helpless, for we all have sinned (Rom. 3:23). The bad news is that we are all hell-bound, due to our unholiness. God is holy, and we are not. Only someone with perfect righteousness can stand before a perfectly righteous God. And since we all have missed the mark of perfection required by a perfect God, there must be some kind of atonement made to restore our fellowship with Him. And that is the Good News.

HIS PERSON

Because of His love for us, the triune God did not leave us alone in our hopeless state. The second Person of the Trinity, Jesus, the Living Word of God, left the sublime, eternal fellowship enjoyed with God the Father and embarked on a rescue mission to redeem His prized creation. The Divine, eternal Truth that shaped and created all of reality, in a supreme act of humility, entered the created order, incarnated as a man. That eternal Person, with His divine nature, embarked on a rescue mission, uniting Himself inseparably with a human nature. George Whitefield once described Jesus' rescue op from a spring perspective: "And as all that proceeded from the springs must be muddy, because the fountain was so, the Lord Jesus Christ came to take our natures upon him, to die a shameful, a painful, and an accursed death for our sakes."[233]

Jesus was conceived by the third Person of the Trinity, the Holy Spirit, and born of a virgin, thus preventing Him from inheriting the sinful nature possessed by the human race. So, in Jesus, the "whole fullness of deity dwells bodily" (Col. 2:9), which is to say Jesus exists as truly God and truly man. His Divine and human natures retained their attributes in harmony, united together without confusion, division, or separation. Despite being tempted in every human way, Jesus lived a sinless life of perfect obedience. When viewed collectively over the whole of His life, Jesus' purity rendered complete righteousness—that which is necessary to stand reconciled before a perfectly righteous God. Thus, being perfectly human to serve as an acceptable Substitute, being perfectly obedient to inhere necessary righteousness, and being perfectly infinite as the God-man Who alone can bear the just punishment for sin committed against an infinite Being, Jesus was the only One capable of serving as the perfect Sacrifice, or Atonement, to satisfy the justice and righteousness of God.

HIS WORK

The work of Jesus is very simply His life and death—as prophesied by prophets of old that the vicarious death of the Savior would bear the wrath of God against the sins of His people. And that is just what Jesus did. Jesus lived the perfect life we could not live, satisfied God's perfect Law we could not satisfy, and yet suffered the sacrificial death that we should have received. In what I call "the Divine exchange," Jesus stood in our place, gorily crucified on a cross, where God the Father placed our sin and punishment upon Him, in order to transfer His perfect righteousness to us (2 Cor. 5:21). Only by this righteousness imputed, not infused, to the account of our souls, are we able to stand before God without fear of our just condemnation. Rather, we can now stand before God with the righteousness of Jesus. The genius of the atonement's redemptive plan speaks to its Divine origin, as it provides something no other world religion can: a solution for our guilt and need for righteousness.

Fortunately, the work of Jesus did not end with His sacrificial death on a cross. Death could not defeat Him, so, as the Bible tells us, "Christ died for our sins in accordance with the Scriptures, that He was buried, that he was raised on the third day in accordance with the Scriptures" (1 Cor. 15:3b-4). After His resurrection, Jesus ascended into Heaven, seated next to the Father's right hand, ruling and making intercession for His people. Therefore, Jesus did for us what we could not possibly do for ourselves. Such is the beauty of the Gospel. When humanity's most natural inclination is to say, "Give me the rules, so I can follow them; I can work to be good enough to save myself," the Gospel says, "No, you can't ... But God, rich in mercy, has done it for you." When the world says, "Peace and contentment can be found if you will just validate yourself to all," the Gospel says, "Everlasting joy and comfort is yours because you no longer have to validate yourself to God, other people, or your pride." The Gospel is the ultimate metanarrative of humanity, bookended with contrasts: by one man, universal sin and universal guilt entered the world. But by Another came infinite righteousness, so that sin may reign no more.

HIS BENEFITS AND HOW WE ACQUIRE THEM

The benefits of Christ's atoning work are called salvation. Salvation is deliverance from the wrath of God, the dominion of sin, and the power of death. The Bible is clear that we do not receive the benefits of Christ by our works or deeds. There is nothing about our salvation in which we have any ability to boast because it is solely by God's grace we can be saved. It is by grace alone that God regenerates us, imparting spiritual life and the ability to discern spiritual truth so that we are capable of responding to the Gospel. And it is by grace God provided a way, the only way, for us to be reconciled with God. That way is by faith in Christ alone. Faith is putting our full belief in Jesus as the Son of God, Who lived the perfect life of righteousness, died a sacrificial death as the perfect sacrifice, and was resurrected as the risen Savior, whereby His righteousness is imputed to us. Yet, even our belief does not escape the auspices of grace, given belief in Christ is, itself, one of God's works (Jn. 6:29).

Faith is the instrument that joins us into eternal spiritual union with Christ so that we are then "in Christ" and receive His righteousness. Thus, not only is Jesus the means to salvation, but more accurately, He *is* our Salvation. Perhaps a better illustration may better show how faith is operative toward our salvation.

Imagine you are fishing in a large river when, suddenly, a large forest fire engulfs the entire watershed. Devastation and death are certain as the raging wall of flames closes in on you. Suddenly, you see one of those amphibious vehicles that can traverse both land and water, making its entry from the land into the stream, where it will find safety from the imminent doom. The cabin of the capsule is shut as it enters the water, and your only hope for survival is to latch onto the tow hitch in the back of the vessel. Trusting in this vessel as the only means of salvation, you turn from the land and throw yourself at the amphibious vehicle, grasping the tow hitch and clinging to it with all your might. Your faith is rewarded as the crew walks back, pulls you off the hitch, and ushers you into the cabin, thereby adopting you as one of their own.

Our faith in Christ is similar to the tow hitch in this analogy. (Granted, the analogy is not perfect, given our natural condition prefers the dying world being consumed around us.) Our faith is not what saves us, just as the tow hitch by itself does not save us. Our faith, like the tow hitch, is the means that unites us to what saves us. Jesus is that Lifeboat, where salvation from the burning world is found. Once we have been born again and see our need for Jesus, and then respond by genuinely exercising our faith in Him, He adopts us into His family forever.

The benefits of Christ are not just something to be enjoyed in the future, but rather a present *and* future benefit. At the moment we place our faith in Him alone and repent (the turning away from the lifestyle that characterized us before Christ), we are justified, or declared righteous in Christ, in a one-time, eternally-binding decree. But the benefits don't end there. At the time we are justified, we are adopted into the Kingdom of God as one of His people. The guarantee of our future heavenly inheritance is the Holy Spirit, Who indwells us from the point of regeneration and guides us in our sanctification—the process of growing more like Christ in this earthly life until the day we are glorified and go into the eternal, blissful presence of God.

This is the Gospel, the Good News that God saves sinners, doing for us what we could never do for ourselves, in spite of ourselves. It is a Gospel of contrasts—where simple meets profound, where good news meets bad news, where wrath meets love, where grace meets justice, where self-sufficiency meets self-surrender, where death meets life, and where God meets us—yet without compromising His holy character. This is the Gospel of Jesus Christ, the best news you could ever hear. This is the Gospel with a Foundation you can stand on.

TRANSFORMED LIVES

Before we close, I want to leave you with three final illustrations from the spring. The Gospel of Jesus Christ is transformational for those who receive it. The Gospel makes us new creations from the inside out. We won't live, act, and look the same as we did before the Gospel came in to renovate our souls. Therefore, as we live anew in the stream, the theology of the spring draws from its waters three final illustrations of what a life in Christ should look like.

First, as members of the citizens of the Kingdom of Heaven, we will find ourselves swimming against the current. The fish that catches the fly fisherman's eye is not the conformist trout that casually makes its way downstream alongside others. The fish that stands out is that one by itself, head down, swimming against the current, making its way upstream. You see that fish and ask yourself things like, "Where is he going? What does he know that the others don't? What gives him such confidence to venture off on his own?" You want to catch that fish swimming against the current because he represents something different from all the rest. We delight in the challenge to trip up this one that is set apart and unlike the others.

Such is often the way the world looks upon the counter-cultural believer. Living counter to the world and swimming against the current is not expected to be easy, but it is no less expected for all believers. The apostle Paul exhorts the converts at Ephesus to "no longer walk as the Gentiles do" (Eph. 4:17). Paul follows that with parallel imperatives "to put off your old self, which belongs to your former manner of life," and, in turn, "put on the new self, created after the likeness of God in true righteousness and holiness" (Eph. 4:22b, 24). The counsel given is normative for all time, reminding us that we have a new identity, and we should live our lives true to it. Paul echoes that sentiment in the opening lines of his letter to the Galatians. Addressing those who have quickly turned from the faith to a different gospel, Paul cuts at our new identity through contrast, noting, "If I were still trying to please man, I would not be a servant of Christ" (Gal. 1:10b). Other passages of Scripture—such as James 4:4, Romans 12:2, and 1 Peter 1:15-16—directly teach and presuppose that the Christian life is one set apart from the world.

Make no mistake, contrary to many false teachers and profiteers, becoming a Christian does not guarantee you an easy life of prosperity. Jesus Himself taught the opposite. He said, "You are not of the world, but I chose you out of the world, therefore, the world hates you" (Jn. 15:19b). Later, He added with no qualification, "In this world you will have tribulation" (Jn. 16:33b). Peter presupposes that believers will suffer, and their suffering is not limited to any place on earth, noting, "Knowing that the same kinds of suffering are being experienced by your brotherhood throughout the world. And after you have suffered a little while, the God of all grace, who has called you to his eternal glory in Christ, will himself restore . . . " (1 Pet. 5:9b-10). Because we are not to conform to the world, and the world loves its own, its reaction toward our non-conformity can become all the more aggressive. If we abide in the world, while truly abiding in the faith, our faith will eventually cost us something. As citizens of Heaven, we respond by keeping our eyes on Christ as we swim against the current.

The second transformative characteristic taught by the spring is modeled by way of negative example: we are not to be bottom-feeders. If you fish enough, particularly in state parks, you will find a familiar presence lurking in the depths of the stream: bottom-dwelling suckers. Suckers come in different species, but one common characteristic they all share is that they are scavengers that suspend themselves motion-less just above the stream floor to suck up anything that happens to float their way. They rarely move or journey too far to feed themselves. Rather, they prefer to be spoon-fed by the spring.

Countless church members go through life the same way. They voice a public profession of faith and turn around to make their life a private profession of pew-sitting. Week in and week out, they plug themselves into the same spot to receive their weekly infusion of "religion." Sadly, their only means of edification comes from the weekly dose of spoon-feeding by their pastor's sermon. These bottom-feeders refuse to meet with other believers outside of a worship service. Worse, they often won't even move the pages of their Bible to read and meditate on its Truth during the week. It is opened only during Sunday sermons.

Believers are not saved to be bottom-feeders. The Bible, our guiding Truth from God Himself, makes use of the milk/solid food metaphor more than once, emphasizing that we are not to be like children stuck on milk but rather to grow in spiritual maturity, being nourished by solid food—that is, deeper matters of doctrine (1 Cor. 3:2; Heb. 5:14). As new creations, indwelt by the Holy Spirit, we are graced with the mind of Christ (1 Cor. 2:16), a mind that we are called to renew by discerning "what is the will of God, what is good and acceptable and perfect" (Rom. 12:2). We cannot discern the will of God if we don't read and study His Word that reveals His preceptive will. Likewise, we cannot know what is pure and how we grow in purity without seeking God's Word (Ps. 119:9), along with the counsel and encouragement of others in a small group environment. The very spirit of the Great Commission of Matthew 28:19 is to "go," which forms a diametric contrast to the disposition of bottom-feeders to "sit."

Our final image of the spring spills over as a byproduct of a bottom-feeder. The consequence of being a bottom-feeder, however, is better reflected by a different spring illustration. The spring's final illustration comes, again, by negative example. There is no spring mural unseemlier to the eye than seeing a beautiful fount, whose winding flow is choked by a clogged channel.

You've seen these clogged channels. They typically are bogged up with dark, still fluid. Water and life may flow in, but nothing flows out. The flow's blockage is sometimes attributed to an accumulation of fallen sticks and brush. Other obstructions, clogging once-ripe rivulets, amass from dead leaves and other debris. The surface is adorned with a thick, ashen film that preserves death in the stream like a natural embalming fluid. The pool may swell as the stream's confluence collects, but the rot of stagnation soon contaminates it. If the mud and sludge lining the rim of this wasteland doesn't deter entry, the blood-sucking mosquitos will. Far from springs of living water, these clogged channels paint a morose distortion of the Christian life.

If we are people truly transformed by the Gospel, we realize this clogged channel of "sit-and-soak Christianity" is not Christianity at all. We are not called to be constipated Christians, who take in God's Word but never release its life-changing Truths. Rather, the believer is tasked to release pent-up doctrine and head knowledge to others by means of discipleship. "Discipleship" is another word that's died the death of a thousand qualifications but simply means the intentional process whereby one mature Christ-follower invests in another through a personal relationship, facilitating their transformation toward Christlikeness. In short, we are to pass on what we have learned.

The Bible contains too many direct admonitions mandating discipleship to list them all. Some of the more salient passages, however, can drive the point home. Jesus places the value of discipleship in a very exclusionary context in John chapter fifteen by drawing the line that we prove to be His disciples by bearing fruit, the outgrowth of our spiritual life (v. 8). Jesus doubles down on this non-negotiable in the first part of verse sixteen, grounding it to the very purpose for our spiritual birth, "You did not choose me, but I chose you and appointed you that you should go and bear fruit . . . " In much the same reason a tree is made an apple tree to mature and bear the fruit of an apple tree, a person is made a Christian to mature and bear Christian fruit.

The apostle Paul undoubtedly seized upon Jesus' teaching in Ephesians 2:10a, where He emphasized that we are saved to be God's "workmanship, created in Christ Jesus for good works." Our salvation does not flow from good works; rather, good works flow from the new spiritual creation born with a heart to please God. Again, there is no such thing as a believer who doesn't bear fruit or who doesn't have good works naturally flowing.

A word of caution is warranted at this point. We should guard against letting our works gravitate toward two extremes. On one hand, our fruit and good works are not impersonal expressions occurring in a vacuum. On the other extreme, we can get too man-centric with our fruit when we cultivate it as rote tasks, or we trumpet our fruit publicly, to be seen by others. Rather, our fruit should first appear as blooms of personal holiness, sprouting naturally from a heart that seeks to please God. The fruit of this blossoming holiness, then, is perceptible by others in general and reproducible in personal relationships specifically.

The apostle Paul's paradigm for reproducing Christlike disciples was that of pouring into others and passing on fruit. Not only did Paul live out this exemplar, he taught it as well. Paul instructs his own disciple, Timothy, to not only "rightly [handle] the word of truth" (2 Tim. 2:15), but also to pass on what Paul had taught him to other faithful believers "who will be able to teach others also" (2 Tim. 2:2). Paul's didactic life, in word and deed, provides normative applications for all believers. So, while "consumer Christianity" pleads with our flesh to sit, soak, and consume without any obligation to others, Scripture and spring converge to proffer a very different answer. The answer is as clear as spring water itself: a life living out the Gospel of Jesus Christ is not a life lived as a clogged stream. As the theology of the spring attests, the life of a believer is not just that of a hearer, but also a doer (Jas. 1:22).

We've been on quite the excursion. You began with an introduction to the spring as a hearer—or reader, to be more precise. Taking your first baby steps into its crisp waters, you were perhaps numbed by the initial confrontation with its truth. But wading in further, the initial shock wore off as you became acclimated to the progression of the truths the spring steadily declared. As the theology of the spring progressively unfolded, its revelations, and the One to whom it ultimately points, could no longer be overlooked. Thus, as we exit the water, may we do so as changed people. May we do so convicted as both readers and doers.

It is my hope that the living discourses from the spring have opened your eyes to the beauty of creation; to the rationality the spring declares; to the systematic interconnectedness that makes abundant life in the spring possible; to the fact that we needn't approach life as a purposeless existence on the dark side of the moon, ravaged by the claws of post-modern disillusionment; to the ability to peer into the spring bosom to see the image of God reflected back; and to the call to get off your chair and go out to meet the spring. The spring invites you into its sanctuary to go fishing, hiking, camping, canoeing, kayaking, snorkeling, tubing, or simply spectating. But most passionately, the spring invites you to its Creator. What are you waiting for?

Reflection Questions

1. Have you ever had that moment in your life where you discovered the foundation you were standing upon was not stable? Where did you turn and why?

2. Consider the statement, "Faith can only be as stable as the object in which it is placed." Do you agree with this statement? Why or why not?

3. What are some reasons why people succumb to becoming clogged channels or bottom-feeders, whether that be in church, work, school, or other social institutions?

4. How does the very nature of the Gospel repudiate self-reliance?

5. It could be said that what keeps us from being courageous enough to swim upstream against the current is not that we don't care enough, but that we care too much. What are some things that you possibly care too much about that prevent you from living counter-culturally and swimming upstream? Have these things subtly become idols in your life?

6. Think of, or list, three ways this book has enabled you to see God differently. How will these three considerations influence you as you move forward?

ENDNOTES

Acknowledgments/Preface

1. Henry Van Dyke, *Fisherman's Luck,* (Whitefish: Kessinger Publishing, LLC, 2004).

2. John Braselton Fillmore Wright, "Precious Memories" (Stamps-Baxter Music Co., 1925).

Chapter One

3. *Dictionary.com, s.v.* "matter," accessed February 13, 2016, http://www.dictionary.com/browse/matter.

4. John H. Gerstner, *Reasons for Faith,* (Morgan: Soli Dei Gloria Publications, 2004), 32.

5. R.C. Sproul, "Anselm," *Tabletalk,* May 2011, 6-7.

6. Montague Brown, "Faith and Reason in Anselm: Two Models," *The Saint Anselm Journal 2.1,* Fall 2004, 16.

7. R.C. Sproul, "Anselm," in *The Consequence of Ideas.* Lecture (Orlando: Ligonier Ministries, 1998).

8. R.C. Sproul, "Augustine," in *The Consequence of Ideas,* Lecture (Orlando, FL: Ligonier Ministries, 1998).

9. Ibid.

10. Jason Lisle, "Evolutionary Math," Institute for Christian Research, accessed March 28, 2013, http://www.icr.org/article/7098.

11. Ibid.

12. Eric Metaxas, "Science Increasingly Makes the Case for God," *The Wall Street Journal*, December 25, 2014.

13. Dinesh D'Sousa, *What's So Great About God?* (Carol Stream: Tyndale House Publishers Inc., 2013), 165.

14. Rich Deem, "The Incredible Design of the Earth and Our Solar System," GodandScience.org, accessed March 5, 2015, http://www.godandscience.org/apologetics/designss.html#rotation.

15. Eric Metaxas, *Miracles* (New York: Dutton, 2014), 52.

16. Ibid, 52.

17. Jerry D. Feder and Gerald L. Vineyard, *Springs of Missouri* (Rolla: Missouri Geological Survey and Water Resources, 1974), 182.

<h2 style="text-align:center">Chapter Two</h2>

18. R.C. Sproul, *Everyone's a Theologian* (York: Reformation Trust, 2014), 4.

19. David Platt, *Follow Me* (Carol Stream: Tyndale House Publishers, 2013), 23.

20. Jerry D. Feder and Gerald L. Vineyard, *Springs of Missouri* (Rolla: Missouri Geological Survey and Water Resources, 1982), 11.

21. H. Dwight Weaver, *The Wilderness Underground: Caves of the Ozark Plateau* (Columbia: University of Missouri Press, 1992), 25.

22. Ibid, 25.

23. Ibid, 11.

24. Steven Austin, Ph. D., *Origin of Limestone Caves,* Institute for Creation Research, accessed March 28, 2013, http://www.icr.org/article/origin-limestone-caves.

25. Paul Blanchard, Personal Interview with author, February 25, 2015.

26. Ibid.

27. *Wikipedia, s.v.,* "Big Spring Discharge," accessed October 5, 2017, https://en.wikipedia.org/wiki/Big_Spring_(Missouri)#cite_note-5.

28. Feder and Vineyard, 86.

29. Steve Kohler, *Two Ozark Rivers* (Columbia: University of Missouri Press, 1984), 50.

30. Weaver, 9.

31. *Wikipedia, s.v.,* "Spring Classifications (Hydrology)," accessed October 5, 2017, https://en.wikipedia.org/wiki/Spring_(hydrology).

32. Feder and Vineyard, 11.

33. "Springs—The Water Cycle," U.S. Geological Survey, accessed February 10, 2015, http://water.usgs.gove/edu/watercyclesprings.html.

34. *National Geographic,* "Aquifer," https://www.nationalgeographic.org/encyclopedia/aquifer/,accessed October 5, 2017.

35. R.C. Sproul, *Defending your Faith: An Introduction to Apologetics* (Wheaton: Crossway Books, 2003), 122.

36. John Gerstner, *Reasons for Faith* (Morgan: Soli Dei Gloria Publications, 2004), 32.

37. William Lane Craig, *Reasonable Faith* (Wheaton: Crossway Books, 1994), 98.

38. Ibid, 100.

39. R.C. Sproul, *Defending Your Faith,* 130.

40. John Gerstner, *Theology in Dialogue* (Morgan: Soli Dei Gloria, 1996), 9.

41. David W. Beck, "God, Existence of," in *The Popular Encyclopedia of Apologetics,* ed. Ergun Caner and Ed Hindson. (Eugene: Harvest House, 2008), 237.

42. Dr. Stephen Meyer, "Session Two—Does God Exist?" Lecture, True U (Carol Stream: 2009).

43. "The Effect Problem," Institute of Christian Research, accessed April 1, 2013, http://www.icr.org/first-law.

44. William Lane Craig, *Reasonable Faith* (Wheaton: Crossway Publishing, 2010), 132.

45. Meyer, "Session Two."

46. Ibid.

47. Jonathan Webb, "Largest Ever 'Age Map' Traces Galactic History," BBC. com, accessed January 8, 2016, http://www.bbc.com/news.

Chapter Three

48. *A River Runs Through It,* directed by Robert Redford (1992; Culver City, CA: Sony Pictures Home Entertainment, 2011), DVD.

49. "Cutthroat Trout." Troutster.com, accessed May 25, 2016, http://troutster.com/trout-species/cutthroat-trout/.

50. Peter Bisson and Patrick Trotter, "History of the Discovery of the Cutthroat Trout," *American Fisheries Society Symposium,* Volume 4, 1988, 8.

51. Ibid, 9.

52. "Brown Trout," Trout Pro Store, accessed May 25, 2016, http://www.troutprostore.com/trout_species.

53. Kramer, Gary. "Wind River Gold." *American Angler.* May-June 2016: 63-65.

54. Michigan Department of Natural Resources. "Lake Trout." Michigan. gov. https://www.michigan.gov/dnr/0,4570,7-153-10364_18958-45670--,00.html (accessed May 25, 2016).

55. Joseph J. Cech, Jr. and Peter B. Moyle, *Fishes: An Introduction to Ichthyology,* 5th ed. (Upper Saddle River: PHI Learning, 2004), 219.

56. Gesine Behrens, "Iran and Turkey are the World-Leading Producers of Trout in Freshwater," accessed October 10, 2017, http://www.agribenchmark.org/agri-benchmark/did-you-know/einzelansicht/artikel//iran-and-tur.html.

57. *Wikipedia, s.v.,* "Rainbow Trout." accessed May 25, 2016, https://en.wikipedia.org/wiki/Rainbow_trout#cite_note-Seafood_Watch-44.

58. Cech and Moyle, 5.

59. Ibid, 3.

60. Dr. Gary Grossman, "Ask Dr. Trout," *American Angler,* March-April 2016, 11.

61. Cech and Moyle, 41.

62. Ibid, 40-41.

63. Thomas Yorke, Phillip Selway, Edward O'Brien, Colin Greenwood, and Jonathan Greenwood. "Optimistic," Radiohead, *Kid A*, Capitol Records, 7-2435-27753-2-3, 2000, CD.

64. James Civiello, telephone interview with author, March 20, 2013.

65. Ibid.

66. Dr. Gary Grossman, "Ask Dr. Trout," *American Angler,* January-February 2016, 15.

67. Jason Randall, "What Trout See," *American Angler,* January-February 2016, 26-29.

68. Cech and Moyle, 182.

69. Ibid.

70. Ibid, 115.

71. Randall, 26-29.

72. Dr. Gary Grossman, "Ask Dr. Trout," *American Angler,* May-June 2015, 14.

73. Ibid, 14.

74. Cech and Moyle, 169.

75. Dr. Gary Grossman, "Ask Dr. Trout," *American Angler,* September-October 2013, 18.

76. Ibid, 18.

77. Cech and Moyle, 190.

78. Dr. Gary Grossman, "Ask Dr. Trout," *American Angler,* September-October 2013, 18.

79. Cech and Moyle, 169.

80. Ross Purnell, "Katmai Rainbows," *Fly Fisherman*, February-March 2015, 16.

81. Cech and Moyle, 205.

82. Jason Randall, "Temperamental Trout," *American Angler*, March-April 2016, 38.

83. Cech and Moyle, 54.

84. Al Caucci and Bob Nastasi, *Hatches* (Woodside: Comparahatch, Ltd., 1975), 98.

85. Jason Randall, "Pupae, Cases, & Tent Wings," *American Angler*, May-June 2015, 26.

86. Henry Ramsay, "Isonychia." *Fly Fisherman*, August-September 2014, 38.

87. William Pflieger, "Sculpin," in *The Fishes of Missouri* (Missouri Department of Conservation, 1997), 252.

88. Cech and Moyle, 83.

89. "Wonderful Worms." Answers in Genesis, accessed March 28, 2013, https://answersingenesis.org/creepy-crawlies/wonderful-worms/.

90. Geoff Chapman, "Orchids . . . A Witness to the Creator," *Creation*, December 1, 1996, https://answersingenesis.org/biology/plants/orchids-a-witness-to-the-creator/, accessed March 28, 2013.

91. Steven Meyer, *Darwin's Doubt: The Explosive Origin of Animal Life and the Case for Intelligent Design* (New York: Harper One, 2013), 159.

92. Ibid, 175, 181.

93. Dr. Stephen Meyer, "Session Seven—Does God Exist?" Lecture, True U (Carol Stream, 2009.)

94. Meyer, *Darwin's Doubt*, 200.

95. Meyer, "Session Seven Lecture—Does God Exist?"

96. Meyer, *Darwin's Doubt*, 196-199.

97. Ibid, 259-261.

98. Ibid, 264.

99. Dr. Gary Grossman, "Ask Dr. Trout." *American Angler,* May-June 2013, 12.

100. Michael Behe, "Evidence for Intelligent Design from Biochemistry," in *Christian Apologetics: An Anthology of Primary Sources,* ed. Khaldoun A. Sweis and Chad Meister (Grand Rapids: Zondervan, 2012), 103.

101. David Klausmeyer, "Hatchery Fish Genetically Change Over Time." *American Angler,* May-June 2016, 14.

102. Mark R. Christie, Melanie L. Marine, Samuel E. Fox, Rod A. French, and Michael S. Blouin, "A Single Generation of Domestication Heritably Alters the Expression of Hundreds of Genes," Nature.com, accessed June 6, 2016, http://www.nature.com/ncomms/2016/160217/ncomms10676/full/ncomms10676.html.

103. Meyer, *Darwin's Doubt,* 273.

104. Marc Ambler, "Epigenetics—An Epic Challenge to Evolution," Creation.com, accessed on May 27, 2016, http://creation.com/epigenetics-challenges-neodarwinism.

105. Ibid.

106. Ibid.

Chapter Four

107. *One God in Three Persons,* ed. Bruce Ware and John Starke (Wheaton: Crossway Books, 2015), 85.

108. Peter King, "Augustine's Trinitarian Examples," The University of Toronto, http://individual.utoronto.ca/pking/articles/KING.Augustine_Trinitarian_Examples.pdf, accessed October 9, 2017.

109. Bryan M. Litfin, *Getting to Know the Church Fathers* (Grand Rapids: Brazos Press, 2007), 112.

110. James R. White, *The Forgotten Trinity* (Bloomington: Bethany House Publishers, 1998), 66.

111. John Calvin, *Institutes of the Christian Religion,* trans. Henry Beveridge (Peabody: Hendrickson Publishers, 2008), 78-79.

112. Louis Berkhof, *Systematic Theology* (Edinburgh: The Banner of Truth Trust, 1958), 91.

113. The Missouri Springs Virtual Resurgence, *"Commonly Asked Questions About Springs",* http://members.socket.net/~joschaper/sprfaq.html, accessed October 10, 2017.

114. Ware, 248.

115. Berkhof, 91.

116. *Blue Letter Bible, s.v.* "Jesus," accessed April 6, 2016,   https://www.blueletterbible.org/lang/lexicon/lexicon.cfm?strongs=g1577.

117. Litfin, 65.

118. Ibid.

119. White, 52.

120. Ibid, 51.

121. Calvin, *Institutes of the Christian Religion,* 70.

122. Ibid, 71.

123. Ibid, 81.

124. Robert L. Reymond, *What is God?* (Ross-shire: Christian Focus Publications, 2007), 323.

125. Jonathan Edwards, *Concerning the Deity of Christ,* vol. 2, *The Complete Works of Jonathan Edwards* (Peabody: Hendrickson Publishing, 2011), 503.

126. *Blue Letter Bible,* "Athanasius: Chapter 3: The Divine Dilemma and Its Solution in the Incarnation," Blue Letter Bible.org, accessed February 3, 2016, https://www.blueletterbible.org/Comm/athanasius/Incarnation/ The_Divine_Dilemma_and_Its_Solution_in_the_Incarnation_ Continued.cfm.

127. R.C. Sproul, *Who Is the Holy Spirit?* (Orlando: Reformation Trust, 2012), 31.

128. Calvin, *Institutes of the Christian Religion*, 82.

129. Anotina Shoumatoff, "Cary's Weathers Lectures on Fog," *The Millbrook Independent*, June 18, 2014.

130. Martha Scholl, Wener Eugster, and Reto Burkard, "Understanding the Role of Fog in Forest Hydrology," *Hydrological Processes*, 2010: 1-8.

131. Ibid, 1.

132. Ibid, 7.

133. R.C. Sproul, *John (St. Andrew's Expositional Commentary)* (Orlando: Reformation Trust, 2009), 299.

134. R.C. Sproul, *Who Is the Holy Spirit?*, 69.

135. J.I. Packer, *Concise Theology: A Guide to Christian Beliefs* (Carol Stream: Tyndale House Publishers, 2001), 155.

Chapter Five

136. Jim Morrison. "An American Prayer," The Doors, *An American Prayer*, Elektra Records, 7559-61812-2, 1978, CD.

137. Frederich Nietzche, R. Kevin Hill Ed., *A Will to Power* (London, Penguin Classics, 2017), 8.

138. Jim Morrison. "Stoned Immaculate," The Doors, *An American Prayer*, Elektra Records, 7559-61812-2, 1978, CD.

139. The Doors. "When the Music's Over," The Doors, *Strange Days*, Elektra Records, 7559-74014-2, 1967, CD.

140. "Westminster Shorter Catechism," Center for Reformed Theology and Apologetics, accessed October 24, 2016, http://www.reformed.org/documents/wsc/index.html?_ top=http://www.reformed.org/documents/WSC.html.

141. "Hezekiah's tunnel," Generationword.com, accessed October 31, 2016, http://www.generationword.com/Israel/jerusalem_sites/hezekiah_tunnel.html.

142. Ibid.

143. Brian Fagan, *Elixir: A History of Water and Humankind* (New York: Bloomsbury Press, 2011), preface—xxiii.

144. Fred Pearce, *Keepers of the Spring: Reclaiming Our Water in an Age of Globalization* (Washington, DC: Island Press, 2004), 38.

145. Ibid, 32.

146. Fagan, 112.

147. Ibid, 46.

148. Ibid, 42.

149. Ibid, 46.

150. Ibid, 139.

151. Ibid, 143.

152. Pearce, 134.

153. Ibid, 5.

154. Ibid, 127.

155. Conevery Bolton Valencius, *The Health of the Country: How American Settlers Understood Themselves and Their Land* (New York: Basic Books, 2002), 4.

156. Loring Bullard, *Healing Waters: Missouri's Historic Mineral Springs and Spas* (Columbia: University of Missouri Press, 2004), 29.

157. Ibid, 28.

158. Valencius, 157.

159. Bullard, 11.

160. Matt Kaplan, *Science of the Magical* (New York: Scribner, 2015), 19.

161. Bullard, 11.

162. Ibid, 17.

163. Ibid.

164. Valencius, 156.

165. Kaplan, 22-23.

166. Ibid, 23.

167. Bullard, 23.

168. *Topix, s.v.* "spring," accessed October 7, 2017, www.topix.com/city/list.

169. Napier Shelton, *Natural Missouri: Working with the Land* (Columbia: University of Missouri Press, 2005), 110.

170. Friends of Shannon County Libraries, *History of Shannon County Missouri,* (Dallas: Taylor Publishing, 1986), 7.

171. Shelton, 112.

172. Friends of Shannon County, 7.

173. Ibid, 13.

174. Shelton, 115.

175. Ibid.

176. Charles Haddon Spurgeon, *Lectures to My Students, Vol. 1-4* (Lexington: DREAM Publishing International, 2017), 134.

Chapter Six

177. *The Twilight Zone,* "A Penny for Your Thoughts," Season 2: Episode 16, Directed by James Sheldon, Written by George Clayton Johnson (CBS Television, February 3, 1961).

178. Julien Green, *God's Fool: The Life and Times of Francis of Assisi* (San Francisco: Harper and Row Publishers, 1985), 163.

179. A.W. Tozer, *The Knowledge of the Holy* (New York: Harper and Row Publishers, 1961), 111.

180. Stephen R. Kellert, *Birthright: People and Nature in the Modern World* (New Haven: Yale University Press, 2012), Introduction, i.

181. D.J. Case and Associates. *Missouri State Park Economics and Benefits: An Update Based on 2011 Visitation* (Mishawaka, IN: 2012).

182. Stephen R. Kellert, *Building for Life: Understanding and Designing the Human-Nature Connection* (Washington, DC: Island Press, 2005), 250.

183. "NPS Reports." National Park Service, accessed March 25, 2013, http://www.nature.nps.gov/stats/viewReport.cfm.

184. "Facts and Figures," Missouri State Parks, accessed November 16, 2016, https://mostateparks.com/page/55072/facts-and-figures.

185. J. Gresham Machen, *Christianity and Liberalism, New Edition* (Grand Rapids: Wm. B. Eerdmans Publishing, 2009), 115.

186. John Owen, *Overcoming Sin and Temptation*, ed. Kelly M. Kapic and Justin Taylor (Wheaton: Crossway, 2015), 206.

187. Ibid, 257.

188. *The Holy Bible, King James Version*, Nashville: Holman Bible Publishers, 1998.

189. Berkhof, 468.

190. John Murray, *Collected Writings of John Murray, Volume 2: Select Lectures in Systematic Theology* (Edinburgh: The Banner of Truth Trust, 1977), 171.

191. Arthur W. Pink, *The Sovereignty of God* (Grand Rapids: Baker Book House, 1976), 131.

192. Owen, 308.

193. Shai Linne. "Regeneration," Shai Linne, *Lyrical Theology Pt. 1: Theology*, Lamp Mode, 7-98576-65782-6, 2013, CD.

194. Owen, 59.

195. Jared C. Wilson, *The Prodigal Church: A Gentle Manifesto Against the Status Quo* (Wheaton: Crossway Books, 2015), 67.

196. Phillip Monahan, "Closer Look: Split-Cane Fly Rods," *American Angler*. March-April 2016, 43.

Chapter Seven

197. Jim Holvay. "Kind of a Drag," The Buckinghams, *Kind of a Drag*, USA Records, 90771-6126-2, 1966, CD.

198. Neil Young. "Old Man," Neil Young, *Harvest*, Reprise Records, 7599-27239-2, 1972, CD.

199. Ibid.

200. Ibid.

Chapter Eight

201. David Dark, *Everyday Apocalypse* (Grand Rapids: Brazos Press, 2002), 143.

202. Jason Randall, "Temperamental Trout," *American Angler*, March-April 2016, 39.

203. Chris Gates, personal interview with author, June 23, 2016.

204. Quote Investigator, "Nobody Goes There Anymore, It's Too Crowded," QuoteInvestigator.com, (accessed July 16, 2016), https://quoteinvestigator.com/2014/08/29/too-crowded/.

205. Carl Richards and Doug Swisher. *Fly Fishing Strategy* (New York: Crown Publishers, 1975), 58.

206. Gregory Koukal, *Tactics: A Game Plan for Discussing Your Christian Convictions* (Grand Rapids: Zondervan, 2009), 47.

207. Hugh Hewitt, *In, But Not Of* (Nashville: Thomas Nelson, 2003), 166.

208. John Calvin, *Calvin's Commentaries: The Second Epistle of Paul the Apostle to the Corinthians* (Grand Rapids: Eerdmans Publishing Company, 1964), 172.

209. Richards and Swisher, 99.

210. Alvin L. Reid, *Radically Unchurched* (Grand Rapids: Kregel Publications, 2002), 120.

211. *Friends*, "The One with Monica and Chandler's Wedding," Season 7: Episodes 23-24, Directed by Kevin Bright, Written by Gregory S.

Malins, Marta Kauffman, and David Crane (NBC Television, May 17, 2001).

Chapter Nine

212. Peter J. Gentry and Stephen Wellum, *God's Kingdom through God's Covenants* (Wheaton: Crossway, 2015), 71.

213. Ibid, 79.

214. Ibid, 87.

215. Ibid, 84.

216. Murray, 38.

217. *The Holy Bible, New King James Version*, Nashville: Thomas Nelson Publishers, 1992.

218. Mark Dever, "Biblical Church Discipline," *Southern Baptist Journal of Theology*, no. 4 (Winter 2000), 29-44.

219. R. Albert Mohler, "Church Discipline: The Missing Mark," *Southern Baptist Journal of Theology*, no. 4 (Winter 2000), 17-28.

220. Thom Rainer, "When People Criticize Church Leadership," *The Pathway* (The Official Newsjournal of the Missouri Baptist Convention), February 22, 2011, 5.

221. Mohler, 23.

222. Philip Mutetei, "The Proper Procedure for Discipline in the Church: Part II," *Africa Journal of Evangelical Theology*, no. 18.2 (1999), 107-128.

223. Ibid, 107.

224. J. Carl Laney, "The Biblical Practice of Church Discipline," *Bibliotheca Sacra* (October-December 1986), 353-364.

225. Mutetei, 118.

226. Mohler, 24.

227. Laney, 359.

228. Jim West, "Nineteenth-Century Baptists and Church Discipline: Case Studies from Georgia," *Baptist History and Heritage*, no. 45:1 (Winter 2010), 80-90.

229. Dever, 35.

230. Kevin Miller, "Church Discipline for Repetitive Sin," *Leadership* (Spring 2009). 39-41.

231. L.R. DeKoster, "Church Discipline," in *Evangelical Dictionary of Theology*, 2nd ed, ed. Walter A. Elwell (Grand Rapids: Baker Academic, 2001), 256.

Chapter Ten

232. W.E. Vine, "Gospel" in *An Expository Dictionary of New Testament Words* (Old Tappan: Fleming H. Revell Company), 167.

233. George Whitefield, "The Observation of the Birth of Christ, the Duty of all Christians; or the True Way of Keeping Christmas," Bible Bulletin Board.com, accessed on December 12, 22, 2016, http://www.biblebb.com/files/whitefield/gw016.htm.

BIBLIOGRAPHY

A River Runs Through It. Directed by Robert Redford. 1992. Culver City, CA: Sony Pictures Home Entertainment, 2011. DVD.

Ambler, Marc. "Epigenetics—An Epic Challenge to Evolution." Creation.com. https://creation.com/epigenetics-challenges-neo-darwinism (accessed May 27, 2016).

Answers in Genesis. "Wonderful Worms." Answersingenesis.org. https://answersingenesis.org/creepy-crawlies/wonderful-worms/ (accessed March 28, 2013).

Austin, Steven, Ph. D. *Origin of Limestone Caves.* ICR.org. http://www.icr.org/article/origin-limestone-caves (accessed March 28, 2013).

Beck, David W. "God, Existence of." In *The Popular Encyclopedia of Apologetics,* edited by Ergun Caner and Ed Hindson, 237. Eugene: Harvest House, 2008.

Behe, Michael. "Evidence for Intelligent Design from Biochemistry." In *Christian Apologetics: An Anthology of Primary Sources,* edited by Khaldoun A. Sweis and Chad Meister, 103. Grand Rapids: Zondervan, 2012.

Behrens, Gesine. "Iran and Turkey are the World-Leading Producers of Trout in Freshwater." Agribenchmark.org. http://www.agribenchmark.org/agri-benchmark/did-you-know/einzelansicht/artikel//iran-and-tur.html (accessed October 10, 2017).

Berkhof, Louis. *Systematic Theology.* Edinburgh: The Banner of Truth Trust, 1958.

Bisson, Peter, and Patrick Trotter. "History of the Discovery of the Cutthroat Trout." *American Fisheries Society Symposium* 4 (1988): 8.

Blue Letter Bible. "Athanasius: Chapter 3: The Divine Dilemma and Its Solution in the Incarnation." Blueletterbible.org. https://www.blueletterbible.org/Comm/athanasius/Incarnation/The_Divine_Dilemma_ and_Its_Solution_in_the_Incarnation_Continued.cfm (accessed February 3, 2016).

Blue Letter Bible, s.v. "Jesus," accessed April 6, 2016, https://www.blueletterbible.org/lang/lexicon/lexicon.cfm?strongs=g1577.

Brown, Montague. "Faith and Reason in Anselm: Two Models." *The Saint Anselm Journal 2.1* (Fall 2004): 16.

Bullard, Loring. *Healing Waters: Missouri's Historic Mineral Springs and Spas*. Columbia: University of Missouri Press, 2004.

Calvin, John. *Calvin's Commentaries: The Second Epistle of Paul the Apostle to the Corinthians*. Grand Rapids: Eerdmans Publishing Company, 1964.

Calvin, John. *Institutes of the Christian Religion*. Translated by Henry Beveridge. Peabody: Hendrickson Publishers, 2008.

Caucci, Al, and Bob Nastasi. *Hatches*. Woodside: Comparahatch, Ltd., 1975.

Cech, Jr. Joseph J., and Peter B. Moyle. *Fishes: An Introduction to Ichthyology*. 5th ed. Upper Saddle River: PHI Learning, 2004.

Center for Reformed Theology and Apologetics. "Westminster Shorter Catechism." Reformed.org. http://www.reformed.org/documents/wsc/index.html?_ top=http://www.reformed.org/documents/WSC.html (accessed October 24, 2016).

Chapman, Geoff. "Orchids . . . A Witness to the Creator." *Creation* (December 1, 1996). https://answersingenesis.org/biology/plants/orchids-a-witness-to-the-creator/ (accessed March 28, 2013).

Christie, Mark R., Melanie L. Marine, Samuel E. Fox, Rod A. French, and Michael S. Blouin. "A Single Generation of Domestication Heritably Alters the Expression of Hundreds of Genes." Nature.com. http://www.nature.com/ncomms/2016/160217/ncomms10676/full/ncomms10676.html (accessed June 6, 2016).

Craig, William Lane. *Reasonable Faith*. Wheaton: Crossway Books, 1994.

Troutster. "Cutthroat Trout." Troutster.com. http://troutster.com/trout-species/cutthroat-trout/ (accessed May 25, 2016).

D.J. Case and Associates. 2012. *Missouri State Park Economics and Benefits: An Update Based on 2011 Visitation*. Mishawaka: May, 2012.

Dark, David. *Everyday Apocalypse*. Grand Rapids: Brazos Press, 2002.

Deem, Rich. "The Incredible Design of the Earth and Our Solar System." GodandScience.org. http://www.godandscience.org/apologetics/designss.html#rotation (accessed March 5, 2015).

DeKoster, L.R. "Church Discipline." In *Evangelical Dictionary of Theology*. 2nd ed, edited by Walter A. Elwell, 256. Grand Rapids: Baker Academic, 2001.

Dever, Mark. "Biblical Church Discipline." *Southern Baptist Journal of Theology*, 4 (Winter 2000): 29-44.

Dictionary.com, s.v. "matter," accessed February 13, 2016, http://www.dictionary.com/browse/matter.

D'Sousa, Dinesh. *What's So Great About God?* Carol Stream: Tyndale House Publishers Inc., 2013.

Edwards, Jonathan. *Concerning the Deity of Christ*, vol. 2, *The Works of Jonathan Edwards*. Peabody: Hendrickson Publishing, 2011.

Fagan, Brian. *Elixir: A History of Water and Humankind*. New York: Bloomsbury Press, 2011.

Feder, Jerry D. and Gerald L. Vineyard. *Springs of Missouri*. Rolla: Missouri Geological Survey and Water Resources, 1982.

Friends. "The One with Monica and Chandler's Wedding." Season 7: Episodes 23-24. Directed by Kevin Bright. Written by Gregory S. Malins, Marta Kauffman, and David Crane. NBC Television, May 17, 2001.

Friends of Shannon County Libraries. *History of Shannon County Missouri.* Dallas: Taylor Publishing, 1986.

Futato, Mark D. "Because it Had Rained: A Study of Gen. 2:5-7 with Implications for Gen. 2:4-25 and Gen. 1:1-2:3" *Westminster Theological Journal 60* (1998): 1-21.

Gentry, Peter J. and Stephen Wellum. *God's Kingdom through God's Covenants.* Wheaton: Crossway, 2015.

Gerstner, John H. *Reasons for Faith.* Morgan: Soli Dei Gloria Publications, 2004.

Gerstner, John H. *Theology in Dialogue.* Morgan: Soli Dei Gloria, 1996.

Green, Julien. *Gods Fool: The Life and Times of Francis of Assisi.* San Francisco: Harper and Row Publishers, 1985.

Grossman, Dr. Gary. "Ask Dr. Trout." *American Angler.* (January-February 2016): 15.

Grossman, Dr. Gary. "Ask Dr. Trout." *American Angler.* (March-April 2016): 11.

Grossman, Dr. Gary. "Ask Dr. Trout." *American Angler.* (May-June 2013): 12.

Grossman, Dr. Gary. "Ask Dr. Trout." *American Angler.* (May-June 2015): 14.

Grossman, Dr. Gary. "Ask Dr. Trout." *American Angler.* (September-October 2013): 18.

Hewitt, Hugh. *In, But Not Of.* Nashville: Thomas Nelson, 2003.

The Holy Bible, New King James Version. Nashville: Thomas Nelson Publishers, 1992.

The Holy Bible, King James Version. Nashville: Holman Bible Publishers, 1998.

Institute of Christian Research. "The Effect Problem." ICR.org. http://www.icr.org/first-law (accessed April 1, 2013).

Kaplan, Matt. *Science of the Magical.* New York: Scribner, 2015.

Kellert, Stephen R. *Birthright: People and Nature in the Modern World.* New Haven: Yale University Press, 2012.

Kellert, Stephen R. *Building for Life: Understanding and Designing the Human-Nature Connection.* Washington, DC: Island Press, 2005.

King, Peter. "Augustine's Trinitarian Examples." Utoronto.ca. http://individual.utoronto.ca/pking/articles/KING.Augustine_Trinitarian_Examples.pdf (accessed October 9, 2017).

Klausmeyer, David. "Hatchery Fish Genetically Change Over Time." *American Angler.* (May-June 2016): 14.

Kline, Meredith. "Because it Had Not Rained." *Westminster Theological Journal 20* (1958), 146-157.

Kohler, Steve. *Two Ozark Rivers.* Columbia: University of Missouri Press, 1984.

Koukal, Gregory. *Tactics: A Game Plan for Discussing Your Christian Convictions.* Grand Rapids: Zondervan, 2009.

Kramer, Gary. "Wind River Gold." *American Angler.* (May-June 2016): 63-65.

Laney, J. Carl. "The Biblical Practice of Church Discipline." *Bibliotheca Sacra.* (October-December 1986): 353-364.

Lisle, Jason. "Evolutionary Math." ICR.org. http://www.icr.org/article/7098 (accessed March 28, 2013).

Litfin, Bryan M. *Getting to Know the Church Fathers.* Grand Rapids: Brazos Press, 2007.

Machen, J. Gresham. *Christianity and Liberalism, New Edition*. Grand Rapids: Wm. B. Eerdmans Publishing, 2009.

Metaxas, Eric. *Miracles*. New York: Dutton, 2014.

Metaxas, Eric. "Science Increasingly Makes the Case for God." *The Wall Street Journal*. (December 25, 2014).

Meyer, Stephen C. *Darwin's Doubt: The Explosive Origin of Animal Life and the Case for Intelligent Design*. New York: Harper One, 2013.

Meyer, Stephen C. "Session Seven—Does God Exist?" Lecture, True U, Carol Stream, IL, 2009.

Meyer, Stephen C. "Session Two—Does God Exist?" Lecture, True U, Carol Stream, IL, 2009.

Michigan Department of Natural Resources. "Lake Trout." Michigan.gov. https://www.michigan.gov/dnr/0,4570,7-153-10364_18958-45670--,00.html (accessed May 25, 2016).

Miller, Kevin. "Church Discipline for Repetitive Sin." *Leadership* (Spring 2009): 39-41.

The Missouri Springs Virtual Resurgence. "Commonly Asked Questions About Springs." http://members.socket.net/~joschaper/sprfaq.html, accessed October 10, 2017.

Missouri State Parks. "Facts and Figures." Mostateparks.com. https://mostateparks.com/page/55072/facts-and-figures (accessed November 16, 2016).

Mohler, R. Albert. "Church Discipline: The Missing Mark." *Southern Baptist Journal of Theology*, 4 (Winter 2000): 17-28.

Monahan, Phillip. "Closer Look: Split-Cane Fly Rods." *American Angler*. (March-April 2016): 43.

Murray, John. *Collected Writings of John Murray, Volume 2: Select Lectures in Systematic Theology*. Edinburgh: The Banner of Truth Trust, 1977.

Mutetei, Philip. "The Proper Procedure for Discipline in the Church: Part II." *Africa Journal of Evangelical Theology*, 18.2 (1999): 107-128.

National Geographic. "Aquifer," https://www.nationalgeographic. org/encyclopedia/aquifer/, (accessed October 5, 2017).

National Park Service. "NPS Reports." Nps.gov. http://www.nature. nps.gov/stats/viewReport.cfm (accessed March 25, 2013).

Nietzche, Frederich., R. Kevin Hill Ed. *A Will to Power.* London: Penguin Classics, 2017.

Owen, John. *Overcoming Sin and Temptation,* Edited by Kelly M. Kapic and Justin Taylor. Wheaton: Crossway, 2015.

Packer, J.I. *Concise Theology: A Guide to Christian Beliefs.* Carol Stream: Tyndale House Publishers, 2001.

Pearce, Fred. *Keepers of the Spring: Reclaiming Our Water in an Age of Globalization.* Washington, DC: Island Press, 2004.

Pflieger, William. "Sculpin." *The Fishes of Missouri.* Missouri Department of Conservation, 1997.

Pink, Arthur W. *The Sovereignty of God.* Grand Rapids: Baker Book House, 1976.

Platt, David. *Follow Me.* Carol Stream: Tyndale House Publishers, 2013.

Purnell, Ross. "Katmai Rainbows." *Fly Fisherman.* (February-March 2015): 16.

Quote Investigator. "Nobody Goes There Anymore, It's Too Crowded." QuoteInvestigator.com. https://quoteinvestigator. com/2014/08/29/too-crowded/ (accessed July 16, 2016).

Rainer, Thom. "When People Criticize Church Leadership." *The Pathway.* (February 22, 2011): 5.

Ramsay, Henry. "Isonychia." *Fly Fisherman.* (August-September 2014): 38.

Randall, Jason. "Pupae, Cases, & Tent Wings." *American Angler*. (May-June 2015): 26.

Randall, Jason. "Temperamental Trout." *American Angler*. (March-April 2016): 38-39.

Randall, Jason. "What Trout See." *American Angler* (January-February 2016): 26-29.

Reid, Alvin L. *Radically Unchurched*. Grand Rapids: Kregel Publications, 2002.

Reymond, Robert L. *What is God?* Ross-shire: Christian Focus Publications, 2007.

Richards, Carl and Doug Swisher. *Fly Fishing Strategy*. New York: Crown Publishers, 1975.

Scholl, Martha, Wener Eugster, and Reto Burkard. "Understanding the Role of Fog in Forest Hydrology." *Hydrological Processes* (2010): 1-8.

Shelton, Napier. *Natural Missouri: Working with the Land*. Columbia: University of Missouri Press.

Shoumatoff, Anotina. "Cary's Weathers Lectures on Fog." *The Millbrook Independent*. (June 18, 2014).

Sproul, R.C. "Anselm." *Tabletalk*. (May 2011): 6-7.

Sproul, R.C. "Anselm." *The Consequence of Ideas*. Lecture, Ligonier Ministries, Orlando, 1998.

Sproul, R.C. "Augustine." *The Consequence of Ideas*. Lecture, Ligonier Ministries, Orlando, 1998.

Sproul, R.C. *Defending your Faith: An Introduction to Apologetics*. Wheaton: Crossway Books, 2003.

Sproul, R.C. *Everyone's a Theologian*. York: Reformation Trust, 2014, 4.

Sproul, R.C. *John (St. Andrew's Expositional Commentary)*. Orlando: Reformation Trust, 2009.

Sproul, R.C. *Who Is the Holy Spirit?* Orlando: Reformation Trust, 2012.

Spurgeon, Charles Haddon. *Lectures to My Students, Vol. 1-4.* Lexington: DREAM Publishing International, 2017.

Topix, s.v. "spring." www.topix.com/city/list (accessed October 7, 2017).

Tozer, A.W. *The Knowledge of the Holy.* New York: Harper and Row Publishers, 1961.

The Twilight Zone. "A Penny for Your Thoughts." Season 2: Episode 16. Directed by James Sheldon. Written by George Clayton Johnson. CBS Television, February 3, 1961.

Trout Pro Store. "Brown Trout." Troutprostore.com. http://www.troutprostore.com/trout_species (accessed May 25, 2016).

U.S. Geological Survey. "Springs–The Water Cycle." Usgs.gov. http://water.usgs.gove/edu/watercyclesprings.html (accessed February 10, 2015).

Valencius, Conevery Bolton. *The Health of the Country: How American Settlers Understood Themselves and Their Land.* New York: Basic Books, 2002.

Van Dyke, Henry. *Fisherman's Luck.* Whitefish: Kessinger Publishing, LLC, 2004.

Vine, W.E. "Gospel." *An Expository Dictionary of New Testament Words.* Old Tappan: Fleming H. Revell Company, 167.

Ware, Bruce A., and John Starke. *One God in Three Persons: Unity of Essence, Distinction of Persons, Implications for Life.* Wheaton: Crossway Books, 2015.

Weaver, H. Dwight. *The Wilderness Underground: Caves of the Ozark Plateau.* Columbia: University of Missouri Press, 1992.

Webb, Jonathan. "Largest Ever 'Age Map' Traces Galactic History." BBC.com. http://www.bbc.com/news (accessed January 8, 2016).

Wiemers, Galyn. "Hezekiah's tunnel." Generationword.com. http://www.generationword.com/Israel/jerusalem_sites/hezekiah_tunnel.html (accessed October 31, 2016).

West, Jim. "Nineteenth-Century Baptists and Church Discipline: Case Studies from Georgia." *Baptist History and Heritage*, no. 45:1 (Winter 2010): 80-90.

White, James R. *The Forgotten Trinity.* Bloomington: Bethany House Publishers, 1998.

Whitefield, George. "The Observation of the Birth of Christ, the Duty of all Christians; or the True Way of Keeping Christmas." Bible Bulletin Board.com. http://www.biblebb.com/files/whitefield/gw016.htm (accessed December 12/22, 2016).

Wikipedia, s.v., "spring (hydrology)." https://en.wikipedia.org/wiki/Spring_(hydrology) (accessed October 5, 2017).

Wikipedia, s.v., "Big Spring (Missouri)." https://en.wikipedia.org/wiki/Big_Spring_(Missouri)#cite_note-5 (accessed October 5, 2017).

Wikipedia, s.v., "rainbow trout." https://en.wikipedia.org/wiki/Rainbow_trout#cite_note-Seafood_Watch-44 (accessed May 25, 2016).

Wilson, Jared C. *The Prodigal Church: A Gentle Manifesto Against the Status Quo.* Wheaton: Crossway Books, 2015.

DISCOGRAPHY

The Buckinghams. "Kind of a Drag." *Kind of a Drag.* USA Records 107, 1966, CD.

The Doors. "An American Prayer." *An American Prayer.* Elektra Records W 52111, 1978, CD.

The Doors. "Stoned Immaculate." *An American Prayer.* Elektra Records 5E-502, 1978, CD.

The Doors. "When the Music's Over." *Strange Days.* Elektra Records, 1967, CD.

Linne, Shai. "Regeneration." *Lyrical Theology Pt. 1: Theology.* Lamp Mode, 2013, CD.

Radiohead. "Optimistic." *Kid A.* Capitol Records dpro 7087 6 15199 0 7, 2000, CD.

Wright, John Braselton Fillmore. "Precious Memories." Stamps-Baxter Music Co., 1925.

Young, Neil. "Old Man." *Harvest.* Reprise Records, 1972, CD.

For more information about
Jacob A. Taggart
&
Theology from the Spring

please visit:

www.theologyfromthespring.com
@jacobataggart

For more information about
AMBASSADOR INTERNATIONAL
please visit:

www.ambassador-international.com
@AmbassadorIntl
www.facebook.com/AmbassadorIntl

If you enjoyed this book, please let us know on social media using
#TheologyFromTheSpring, and please consider leaving us a review on
Amazon, Goodreads, or our website.